business

Globalization and Business Politics in Arab North Africa
A Comparative Perspective

Can production for global markets help business groups to mobilize collectively? Under what conditions does globalization enable the private sector to develop independent organizational bases and create effective relationships with the state? Focusing on varied Moroccan and Tunisian responses to trade liberalization in the 1990s, Melani Cammett argues that two constitutive dimensions of business–government relations shape business responses to global economic opening: first, the balance of power between business and the state before economic opening; and second, preexisting business class structure. These two dimensions combine to form different configurations of business–government relations, including "distant" and "close" linkages, leading to divergent interests and, hence, strategic behavior by industrialists. The book also extends the analysis to additional country cases, including India, Turkey, and Taiwan, and examines how different patterns of business–government relations affect processes of industrial upgrading.

Melani Cammett is Associate Professor of Political Science and Director of the Middle East Studies Program at Brown University. She specializes in the political economy of development and the Middle East. She earned her Ph.D. in 2002 from the Department of Political Science at the University of California at Berkeley and served as an Academy Scholar at the Harvard Academy for International and Area Studies from 2005 to 2006 and 2007 to 2008. Cammett has published scholarly articles in *Studies in Comparative International Development, Comparative Politics, World Development, Global Governance,* and other journals. She is also completing a new book entitled *Servicing Sectarianism: Welfare and Politics in Weak States,* which explores how ethnic and religious parties allocate welfare goods focusing on sectarian organizations in Lebanon and other countries in the Middle East and South Asia. Her research has received support from the Smith Richardson Foundation, U.S. Institute of Peace, Academy Scholars Program at Harvard, Social Science Research Council, American Institute for Maghrib Studies, Salomon Faculty Research Grant at Brown University, and Institute for International Studies at University of California Berkeley. Cammett also holds an M.A.L.D. from the Fletcher School of Law and Diplomacy (1994), received a Fulbright Fellowship in Jordan, and has consulted for development policy organizations.

"For nearly two hundred years, students of politics have debated what determines when and how capitalists influence state policy. In drawing on the experience of developing country manufacturers – the textile industries of Morocco and Tunisia – Melani Cammett both deepens the theoretical sophistication and broadens the empirical reach of these debates. Incorporating how the opportunities and challenges of the export market shape both business horizons and government incentives, she draws subtle portraits of the changing outlooks of the business communities of Tunisia and Morocco. In doing so, she deftly outlines when and why industrialists mobilize, and when and why they are effective. This book is valuable not only for what it tells us about North African textile exporters but also for what we learn about the global dynamics of business-state relations in the twenty-first century."

– Lisa Anderson, Columbia University

"As developing countries open to the world economy, the organization and political activity of local business communities, and their relationship with national governments, have become ever more important. *Globalization and Business Politics in Arab North Africa* is a serious contribution to our understanding of this central feature of the political economy of developing nations. In it, Melani Claire Cammett carries out a careful and nuanced study of the economics and politics of the crucial textile and garment industries in Tunisia and Morocco as the two countries are drawn into the world economy. She contrasts the relative political passivity of the Tunisian industrialists with the striking activism of their counterparts in Morocco. Cammett invokes a sophisticated mix of economic, political, and sociological factors to explain the differences in the behavior of the two countries' industrialists. Along the way, she provides us with a detailed analysis of the global textile and apparel trade, and of the developing world's place in it, and an extension of her two-country comparison to other developing nations. *Globalization and Business Politics in Arab North Africa* will be of great relevance to all those interested in the political economy of development."

– Jeffry Frieden, Harvard University

"An impressive scholarly contribution. Cammett's careful and theoretically informed study, based on in-depth fieldwork in Tunisia and Morocco, provides not only valuable analytical insights but also important real-world lessons about how, why, and with what domestic political implications industrialists in developing countries respond to globalization and trade liberalization."

– Mark Tessler, University of Michigan

Globalization and Business Politics in Arab North Africa

A Comparative Perspective

MELANI CLAIRE CAMMETT

Brown University

CAMBRIDGE
UNIVERSITY PRESS

CAMBRIDGE UNIVERSITY PRESS
Cambridge, New York, Melbourne, Madrid, Cape Town, Singapore,
São Paulo, Delhi, Dubai, Tokyo, Mexico City

Cambridge University Press
32 Avenue of the Americas, New York, NY 10013-2473, USA

www.cambridge.org
Information on this title: www.cambridge.org/9780521156264

First published 2007
First paperback edition 2010

Printed in the United States of America

A catalog record for this publication is available from the British Library.

Library of Congress Cataloging in Publication Data

Cammett, Melani Claire.
Globalization and business politics in Arab North Africa : a comparative perspective.
Melani Claire Cammett.
    p. cm.
Includes bibliographical references and index.
ISBN 978-0-521-86950-8 (hardback)
1. Business enterprises – Morocco. 2. Business enterprises – Tunisia. 3. Morocco –
Economic policy. 4. Tunisia – Economic policy. 5. Globalization. I. Title.
HC810.C36 2007
338.9611 – dc22   2006037803

ISBN 978-0-521-86950-8 Hardback
ISBN 978-0-521-15626-4 Paperback

For Alex, Lena, and Angelo

Contents

List of Tables and Figures		*page* ix
Acknowledgments		xi
List of Abbreviations		xv
Map of Morocco		xviii
Map of Tunisia		xix

I THE FRAMEWORK

1   Rethinking Globalization and Business Politics   3
    The Theory: Political Opportunities, Class Identity, and the
    Social Foundations of Business Collective Action   13

2   Globalization and Integration in International Apparel
    Manufacturing Networks: The New Politics of Industrial
    Development   25
    Features of Textile and Apparel Manufacturing   26
    The Shifting Global Production Context   28
    Waves of Off-Shore Délocalisation   29
    Trends in Global Supply Chain Management   41
    Industrial Development Strategy in the Contemporary Global
    Economy: Clusters in Global Value Chains   47

II THE INSTITUTIONAL CONTEXT

3   Business and the State in Tunisia: Statist Development,
    Capital Dispersion, and Preemptive Integration in World
    Markets   55
    State-Building and Economic Elites in Tunisia   55
    Who Made the Rules? The New Administrative Elite   62

State Policies and Class Formation: The Development of a
Tunisian Industrial Class   65
A Critical Juncture: Early Integration in Global Markets and
the Emergence of the Dual Market   72

4   Business and the State in Morocco: Business Penetration of
    the State and the Genesis of the "Fat Cat"   80
    Business–Government Relations in Postindependence Morocco   80
    The Institutionalization of the Protected Economy   89

III GLOBALIZATION AND INSTITUTIONAL CHANGE

5   Business as Usual: State-Sponsored Industrialization and
    Business Collective Inaction in Tunisia   107
    Preferences and Lobbying: Intentions versus Action   107
    State Repression, Organizational Weakness, or Preemptive
    Incentives? Competing Accounts of Tunisian Business
    Complacency   116
    The Social Foundations of Business Behavior   135

6   Fat Cats and Self-Made Men: Class Conflict and Business
    Collective Action in Morocco   148
    The Construction of an Interest Group   149
    The Catalyst for Mobilization: From Class Identity to Class
    Formation   168
    Producer Mobilization and New Modes of Business Politics   178

7   Globalization, Business Politics, and Industrial Policy in
    Developing Countries   190
    Dismantling Protectionism and Business Politics beyond North
    Africa   194
    Business Politics and Industrial Development in the
    Contemporary World Economy   209

Appendix A: Methodological Note and List of Interviewees   219
Appendix B: Standardized Questionnaire for Textile and
Apparel Industrialists and Factory Managers   229
Bibliography   233
    Journals and Newspapers   233
    Government Publications   234
    Books, Articles, and Reports   234
Index   255

Tables and Figures

TABLES

1.1 Periodization of Global Economic Integration and Trade
    Liberalization in Morocco and Tunisia   *page* 10
1.2 Globalization and Business Collective Action: Theoretical
    Approaches and Predictions   15
1.3 Globalization, Preexisting Business–Government Relations,
    and Business Collective Action   22
2.1 Average Hourly Wage Rates for Apparel Assembly in Select
    Countries, 1980 and 1990 (in US$)   38

FIGURES

2.1 The Structure of the Apparel Supply Chain   27
2.2 Apparel Exports from Developing and Postsocialist
    Countries, 1970–2005   32
2.3 Exports as a Percentage of GDP in Tunisia and Morocco,
    1970–2005   33
3.1 Growth of Industrial Production and Exports in Tunisia,
    1971–1979   74
3.2 Factories in the Tunisian Textile Sector by Branch,
    1966–1978   75
4.1 Development of Apparel Manufacturing in Morocco,
    1983–1997   100
5.1 Trade Policy Preferences of Textile and Apparel
    Manufacturers in Tunisia   108

5.2 Lobbying Methods of Textile and Apparel Manufacturers
    in Tunisia   110
6.1 Trade Policy Preferences of Textile and Apparel
    Manufacturers in Morocco   160
6.2 Lobbying Methods of Textile and Apparel Manufacturers
    in Morocco   179
7.1 Total Apparel Exports – Morocco and Tunisia, Selected
    Years   214

Acknowledgments

This book could not have been completed without the guidance, support, and advice of many individuals and institutions in the United States and abroad. My advisors at the University of California, Berkeley, provided invaluable guidance throughout the research and writing of the dissertation and, later, book. Kiren Aziz Chaudhry was a great source of intellectual and political inspiration. Her support, critical perspective, and engagement in the project have taught me the meaning of the word "mentor." I am also deeply indebted to Ruth Berins Collier and Richard Walker, who brought their own areas of expertise and insights to improve the substance and framework of the project. At key moments, all three reminded me of the importance of this research and, more broadly, of what we do as scholars. The early input of Christopher Ansell was also important in helping me to hone in on some of the key issues raised in this research.

The encouragement and constructive criticism of many colleagues and friends shaped my ideas in fundamental ways. Julia Lynch and Lauren Morris MacLean provided feedback that went beyond the process of researching and writing this book. I am also grateful to Giovanni Capoccia, Andrew Schrank, Richard Snyder, and two anonymous reviewers for their extensive commentary on the manuscript and related projects. Others, too, offered valuable feedback on parts of the manuscript, including Regina Abrami, Michele Penner Angrist, Eva Bellin, Jim Clem, Neta Crawford, Bryan Daves, Jorge Dominguez, Rick Doner, Ken Foster, Jeffry Frieden, Patrick Heller, Yoshiko Herrera, Nahomi Ichino, Pauline Jones Luong, Jim Mahoney, Khalid Medani, Elliot Posner, Marsha Pripstein Posusney, Dietrich Rueschemeyer, Ben Ross Schneider, Ken Shadlen,

Eduardo Silva, Aseema Sinha, Hillel Soifer, Barbara Stallings, and Robert Vitalis. The thorough editorial work of Kris Rusch, as well as research assistance and suggestions by Fulya Apaydin, Akshay Krishnan, Hannah Weitzer, and Myungji Yang, improved the manuscript substantially. Portions of the arguments in this book have appeared elsewhere, notably in the journals *Comparative Politics, World Development*, and *Competition and Change*.

Numerous people and institutions in Morocco and Tunisia facilitated my field research. I am grateful for the assistance of Daoud Casewit and Saadia Maski at the Moroccan-American Commission for Educational and Cultural Exchange (MACECE), Thor Kuniholm at the Tangier-American Legation Museum (TALM), and Jeanne Mrad at the Centre d'Etudes Maghrébines à Tunis (CEMAT). My gratitude to Jeanne goes far beyond the logistical support provided by my affiliation with CEMAT. In Morocco, scholars from the University Hassan II in Casablanca and the University Mohamed V in Rabat, including Mohamed Saïd Saâdi, Abdelkader Berrada, Abdelhay Moudden, and Mouna Cherkaoui, provided important perspectives on my research and facilitated access to useful data sources. Sociologists, historians, and economists from the University of Tunis, notably Abdeljelil Bédoui, Mohamed Ben Romdhane, Lilia Ben Salem, Tahar Labib, Azzam Mahjoub, and Hédi Timoumi, generously offered their views and suggestions. I am also grateful to scholars at the Institut des Recherches sur le Maghreb Contemporain (IRMC) in Tunis for granting me access to their resources and sharing their expertise with me. Scholars of the Maghreb, notably Christopher Alexander, Miriam Catusse, Eric Gobe, Abdellah Hammoudi, Clement Henry, and Béatrice Hibou, also provided valuable introductions in Morocco and Tunisia, and I thank Hugh Roberts for introducing me to the region.

I am indebted to the hundreds of businesspeople, producer association officials, labor union leaders, workers, journalists, and government officials who agreed to be interviewed for my research. Overcoming suspicions about my true identity and intentions as well as fears about the consequences of their participation, these individuals generously provided the data that constitute the empirical foundations of the project. Although the leaderships of the Association Marocaine des Industries du Textile et de l'Habillement (AMITH) and the Fédération Nationale du Textile (FENATEX) were undoubtedly convinced that I was an undercover agent either for Gap International or the Central Intelligence Agency, officials from these organizations nonetheless provided essential access to their documentation and members. The strengths of the project stem from the insights of all of these individuals, while any errors are solely of my own commission.

Generous funding from several institutions allowed me to carry out the project. The International Predissertation Fellowship Program and the International Dissertation Research Fellowship of the Social Science Research Council, as well as the American Institute for Maghrib Studies, supported the overseas field research that constitutes the backbone of the project. Support from the Berkeley Fellowship and the Simpson Fellowship of the Institute for International Studies at the University of California, Berkeley, enabled me to synthesize and write up the findings. Grants from Brown University and the Academy Scholars Program at Harvard University gave me the resources and time to refine the manuscript, and it has been a pleasure to work with Lewis Bateman at Cambridge University Press.

Finally, John Cammett and Sandi Cooper, my parents, doubled as sources of moral support and critical academic assessment, and I thank them for helping me to keep the project in political perspective. For his encouragement, endurance of long separations, and delight at discovering new places, I thank Angelo.

Abbreviations

AKP	Adalet ve Kalkinma Partisi (Justice and Development Party, Turkish)
AMIT	Association Marocaine de l'Industrie du Textile
AMITH	Association Marocaine de l'Industrie du Textile et de l'Habillement
API	Agence pour la Promotion de l'Industrie
AT	*Admissions Temporaires*
ATC	Agreement on Textiles and Clothing
CEI	Confederation of Engineering Industry
CEPEX	Centre pour la Promotion des Exportations
CETTEX	Centre Technique du Textile
CGEM	Confédération Générale des Enterprises du Maroc
CII	Confederation of Indian Industry
CMPE	Centre Marocain pour la Promotion des Exportations
DEIK	Diş Ekonomik Ilişkiler Kurulu (Association of Foreign Economic Relations, Turkish)
DPP	Democratic Progressive Party
EC	European Community
EDI	Electronic Data Interchange
EPZ	Export Processing Zone
EU	European Union
EUAA	EU Association Agreement
FAMEX	Fonds d'Accès aux Marchés d'Exportations
FDI	Foreign Direct Investment
FENATEX	Fédération Nationale du Textile

FICCI	Federation of Indian Chambers of Commerce and Industry
FOMAN	Fonds National de la Mise à Niveau
FOPRODEX	Fonds de Promotions des Exportations
FOPRODI	Fond pour la Promotion du Developpement Industriel
FORTEX	Fonds de Soutien aux Entreprises du Secteur du Textile-Habillement
FRM	Floor-Ready Merchandise
GATT	General Agreement on Tariffs and Trade
GDP	Gross Domestic Product
IACE	Institut Arabe des Chef d'Entreprise
ICT	Information and Communication Technologies
ILO	International Labor Organization
IMF	International Monetary Fund
INC	Indian National Congress
ISI	Import-Substitution Industrialization
KMT	Kuomintang
LVE	*La Vie Economique*
MDS	Mouvement des Démocrates Socialistes
MFA	Multi-Fiber Agreement
MNC	Multinational Company
MNP	Mouvement National Populaire
MP	Mouvement Populaire
MUSIAD	Mustakil is Adanleri Dernegi (Turkish)
NAFTA	North American Free Trade Agreement
NTB	Nontariff Barrier
OADP	Organisation de l'Action Démocratique et Populaire
OCP	Office Chérfienne des Phosphates
ONA	Omnium Nord Africain
PJD	Party of Justice and Development
PMN	Programme pour la Mise à Niveau
PND	Parti National Démocratique
PPS	Parti du Progrés et du Socialisme
QR	Quick Response
RCD	Rassemblement Constitutionel Démocratique
RNI	Rassemblement National des Indépendants
SAP	Structural Adjustment Program
SFTC	Sectoral Foreign Trade Corporation
SICAF	Société d'Investissement du Capital Fixe
SITEX	Société Industrielle des Textiles (Tunisia)

SKU   Stock-Keeping Unit
TD   Tunisian Dinars
TUSIAD   Türk Sanayicileri ve Işadamlari Derneği (Association of
             Turkish Industrialists and Businessmen)
UC   Union Constitutionnelle
UCC   Uniform Commercial Code
UGTT   Union Générale des Travailleurs Tunisiens
UMT   Union Marocaine du Travail
UNESCWA   United Nations Economic and Social Commission for
             Western Asia
UNIDO   United Nations Industrial Development Organization
UPC   Universal Product Code
USFP   Union Socialistes des Forces Populaires
UTAC   Union Tunisienne de l'Artisanat et du Commerce
UTICA   Union Tunisienne de l'Industrie, du Commerce et de
             l'Artisanat
VETMA   Salon du Vêtement Marocain
WTO   World Trade Organization

Morocco. *Source*: Courtesy of the University of Texas Libraries, the University of Texas at Austin.

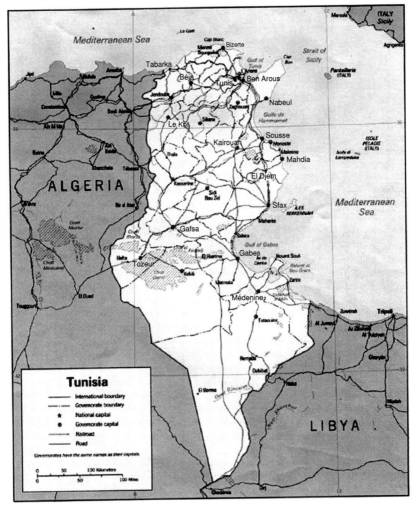

Tunisia. *Source*: Courtesy of the University of Texas Libraries, the University of Texas at Austin.

PART I

THE FRAMEWORK

I

Rethinking Globalization and Business Politics

> We asked [industry executives and retailers] their sourcing plans beyond 2005. The answer was they would source from China and not-China. They would source 70 percent to 80 percent from China and 20 percent to 30 percent from not-China. So, right there, you do not have globalization. You have China and the heart-stopping fear wondering whether your nation is to be one of the 20 percent or 30 percent in the land of not-China.
>
> Mike Todaro, Managing Director, American Apparel Producers' Network (Todaro 2003)

> In the past, I was well received by European clients, but now they give me "seven minutes." I am forced to wait in line with Indians, Pakistanis, Chinese, Asians to show my wares. Then I am given seven minutes to present my line and that's it.
>
> Author interview, textile firm owner, Ain Sebaa, Morocco, January 18, 2000.

These are hard times for manufacturers in developing countries, particularly for countries that are "not-China." Since the 1970s, more and more Asian, Latin American, and Middle Eastern countries have staked their industrial development strategies on exports of low-value-added manufactures such as apparel, making competition for world market share especially fierce. In the 1980s and 1990s, many countries were obliged to dismantle protectionist trade policies as part of structural adjustment programs (SAPs) and international trade agreements, threatening domestic manufacturing bases and pressuring local firms, business associations, and governments to find viable ways to promote industrial upgrading in an open economy. Most recently, the abrogation of the Multi-Fiber Agreement (MFA) in January 2005 has frightened producers and

policymakers throughout the developing world. The accord, which established a system of export quotas for developing country textile and apparel
exports, ensured access to lucrative U.S. and European markets for manufacturers in countries that otherwise could not compete against low-cost
Asian exports.

This book analyzes when and how business groups in developing countries mobilize collectively in response to global economic integration and
trade liberalization.[1] The book also examines the effects of business mobilization on domestic political economies: How can business mobilization
alter established patterns of business–government relations? How does
the nature of business–government linkages affect processes of industrial
upgrading?

Business in developing countries is often decried as parasitic and either
incapable of or unwilling to improve its productive potential because
of rent-seeking behavior or clientelist relations with state officials (Bates
1981; Bratton and van de Walle 1994; Callaghy 1984; Heydemann 2004;
Krueger 1974; Mamdani 1996). In other depictions, the state so thoroughly dominates economic life as owner of the means of production
or largest employer that little opportunity exists for private investment
(Waterbury 1991). Can integration in global markets help business groups
to mobilize collectively, achieve independent organizational bases, and
create more formal, institutionalized modes of business politics?[2] Understanding how producers in developing countries respond to economic
change and forge linkages to state agencies is critical, particularly in an
era when private-sector development is at the core of policy prescriptions
to promote competitiveness in world markets.[3]

---

[1] Business mobilization refers to collective action by private capital holders to lobby the
state for shared policy interests. Mobilization can take many forms, including establishing or strengthening formal producer associations, drafting and disseminating joint
position papers and policy statements, joining foreign chambers of commerce, meeting
with government officials in direct delegations, broadcasting policy goals and demands
through print and broadcast media, and controversial tactics such as waging coordinated campaigns to shut down factories or withhold taxes in protest of government
policies.

[2] The formalization of business representation refers to a shift in the formulation, aggregation, and transmission of business policy interests from individual, personalistic channels
to more transparent, regularized, and often group-based approaches.

[3] Private-sector development has become a key component of development thinking in
the World Bank and other international institutions and donor agencies (Schulpen and
Gibbon 2002, 1; World Bank 2002, 21–23). The approach calls for reduced state intervention in the economy, privatization, and an emphasis on market forces, all of which
demand a greater role for private provision of goods and services in developing economies

The experiences of manufacturers in Tunisia and Morocco are emblematic of the constraints facing producers in many developing countries beyond the Middle East. Since the 1980s, Tunisia, and later Morocco, carved out important places in the global apparel supply chain. In 1981, Tunisia was the ninth-largest apparel exporter to the European Union (EU), and Morocco did not even rank in the top twenty. By 1998, Tunisia ranked fourth and Morocco fifth in the list of top apparel exporters to the EU, the world's largest importer of both textiles and apparel (Gibbon 2000; Stengg 2001). But trade liberalization, the adoption of bilateral free trade agreements with the EU, and the dismantling of the MFA threaten the very existence of domestic and export-oriented firms in these countries. How have Tunisian and Moroccan producers responded to economic change?

Tunisia and Morocco are well matched for comparing private-sector responses to globalization. The two countries share a history of French colonization, common linkages to international markets, and a predominance of the same manufacturing industries, including textiles, apparel, footwear, food processing, light electronics, and chemical processing.[4] Both countries conduct over 70 percent of their trade with Western Europe;[5] agriculture, agribusiness, and phosphate mining are crucial components of their national economies (while neither country is a significant petroleum exporter); the industrial sector generates over 30 percent of gross domestic product (GDP);[6] and the textile and apparel industries account for over 40 percent of industrial goods exports (European Commission 2004). Further, Tunisia and Morocco had parallel experiences of integration in the international economy and underwent comparable episodes of economic liberalization. In the mid-1980s, both adopted an

and involve more than promoting firms and private investment through targeted incentives. The state remains critical for private-sector development by promoting an attractive "business climate," regulating transactions and upholding "good governance," or a commitment to transparency and accountability in administrative procedures and economic management, but the approach emphasizes private initiative in driving growth and reducing poverty (Klein and Hadjimichael 2003, 8; OECD 1995, 10; World Bank 2002, 4). What private-sector–led development means in practice, however, is not obvious, in part because its goals are formulated abstractly and in part because there is no single recipe for developing the private sector (Schulpen and Gibbon 2002, 4; World Bank 2002 [April 9, 2002], 4; World Bank 2003, 159–60).

4 Both countries achieved independence from France in 1956.
5 In 2001, 79.8 percent of Tunisian exports and 72.4 percent of Moroccan exports went to the EU (Eurostat 2003).
6 In 2004, the industrial sector accounted for 35.7 percent of GDP in Morocco and 30.7 percent of GDP in Tunisia (CIA World Factbook 2005).

SAP and signed the General Agreement on Tariffs and Trade (GATT) accords; and in the mid-1990s, both established nearly identical bilateral free trade agreements with the European Union, called the EU Association Agreements (EUAA).[7] Tunisia and Morocco also confronted similar economic environments: as they liberalized, European manufacturers intensified international subcontracting relationships to cut costs, providing ample opportunities for North African businesspeople to participate in global manufacturing chains.

Given comparable relationships to world markets and liberalization experiences, standard trade theory would predict that Tunisian and Moroccan manufacturers would organize similar struggles over economic liberalization: exporters would support trade liberalization in order to gain access to cheaper, higher-quality inputs on world markets, whereas domestic, import-substituting manufacturers would oppose liberalization to block foreign competition. But this prediction has not been borne out. In fact, Tunisian and Moroccan business responses to economic change varied markedly. Tunisian industrialists avoided collective lobbying efforts, instead focusing on firm-based upgrading or exit strategies, and conveyed policy preferences largely through informal channels. As a result, the state-dominated system of economic policymaking, in which firms were, by and large, "policy takers" and the state preemptively forged industrial policy, remained relatively stable in Tunisia. In contrast, Moroccan producers organized powerful collective lobbying efforts through producer associations and increasingly expressed policy goals through public channels such as the media and regularly scheduled official business–government meetings. Collective action brought about shifts in modes of Moroccan business politics in the 1990s. New forms of business representation and business–government relations permitted expanded access to economic opportunities for a larger segment of industrial capital holders. At the same time, formal business associations became increasingly important sites of business mobilization. These were notable shifts in a system renowned for crony capitalist ties between the state and a small elite that controls vast holdings in multiple sectors of the economy. What explains the varied responses of Tunisian and Moroccan industrialists in the same economic sectors to similar experiences of trade liberalization and integration in global manufacturing chains?

I argue that material interests drove the distinct responses of Tunisian and Moroccan industrialists to global economic integration, and

---

7 In March 2004, Morocco signed a free trade agreement with the United States, and Tunisia is presently negotiating a similar accord.

that these interests were shaped by varied historical patterns of business–government relations constituted during postindependence state-building processes and consolidated in the 1970s. Industrialists in the two countries had similar policy preferences, but how they acted on these preferences was contingent on their expectations about state responses to business mobilization, perceptions of state support for their interests, and their perceptions about whether other factions of the industrial class posed credible threats to their interests.

Business responses to global economic integration and trade liberalization vary according to two constitutive dimensions of business–government relations: first, the balance of power between business and the state before economic opening, and second, preexisting business class structure. These two dimensions combine to form different configurations of business–government relations. I focus on two possible configurations, "distant" and "close" business–government relations. Distant business–government relations result from a combination of state dominance in the business–government power relationship and dispersed capital structure, or low capital concentration. The two constitutive dimensions of business–government relations are distinct yet interrelated because state dominance may foster or perpetuate a dispersed capital structure. Close business–government relations arise when business penetrates state decision-making channels and when states do not control capital (while capital is concentrated). These two conditions are conceptually distinct, yet in practice they are often correlated because a concentrated private elite is more likely to penetrate state decision-making processes. This typology of business–government relations can be applied to other logical combinations beyond the distant and close ideal types. For example, capital concentration and business dominance in the business–government power relationship do not necessarily correspond. State dominance can coexist with a concentrated capital structure, as in the case of pre-democratic South Korea.[8] Understanding the distant and close configurations of business–government relations requires more attention to both constitutive dimensions.

Two factors shape the business–government balance of power: state control over business and business penetration of the state. States can control business political behavior through repression or incentives, or "sticks" and "carrots" (Collier and Collier 1979). Sticks include outright repression through force or coercion, or indirect approaches such as threatening tax audits, applying laws arbitrarily, fabricating violations

---

[8] Kang (2002) refers to this kind of business–government relationship as "mutual hostage."

of official regulations, and using smear tactics such as exposing real or fictitious improprieties on the part of firm owners and their family members. While such coercive or arbitrary tactics are relatively uncommon in most advanced, industrialized countries, they are still used in many developing or postsocialist countries.[9] Carrots include incentives that provide benefits to firms such as tax exemptions, access to subsidized credit, or participation in policymaking or advisory councils, which can have both symbolic and material benefits for firms and industries. Carrots may reflect a state strategy of preempting or undercutting business opposition or, put differently, of buying business political quiescence.

But states do not solely determine the business–government balance of power. Business penetration of the state can limit state capacity or motivation to control business political behavior. In many developing countries, state-builders established close alliances or overlapped substantially with private capital holders, enabling economic elites to shape policies through personal ties to officials or by holding public office themselves. In these instances, public and private actors are not strictly separable and instead ties between state officials and an elite faction of private capital holders are close.

Pre-reform capital structure also shapes the level and mode of business collective action. I focus on two broad configurations of capital structure: dispersed and concentrated. Where private capital structure is dispersed throughout the economy and the state has not privileged one faction of industrialists over another, I argue that business collective action is less likely. What is the logic of this expectation? Integration in global production networks and trade liberalization increases incentives to invest in the export sector. In political economies where states ensure that capital is dispersed throughout the economy and across the export and domestic markets, further integration into the global economy and trade liberalization reinforces and expands the existing exporter class. State sponsorship of the export and import-substitution industrialization (ISI) sectors undercuts the organizational foundations for collective business lobbying.[10] Relatedly, evenhanded state policies toward the two spheres of the

---

[9] A well-known contemporary example is the imprisonment of the Russian oil tycoon Michael Khodorkovsky by the government of President Vladimir Putin, allegedly in response to Khodorkovsky's political ambitions.

[10] The argument applies to political economies where the state fostered industrial class development and sponsored the rise of an export class. In some semiopen economies with long-standing coexistent export and ISI sectors, exporters used private capital amassed in other sectors, such as agriculture, to launch export ventures. For example, in the

economy preempt the construction of privileged ties between the state and a particular faction of the industrial class, reducing the chance that business groups will mobilize collectively against each other's demands. Because industrialists do not mobilize to pursue policy interests, they do not spur shifts in established patterns of business–government relations.

Where capital structure is concentrated and domestically oriented industrialists enjoy tight relations with the state, I argue that trade liberalization and global economic integration induce collective business mobilization. These patterns of class structure and business–government relations are typical of countries that pursued classic ISI development strategies, in which the discretionary distribution of production and import licenses tended to create privileged domestic bourgeoisies with close ties to state officials (Bruton 1998; Waterbury 1994; Waterbury 1999). Close links between ISI elites and the state establish the context for conflict among industrialists. With trade liberalization and increased incentives to participate in global manufacturing chains, an export class arises. Where this new export class is sociologically distinct from existing protectionist elites who, historically, have monopolized local economic opportunities and have cultivated close ties with top political officials, new exporters feel marginalized.[11] A shared sense of marginalization forms the basis of a collective identity in opposition to ISI elites, facilitating group mobilization to promote liberalization and gain access to economic opportunities. Collective action is likely to occur through formal business associations because these relatively new capital holders are not part of established, clientelist networks of privilege (Shadlen 2004). In turn, group mobilization by exporters can spur a reaction from ISI elites.

A clear periodization of economic liberalization is essential to understanding the historical development of distant and close business–government relations in Tunisia and Morocco, respectively, and parallels the experiences of other developing countries (Chaudhry 1994; Frieden 1981; Haggard 1990; Kahler 1985). I divide processes of economic opening

Dominican Republic (Schrank 2005) and Mauritius (Alladin 1993; Bowman 1991; Darga 1998; Gibbon 2000; Nathan Associates 2003), agricultural elites used their own capital to diversify into manufactured exports and therefore were less indebted to the state.

[11] This argument rests on the premise that exporters are, by and large, sociologically distinct from domestic economic elites. I do not expect the argument to hold in places where ISI elites dominate export sectors as they divest from activities targeting the local market. Instead, the claims are most relevant where ISI elites continue to focus on holdings in domestic sectors or where they favor export sectors or services with high barriers to entry, which most small investors cannot penetrate.

TABLE 1.1. *Periodization of Global Economic Integration and Trade Liberalization in Morocco and Tunisia*

Country	Pre-Liberalization (1970s)	Liberalization I (1980s)	Liberalization II (1990s)
Morocco	Protected (ISI)	Semiopen: Parallel export and ISI sectors	Deepened liberalization
Tunisia	Semiopen: Parallel export and ISI sectors	Semiopen: Expanded export sector	Deepened liberalization

into three distinct moments during the latter half of the twentieth century: Pre-Liberalization, Liberalization I, and Liberalization II. Tunisia and Morocco began the liberalization process from different starting points and adopted distinct trajectories, as table 1.1 depicts.

In the first period, which prevailed roughly from the 1950s through the 1970s, divergent patterns of business class formation were consolidated in the two countries. In Tunisia, the state established a semiopen economy, which consisted of two parallel economic spheres with separate legal and fiscal regulatory regimes: export processing zones (EPZs), often referred to as "off-shore" zones, and an insulated domestic market, or the "on-shore" economy. By the late 1960s, given the limits of Tunisia's small domestic market, policymakers were convinced of the need for an export orientation. In Morocco, the state instituted classic ISI policies, consolidating and expanding the holdings of urban commercial and proto-industrial elites.

The first phase of liberalization occurred in the 1980s in large part as a response to the Debt Crisis, which forced many developing countries to undertake SAPs that compelled a measure of trade and financial liberalization (Frieden 1981; Kahler 1985). In this period, liberalization was not as far-reaching as international financial institutions and other advocates had hoped, and many economies remained substantially closed, especially with respect to key sectors of the economy.[12] In Tunisia, liberalization in the 1980s reinforced the preexisting semiopen economy, allowing the domestic market to remain substantially protected while giving

---

[12] This is not to deny the very real impact of economic liberalization, especially on the poor and middle classes. "Bread riots" in various parts of the developing world during the 1980s and beyond attest to the effects of dismantling food subsidies and other measures as part of structural adjustment.

a further boost to export activities. For Morocco, the initial liberalization phase institutionalized a dual market system with parallel on-shore
and off-shore economies, establishing a new class of exporters alongside
traditional ISI elites.[13]

In the second phase of liberalization, which began in the 1990s, many
developing countries deepened their commitments to global economic
integration in large part through participation in bilateral and multilateral
trade agreements. A new round of regional free trade agreements linked
industrialized and developing countries, including the North American
Free Trade Agreement (NAFTA) in 1994 and the Euro-Mediterranean
Association Agreements between the European Union and the Middle
East/North Africa region following the Barcelona Declaration of 1995. In
addition, developing countries signed on to the WTO Accords en masse
beginning in the mid-1990s, committing themselves to marked reductions
in trade barriers. The first two phases of market construction in the 1970s
and 1980s established distinct industrial class structures in Tunisia and
Morocco, setting the stage for varied business responses to deepened liberalization and global economic integration in the 1990s.

How do the two constitutive dimensions of business–government relations just outlined illuminate divergent patterns of business mobilization in the 1990s in Tunisia and Morocco? Variation in the business–
government power relationship shaped producer beliefs about the viability of and need for collective action. Both Tunisia and Morocco are aptly
characterized as authoritarian, but the Tunisian state brooks little independent opposition (even from its allies in the business community) and
has provided extensive fiscal and regulatory incentives to firms in both the
ISI and export sectors since the 1970s. State repression and preemptive
provision of economic incentives, as in Tunisia, decrease the chances of
business collective action. In Morocco, the penetration of state decision-
making channels by a domestic elite meant that collective action by business interests, at least through formal organizations, was rarely needed
until a new export class emerged during waves of liberalization in the
1980s and 1990s.

Capital structure and perceived ties between the state and segments of
the industrial class also molded the interests and strategies of Tunisian and

---

[13] In Morocco, the categories of ISI and export elites were not purely distinct in both
their sociological and economic dimensions. Some established ISI elites diversified their
portfolios by investing in export activities. Nonetheless, trade liberalization and increased
opportunities in global markets encouraged new investors to emerge, particularly in
activities with low barriers to entry, such as apparel.

Moroccan industrialists. In a political economy dominated by ISI elites with close ties to the state, as in Morocco, exporters felt marginalized and therefore were compelled to mobilize collectively to defend shared interests. In Tunisia, which was characterized by capital dispersion and evenhanded state support for different segments of the private sector, industrialists faced lower incentives to act collectively.

These divergent patterns of capital structure arose from variations in the importance of wealthy, urban elites in the anticolonial struggle as well as in domestic market size, which shaped official perceptions about the viability of pursuing ISI after independence.[14] In Tunisia, a repressive, single-party state emerged after independence that closely controlled interest-group representation. At the same time, state policies increasingly anticipated the interests of diverse segments of the industrial class by setting up a semiopen economy in which the domestic market was protected alongside an off-shore export sector. Between 1972 and 1974, industrial policies forged a bifurcated industrial class, in which import-substituting and export-oriented investors enjoyed relatively equal treatment. Furthermore, legal regulations inhibited the rise of multisectoral holding companies, deterring capital concentration in the local private sector. Tunisia's dispersed capital structure and state sponsorship of the postindependence industrial class resulted from two primary factors: first, the small size of the domestic market, which had convinced policymakers by the late 1960s of the need to pursue export markets; and second, struggles around state- and market-building in the transition to independence, in which large commercial capital holders and elite families were marginalized.[15] During waves of trade liberalization in the 1980s and 1990s, industrialists from both the export and domestic sectors looked to the state to defend their interests and did not regard each other as obstacles to their policy interests, undercutting the impulse to organize independently.[16]

In Morocco, the monarchy tolerated more expression of dissent and permitted the rise of multiple political parties and interest groups

---

[14] I view industrial class structure as a product of postindependence state sponsorship as well as historical legacies of struggles around state- and market-building in the transition to independent statehood. Thus, the arguments may be more relevant to Africa, the Middle East, and parts of Asia, where postcolonial states fostered the rise of local industrial classes, than to Latin America, where business groups were well established when states introduced ISI policies (Schneider 2005, 203).

[15] See Katzenstein (1985) on outward orientation in the small economies of Europe.

[16] Bellin (2002) makes a similar argument in her discussion of state sponsorship of business in Tunisia.

(although most were co-opted by the state). Thus, when trade liberalization in the 1980s gave rise to a new class of small exporters in industries with low barriers to entry such as apparel assembly, these emergent exporters had the opportunity to mobilize politically. But successful collective action is founded on more than the *possibility* for mobilization. To act collectively, apparel exporters from diverse social origins first needed a shared class identity, or an awareness of common interests and a commitment to work together to pursue these interests. For new exporters, the belief that a well-connected elite – whose diverse holdings included import-substituting firms in the textile sector – blocked their interests was an important catalyst for group-based mobilization. Mobilization arose out of a shared sense of marginalization in a political economy in which big business groups had constructed close ties to the palace and other key decision-making sites in the state apparatus since independence. Morocco's concentrated capital structure arose from the fact that wealthy, urban elites played a key role in the nationalist movement, compelling the postindependence monarchy to reward them with protectionist policies. Furthermore, policymakers also believed that the national market was sufficiently large to sustain an ISI development strategy.[17]

THE THEORY: POLITICAL OPPORTUNITIES, CLASS IDENTITY, AND THE SOCIAL FOUNDATIONS OF BUSINESS COLLECTIVE ACTION

Despite the importance of understanding business politics for understanding larger questions of political and economic change, we know surprisingly little about how business actually responds to globalization in

---

[17] Labor peace is critical for participation in global manufacturing chains; high levels of labor mobilization could compel manufacturers to organize collectively. On the surface, labor activism was greater in Morocco than in Tunisia and therefore could have contributed to varied patterns of business collective action in the two countries. But official strike data suggest that labor activism is comparable, particularly since the late 1980s, and in many years the International Labor Organization (ILO) recorded substantially more strikes in Tunisia than in Morocco (ILO, *Yearbook of Labor Statistics*, various years). More importantly, given the limits of official data, laws and actual implementation vary widely, and discussions with Tunisian and Moroccan firm owners and labor leaders in the labor-intensive apparel sector indicate that unions and workers are active in both countries, despite legal and regulatory differences. Employers in Morocco routinely flout labor laws, while workers frequently engage in wildcat strikes (appendix A: I-40M; I-75M; I-81M; I-86M; I-87M; I-99M; I-100M; I-101M; I-111M; I-115M; I-66T; I-71T; I-73T; I-74T; I-76T; I-78T; I-79T; I-80T).

developing countries.[18] In the new development orthodoxy, the private sector is expected to take greater responsibility for national investment and development, but business mobilization is not automatic. Thus, to understand the impact of globalization on business politics requires a close analysis of the politics of collective action in the private sector.

Political mobilization requires the construction of alliances or coalitions among groups of otherwise disparate individuals, whether organized through formal institutions or informal social networks. What are the foundations of these alliances? My political-sociological approach builds on the literature of globalization and domestic politics, which comprises diverse understandings of how social actors aggregate in response to opportunities and constraints from integration in global markets. Table 1.2 depicts the predictions of different theoretical approaches to business collective action and assesses them against empirical evidence from the Moroccan and Tunisian cases.

Models that emphasize the economic determinants of political responses to globalization provide a useful initial explanation by predicting that trade orientation (Frieden and Rogowski 1996) or barriers to entry found in distinct industrial activities (Shafer 1994) shape producer preferences vis-à-vis trade policy and capacity to organize for or against economic reform. Selecting the same industrial sectors (textiles and apparel) facilitates a test of sectoral models. I chose these sectors because of their importance to the national development strategies of most developing countries in the contemporary world economy and because of their weight in both the Tunisian and Moroccan economies. In 1998, soon after Tunisia signed the EU Agreement, textiles and apparel generated 39 percent of industrial employment, 55 percent of industrial exports, and 25 percent of industrial production in Tunisia (Gherzi Organisation 1999, iii). Likewise, in Morocco, the combined textile and clothing industries represented 40 percent of employment in the industrial sector, 37 percent of total exports, and 15 percent of industrial production (Economist Intelligence Unit 1998, 32). Sectoral models, whether based on trade orientation or production characteristics, generate testable predictions about industrialist reactions to trade liberalization. In many developing countries, the textile sector targets the local market almost exclusively, while

---

[18] Chapter 7 explores the implications of business collective action for industrial development. Another body of research, which I do not address in this analysis, problematizes the role of business, and particularly the industrial bourgeoisie, in driving (or not driving) political liberalization (Bellin 2002; Luebbert 1991; Moore 1965; Rueschemeyer, Stephens, and Stephens 1992).

TABLE 1.2. *Globalization and Business Collective Action: Theoretical Approaches and Predictions*

Theoretical Approach	Predictions	Empirical Anomalies
Sectoral I (trade orientation)	Exporters (apparel): Pro-liberalization	Different cross-national collective action (CA) patterns in same industries
	ISI producers (textiles): anti-liberalization	Mechanism of group formation Firm-level preferences v. interest-group behavior
Sectoral II (industry characteristics/ barriers to entry [BTE]	High BTE/concentrated capital (textiles): CA	Different cross-national CA patterns in same industries
	Low BTE/dispersed capital (apparel): no CA	Mechanics of group formation
Varieties of capitalism/historical institutionalism	Close business–government relations (BGR):	Static national models
	Big ISI capital blocks reform/small firms not organized Distant BGR: state control, low business CA	Global economic change and domestic institutional change/class formation

the apparel sector, dominated by subcontractors who assemble apparel for overseas clients as well as foreign direct investment, is overwhelmingly export-oriented. In general terms, apparel exporters were the "winners" and textile producers were the "losers" when most developing countries undertook trade liberalization. A trade-based globalization model (Frieden and Rogowski 1996) would predict antiglobalization lobbying by textile producers and pro-liberalization lobbying by apparel manufacturers. A model based on asset characteristics (Shafer 1994) would predict greater collective action in the textile sector, which is a comparatively capital-intensive activity with higher barriers to entry, and hence fewer investors, than in apparel assembly, which has lower barriers to entry and thus more investors.

Sectoral approaches fail to capture cross-national (and subnational) variation in business responses to analogous economic changes and do not adequately theorize processes of collective action. As seen in the cases of Morocco and Tunisia, analogous business groups display varied cross-national responses to parallel liberalization experiences in the same industrial sectors. Furthermore, variants of sectoral approaches are grounded in an Olsonian logic of collective action (Olson 1965) and therefore cannot explain how successful collective action arises among numerous, small-scale subcontractors, as occurred in Morocco.[19] The capacity of business to launch collective lobbying efforts is contingent on political or institutional factors, such as the availability of organizational channels through which to aggregate and convey collective interests, the existence of informal public–private networks that facilitate information exchange, and, at the most basic level, whether the business–government power relationship affords the opportunity for social mobilization.

Institutionalist models of national responses to global economic change (Berger and Dore 1996; Hall 1986; Hollingworth and Boyer 1998; Vogel 1996; Zysman 1983), most recently developed in the literature on "varieties of capitalism" (Hall and Soskice 2001), offer a richer understanding of how context-specific institutions, understood as laws, regulatory frameworks, organizations, and established patterns of state–society linkages, shape individual preferences and interests. Such approaches emphasize that preferences cannot be deduced from economic profiles. Instead, national institutions constrain the choices available to policymakers and social actors, leading to variation in both the preferences and political behavior of business groups in response to similar global economic constraints and opportunities (Hall and Taylor 1996; Immergut 1998; Thelen and Steinmo 1992). Institutionalist approaches would correctly predict different cross-national private-sector responses to economic change based on distinct pre-reform institutional configurations. For example, in Morocco, institutionalist models might highlight how established elite networks of state–business interests constructed during the period of ISI development would attempt to block economic reform. Conversely, given the absence of effective associations, institutionalist models might accurately predict little business collective action in Tunisia in response to economic liberalization.

But institutionalist accounts, which are primarily based on evidence from advanced, industrialized countries, tend to downplay the transformative effects of global economic integration and neglect the international sources of domestic institutional change (Chaudhry 1993; 1997). Historically constituted patterns of state–society relations can evolve, as the emerging literature on institutional change suggests (Streeck and Thelen

---

[19] For a critique and reformulation of Olson's framework, see Oliver (1988).

2005). For developing countries, many of which undertook economic liberalization programs, the structure, interests, and political strategies of
private capital holders may shift, in turn altering the institutional context
in which they operate. Institutionalist approaches premised on the dura-
bility of national institutions cannot adequately account for the emergence
of new producer groups and new patterns of state–society relations, as
seen in Morocco, where new export entrepreneurs organized an effective
lobbying group and compelled shifts in established patterns of business–
government relations.

Models based on advanced, industrialized varieties of capitalism also
minimize the role of state repression and co-optation in shaping business responses to economic change (Schneider 2005).[20] The developing
world hosts more authoritarian regimes than are found among industrialized countries, facilitating a state's capacity to coerce and co-opt business
elites. Through direct tactics, such as the threat of coercion, and indirect
channels, including selective incentives such as participation in government commissions or tax breaks, the state can shape the policy interests of
business and its ability to respond to economic change. Statist institutionalist frameworks therefore provide a useful correction to institutionalist
models based on the industrialized West.

Statist models of business responses to economic change in the developing world highlight how state "carrots and sticks" mold the capacity
and motivation of business to organize collectively (Bellin 2002; Schneider 2005). Such approaches, however, do not sufficiently explore how
features of the private sector itself shape collective action by business.
The capacity of business to mobilize collectively is also contingent on the
strategies that businesspeople use to organize through new or existing
institutions, as well as their beliefs about the capacity of other business
groups with opposing policy preferences to hinder the pursuit of their
interests. Business politics and business–government relations are the
product of historical *interactions*. In Morocco and Tunisia, postindependence industrial class structure and business ties to public officials emerged
out of earlier struggles over state-building during and after colonialism.
These struggles created enduring institutional legacies in the form of state
policies, regulations, and patterns of interest-group representation that

---

[20] As the concept of coordinated-market economies in the varieties of capitalism literature
shows (Hall and Soskice 2001), states also shape business responses to economic change
in advanced, industrialized countries, but the nature of business–government ties and
methods of influencing business politics can vary.

set the parameters for the capacity (or incapacity) of businesses to act collectively.[21]

Collective action is at the heart of business responses to global economic integration. Yet analyses of how globalization affects domestic politics have largely overlooked the internal mechanics of business mobilization. By pointing to three variables that interact to bring out mass collective action, including "political opportunities," "mobilizing structures," and "framing" (McAdam 1999; McAdam, McCarthy, and Zald 1996, ch. 1; McAdam, Tarrow, and Tilly 2001), the literature on social movements provides a useful starting point. Studies of business politics emphasize the first two factors. Political opportunities are central to studies of how political regimes organize state–society relations in corporatist structures (Collier and Collier 1991; Schmitter 1974) and to analyses of how state incentives shape the organization of business groups and their ability to contribute to national economic development (Evans 1995; Schneider 2005). But a state-centric approach based on political opportunities provides a partial account. The rules and structure governing and organizing business representation are also a product of private-sector initiatives (Moore 2001; Moore 2004; Shadlen 2002). Still, focusing on the intricacies of associational politics does not address how businesspeople form groups in the first place. Explanations based on political opportunities and mobilizing structures still leave questions unanswered about *how* manufacturers actually mobilize.

I argue that struggles among different groups within the industrial class that have varying ties to the state are key to understanding distinct cross-national patterns of business politics. *By establishing the context for the rise of oppositional class identities, the sociological origins of diverse segments of industrial capital shape collective private-sector responses to economic opening.* Before mobilizing collectively, firm owners and managers must think of themselves as a group with mutual interests. In Morocco, a shared sense that "fat cats" in the textile sector, who had benefited from decades of protectionism, were blocking the policy goals of "self-made men" in the export-oriented apparel assembly industry constituted the basis of a group identity rooted in shared material interests and facilitated collective action among firm owners from diverse social backgrounds. Most studies of business politics explicitly or implicitly presume that capital holders possess and perceive shared economic interests and

---

[21] Schrank (2006) and Waldner (2003) critique institutionalist accounts of the political economy of development for neglecting the social foundations of institutions.

therefore collective action is not difficult to achieve. However, how people view their economic interests and circumstances cannot be deduced a priori (Herrera 2005). Of course, economic gain is the ultimate objective of most business lobbying, but the profit motive does not automatically create collegiality. Not all producers who ostensibly share the same economic interests choose to work together toward common goals (Bowman 1989).

In distinct ways, the literatures on class formation and social movements emphasize the importance of "groupness." Classes do not automatically emerge from the structure of production (Thompson 1963). How members of a class perceive their social position is a critical intervening step.[22] Individual interpretations of material conditions, a process shaped by class "dispositions" (Katznelson 1986), determine whether and how people act as a group. Through the development of a shared group identity, individuals are able to overcome differences that might otherwise prevent them from collaborating toward shared goals (Beckert 2001).[23] Thus, it is difficult to speak of innate or objective group interests – even for seemingly straightforward issues such as trade policy – and actual political behavior does not always reflect stated actor preferences.

For these reasons, it is analytically useful to distinguish between "preferences," or the individual views of social actors, and "interests," or publicly expressed goals collectively pursued through formal or informal political channels (Immergut 1997, 339). As chapters 5 and 6 detail, Tunisian and Moroccan industrialists articulated similar policy preferences on trade policies but translated these preferences into organized interests in distinct ways. Firm-level interviews with Tunisian and Moroccan textile manufacturers and apparel exporters largely confirmed the predictions of basic sectoral models regarding trade policy preferences. Textile manufacturers, who arose and flourished in the context of protective trade regimes in both countries, opposed economic liberalization. The progressive erosion of the sheltered national market would logically compel them to agitate for delayed implementation of tariff cuts, if not total abrogation of free trade agreements. Conversely, apparel assemblers,

---

[22] Recall Marx's famous distinction between a "class in itself" and a "class for itself." Class analysis is increasingly being contested in the face of non–class-based politics (Crompton 1993; Sayer and Walker 1992; Wright 1997) but retains important insights for many social phenomena and particularly for studies of how globalization affects social structures and institutions.

[23] See also the social movement's literature on "framing" (Deaux and Reid 2000; Gamson 1992; Klandermans and deWeerd 2000; McAdam et al. 1996; Melucci 1989; Snow and Benford 1992; Snow et al. 1986; Snow and McAdam 2000; Stryker 2000).

who succeeded as a result of increased subcontracting opportunities with European buyers as well as the creation of duty-free zones, favored trade liberalization and, accordingly, would be expected to support tariff reductions. Yet, despite nearly identical preferences articulated by analogous producers, Moroccan and Tunisian industrialist behaviors differed.[24] A key faction of Moroccan textile manufacturers organized powerful lobbying efforts to stave off liberalization, and apparel manufacturers organized effectively to block the antireform efforts of the protectionist textile lobby.

Group interest formulation, an important step toward collective action, is ultimately an interactive, collective process that depends heavily on how issues are framed (Campbell 1997; Dopfer 1994; Miller 1998). Beliefs about how the actions of other industrialists will affect the chances of realizing one's policy goals, which are likely to vary cross-nationally, may compel actors with the same "objective" policy preferences to adopt different strategies toward the same problem. For example, in Tunisia, exporters did not view local industrialists as a significant antiliberalization lobbying bloc and furthermore viewed the state as an ally, obviating the perceived need for collective action. Conversely, "self-made" Moroccan export subcontractors viewed domestic producers as an obstacle to deepened integration in global production chains because of a history of close ties between ISI elites and the state. This compelled collective action among exporters in pursuit of shared pro-liberalization policy interests.[25] If individuals are the building blocks in models of institutional creation and change (Hall and Soskice 2001; Katznelson 2003; North 1990; Pierson 2000), then strategies for adjustment to economic change and policy outcomes can vary markedly when analogous actors adopt divergent interests.

Leadership and organizations inevitably play a key role in fostering and disseminating group identity and interests. Ideas do not spread spontaneously, and "objective" material conditions alone do not create class behavior or even consciousness (Gramsci 1995, 181). Working through organizations such as the Moroccan textile and apparel association, leaders create group consciousness. Leadership is all the more important when individuals lack preexisting social networks or overlapping organizational memberships, as was the case for many Moroccan apparel subcontractors.

---

[24] Appendix A includes the list of interviewees and a short note on the interview methodology, and appendix B provides the questionnaire that guided the interviews.

[25] Furthermore, interaction with other producers, particularly from other industries, may compel industrialists to reevaluate their prior assumptions, enabling them to develop new perspectives on adjustment to economic opening (Campbell 1997, 17–18).

To create the group consciousness needed for collective action, leaders with agendas promote images and ideas that resonate with members of a potential group (Young 1976).

Group identity is often forged in opposition to others through a reactive process of group differentiation (Kocka 1981). Awareness of distinct relationships to material changes can generate a discourse of "self" versus "other," such as the opposition of self-made men versus fat cats in Morocco, which fosters cohesion among the bearers of these identities. To be sure, the construction of a group identity alone does not explain collective action. After achieving the requisite "groupness," members of a collectivity need organizational tools – whether in the form of formal interest associations or informal social networks – as well as a political environment that provides a modicum of civil liberties. Thus, group identity does not supplant institutional factors as a source of business mobilization, such as state policies or associational structure. But forging a group identity is a critical yet overlooked explanation for group formation and mobilization in response to global economic integration.

Processes of constructing group identity vary by context. I distinguish between modes of business collective identity formation in places where a concentrated economic elite emerged and established close ties with the state, such as Morocco, and contexts where capital is more dispersed and the state did not privilege one segment of the industrial class over another, such as Tunisia. Table 1.3 depicts the progression of the argument.

In Morocco, import-substituting industrialists enjoyed an increasingly privileged position in the postindependence political economy thanks to the role of urban bourgeois interests in the nationalist movement and subsequent efforts by the monarchy to buy their support. The size of the domestic market also influenced this outcome: policymakers believed that the national market was sufficiently large to sustain an ISI development strategy; in domestic protected economies with dominant ISI elites, cleavages between domestic producers and exporters are particularly acute. The initial round of economic liberalization in the 1980s and integration in global manufacturing circuits (Liberalization I) created a *new* class of export-oriented subcontractors linked to global manufacturing chains. This first phase of economic opening institutionalized a dual market system in which the domestic and export spheres remained separate and the local market was sheltered from export or foreign penetration. To boost their competitiveness in world markets, exporters then began to press for more comprehensive dismantling of protective trade barriers and, as a result, tensions built up between domestic and export producers.

TABLE 1.3. *Globalization, Preexisting Business–Government Relations, and Business Collective Action*

T_0: Colonial Legacies	T_1: Postindependence Configuration of Business–Government Relations (BGR)	T_2: Liberalization	T_3: Political Dynamics of Economic Opening	T_4: Business Responses to Economic Opening
Elites marginalized in anticolonial movement	Distant BGR	Existing class structure reinforced; expanded export class	State-controlled adjustment, producers reliant on state	Low collective action
Small national market	Dispersed capital structure			
Elites central to anticolonial movement	Close BGR	New export class	Oppositional producer–group identities	High collective action
Big national market	Concentrated capital structure			

Paradoxically, the very existence of an entrenched ISI elite and the *perception* that it wielded undue influence on policymaking galvanized emergent exporters to push forcefully for fuller economic opening. Collective action, first initiated by exporters, ultimately produced more vocal and well-structured "developmental" business associations, and the Moroccan private sector became an important proponent of industrial upgrading based on clustering and sectoral integration.[26]

In Tunisia, where capital was more dispersed and the state cultivated coexistent domestic and export sectors, the politics of trade liberalization unfolded differently. A strong ISI class did not emerge, while exporters achieved a firm foothold in the domestic political economy before the

---

[26] "Developmental" business associations help firms to upgrade production, facilitate the resolution of collective action problems among firms, push the state to improve public goods such as infrastructure and reduce corruption, help members to gain access opportunities on international markets, and generally avoid particularistic lobbying (Doner and Schneider 2000).

government committed to economic liberalization programs with international financial institutions in a second phase of liberalization in the 1990s. The first round of liberalization merely reinforced the semiopen system and therefore did not incite internal business conflict and mobilization. Even when liberalization progressed in the second round of economic reform, neither domestic nor export manufacturers, who were threatened by global economic integration in distinct ways, organized collective lobbying efforts to oppose policy changes. Because the state did not historically favor one segment of the industrial class, exporters did not perceive domestic producers as an obstacle to further participation in the global economy, while import-substituting manufacturers did not blame export subcontractors for their economic troubles.

Given sufficient political opportunity for business mobilization, historical legacies of class formation – which shape producer beliefs about who has access to economic opportunities and what kinds of ties they have to state officials – set the context for collective business responses to global economic integration. The growing emphasis on the role of the private sector in spearheading national development (Porter 1990; Schulpen and Gibbon 2002; World Bank 2002) calls for greater analysis of when and how business groups organize and adopt a proactive role in national politics in developing countries. Business is now seen as a critical – if not *the* critical – actor in creating market economies and integrating cash-starved developing countries into global production circuits. But business mobilization is far from automatic. Analyzing business responses to global integration takes on renewed importance in an age of private-sector–led development. Chapter 7 explores the implications of different patterns of business collective action in more detail and extends the findings to additional country cases.

The book is organized in four parts. The first part, which includes chapters 1 and 2, presents the argument and specifies the processes of globalization and economic opening that constitute the starting point of the analysis. Chapter 2 conceptualizes the initial independent variable – integration in global manufacturing chains and trade liberalization – and uses the apparel supply chain as a lens into changes in global manufacturing. This chapter also elaborates on Moroccan and Tunisian integration into world markets as a foundation for the subsequent discussion of business responses to economic change. In part two, chapters 3 and 4 specify the two main explanatory variables in greater detail through historical analyses of regime type and class formation in postindependence Tunisia and Morocco, respectively. In part three, chapters 5 and 6 show how the processes and institutions described in previous chapters shaped contrasting modes of Tunisian and Moroccan business politics in the 1980s and 1990s in response to common experiences of integration in global manufacturing circuits. Chapter 7 summarizes the findings, tests the argument against additional developing country cases, and discusses the implications of the findings for adopting contemporary industrial development strategies.

2

Globalization and Integration in International Apparel Manufacturing Networks

The New Politics of Industrial Development

The textile and apparel sectors are important sites for examining how integration in globalized manufacturing affects business politics in developing countries. The apparel industry engages almost every country in the world and is at the forefront of globalization processes. Since the 1970s, more and more developing countries have participated in textile and apparel manufacturing chains, and competition for market share is acute. Trends in textile and apparel production and sourcing since the 1980s have created a new global production context, introducing new inducements for producers in developing countries to integrate in global manufacturing chains and to form alliances with local producers. Large multinational retailers and buyers now encourage developing countries to adopt full-package production, a subcontracting arrangement in which manufacturers receive detailed specifications from buyers, acquire all inputs, and coordinate most phases of production (Bair and Gereffi 2001; Scott 2002). In response, developing country officials and producers emphasize their national and regional capacity to carry out full-package production and promote industrial development based on clustering.[1] This chapter traces the evolving global production context of the apparel supply chain to show how it has reshaped the repertoire of industrial development strategies for producers and officials in developing countries such as Morocco and Tunisia. The structure of global apparel manufacturing frames debates about industrial upgrading but does not

---

[1] Clusters are concentrations of firms in related upstream and downstream industries with supporting research and educational institutions and a favorable policy environment (Porter 1990).

determine the policies and strategic behavior of actors in developing countries. As chapters 5 and 6 show, producers and business associations in the two countries responded differently to these shared global constraints and opportunities.

This chapter first specifies the shifting geography of the apparel supply chain since the 1970s and provides a brief overview of Moroccan and Tunisian trade liberalization to show how producers in the two countries integrated into global manufacturing chains. The chapter then argues that technological changes and new sourcing patterns of large multinational retailers have altered the context for industrial development, posing particular challenges for non-Asian developing countries in the current period.

FEATURES OF TEXTILE AND APPAREL MANUFACTURING

The textile and apparel sectors have received extensive scholarly attention because they play a fundamental role in driving industrialization and are major employers globally. Textiles and apparel are distinct industries intertwined through a web of forward and backward linkages that constitute the apparel supply chain (see figure 2.1).

The apparel supply chain involves five main components: raw materials such as cotton, wool, and silk or synthetic fibers derived from petroleum products; textile inputs, such as thread and fabric; local or overseas apparel factories that assemble finished goods; intermediaries or traders who arrange for apparel to reach sales destinations; and retail markets, such as department stores, chains, specialty shops, or small boutiques (Applebaum and Gereffi 1994, 45). The textile and apparel sectors are also linked to other activities, notably synthetic and natural fiber manufacturing, which processes the materials used to manufacture thread and cloth; the textile machinery and equipment industries; and the chemicals sector, which supplies products for processing and finishing textile goods. In addition, apparel manufacturing involves design and marketing, which are generally carried out by larger retailers in industrialized countries, and packaging. Few countries possess capabilities in all segments of the apparel supply chain (Toyne et al. 1984), but cost pressures in one area greatly influence the other parts of the supply chain.

Textile manufacturing, which includes thread spinning, cloth weaving, and cloth finishing through dyeing and printing, is more capital-intensive than the apparel sector; hence, its ownership structure tends to be more concentrated. The actual manufacturing processes for spinning,

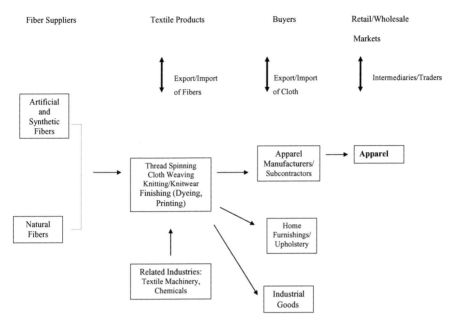

FIGURE 2.1. The Structure of the Apparel Supply Chain.

weaving, and finishing are relatively complex and require particular technical expertise; expensive, specialized machinery; and access to significant quantities of water and electricity and elaborate ventilation systems. Making cloth and thread from synthetic fibers requires even more complicated equipment (appendix A, I-59M; Clairmonte and Cavanaugh 1981, 13–14, 18). Fabric weaving is less complex than the other industries in the textile sector. Although a handful of large multinationals dominate global textile production, thousands of smaller firms that manufacture limited quantities have found a place in the industry (Toyne et al. 1984, 14).[2] The largest and most internationally competitive firms are located in the advanced, industrialized countries, although the East Asian newly industrialized countries have become major textile manufacturers in the last two decades and tend to have vertically integrated spinning and weaving capabilities.

The apparel sector, in contrast, is much more fragmented than the textile sector, with many small factories and a significant home-based component. Apparel assembly is labor-intensive, relying on low-wage labor

[2] See Clairmonte and Cavanaugh (1981) for a detailed discussion of the global trend toward concentration and vertical integration in the textile industries in the 1970s.

and requiring minimal start-up capital and few specialized skills. In the case of apparel made from woven cloth, the sewing machine is the primary piece of capital equipment (although cutting fabric in preparation for assembly, a task that entails great precision, calls for some specialized machinery). Making knitwear is more capital-intensive than assembling apparel from woven cloth because manufacturers require knitting machines, which demand some technical knowledge, particularly circular knitting machines that produce finished apparel such as pullovers and sweaters.

The distinct natures of textile and apparel manufacturing processes generally attract different kinds of players. In textiles, large capital holders and multinational corporations dominate the field. In Morocco, big business and the state control most textile manufacturing. In Tunisia, the state dominates the sector, although some wealthy families have textile firms. The lower barriers to entry characteristic of apparel production permit many entrepreneurs to venture into the industry, as the comparatively dispersed capital structures of the Moroccan and Tunisian apparel sectors attest. National context introduces some variation: within the European Community (EC) countries, for example, a few large firms traditionally dominated the British textile sector, while a larger number of small and medium-sized firms operated in Italy and West Germany (Toyne et al. 1984, 88, 105–106).

THE SHIFTING GLOBAL PRODUCTION CONTEXT

Over the course of the last three decades, the apparel industry has become one of the most globalized industries in the world, with manufacturing for a single retailer spread across dozens of countries. Because clothing is one of the first areas in which consumers cut back spending in times of recession, manufacturers have searched for ways to reduce costs. The quest for cheaper production strategies was a primary impetus for the trend toward the globalization of apparel manufacturing after World War II.

An overview of textile and apparel production and employment trends reveals fundamental shifts in the geography of these sectors. In the early twentieth century, Britain controlled approximately 70 percent of the world textile trade, but by the 1960s the national industry had declined precipitously, prompting British textile industrialists, along with their counterparts in other industrialized countries such as the United States, to press for protective trade barriers (Dickerson 1991, 104). Beginning in the late 1950s, production gradually shifted away from Western countries toward Japan and other Asian countries, and production of textiles began to grow more rapidly in developing countries than in the developed world.[3] Nevertheless, during the 1950s and 1960s, advanced industrialized countries maintained steady levels of production in textiles and apparel and accounted for most textile and apparel trade until the 1970s, when the balance shifted dramatically in favor of the developing world. To manage the textile trade and shield their own threatened industries, developed countries instituted a series of international agreements regulating textile exports from newly industrialized countries. The next section traces various "waves" of *délocalisation,* or relocation of firms from industrialized to developing countries, as well as international treaties regulating the textile and apparel trades from the 1970s through the 1990s.

WAVES OF OFF-SHORE DÉLOCALISATION

In the early 1970s, manufacturers in the industrialized countries began to search for lower-cost, off-shore production sites. The bulk of firm relocations in the apparel sector took place in three waves (appendix A: I-42M; I-48M), each of which provided new opportunities and challenges to producers and governments in developing countries.

The First Wave: Early 1970s

The first wave of *délocalisation* occurred in the early 1970s as apparel producers in Western Europe and the United States transferred production to sites with lower labor costs in response to worldwide recession and the consequent reduction in consumer purchasing power. During this period, developing country exports of clothing boomed, growing more than 20 percent annually from 1968 to 1978 and doubling as a share of world trade in the sector from 22 percent to 41 percent (Hoffman 1985, 371). Hong Kong, South Korea, and Taiwan alone accounted for more than 75 percent of all developing country exports in apparel, and their example was an important model for other countries. After gaining

---

[3] Japan had already developed a significant textile industry after World War I, but its defeat in World War II meant it had to rebuild its industry beginning in the 1950s (Aggarwal 1985, 44). Clairmonte and Cavanaugh (1981, 177) argue that the "tragedy of Lancashire," or the decline of the British cotton-spinning industry in the 1930s and 1940s, was largely due to a surge in Japanese high-quality, low-cost production. Later, Japanese off-shore investment played an important role in promoting the development of textile and apparel manufacturing throughout East Asia.

self-sufficiency, the East Asian countries became net exporters of textile products, threatening established producers in Western Europe and North America (Clairmonte and Cavanaugh 1981, 165; Olsen 1978, 123–125; Toyne et al. 1984, 60–61). Indeed, apparel exports from the industrialized world experienced almost no growth during the 1970s, marking the beginning of the decline of the sector in these countries (Dickerson 1991, 113–114; Toyne et al. 1984, 90). Industrialized countries were forced to downplay the labor-intensive components of the garment manufacturing chain, notably apparel assembly, while boosting their productivity and focusing increasingly on higher-tech synthetic fibers.[4] Employment trends also reflected the decline of textile and apparel manufacturing in the developed world, where jobs in textiles declined by 30 percent between 1973 and 1985 and employment in the clothing industry dropped by 18 percent. Meanwhile, developing countries almost doubled their share of worldwide employment in apparel manufacturing (Commission Economique et Monetaire 1977; Dickerson 1991, 118–119, 130). Tunisia was one of the earlier developing countries to profit from the outsourcing of low-wage industries thanks to the "1972 Law," which offered incentives to export-oriented companies, most of which carried out assembly work for European firms.

The gradual shift in the terms of trade compelled the United States and Europe to institute a series of multilateral accords to regulate the textile industry.[5] Signed in 1973, the Multi-Fiber Agreement (MFA) established an elaborate system of quotas organized by product and country and created the Textiles Surveillance Body to enforce the agreement and mediate disputes (Aggarwal 1985, 127–128; Clairmonte and Cavanaugh 1981, 187; Olsen 1978, 1250–1256). Although the MFA was created to curb mounting restrictions on the textile trade by introducing an organized regulatory system, the agreement became a vehicle for national restrictive policies. European manufacturers lobbied vigorously to strengthen import restrictions on textile and garment products, and subsequent renewals of the MFA reflected this trend (Aggarwal 1985, 14, 181–182; Commission Economique et Monetaire 1977; Spinanger 1991, 544).[6] The primary effect of the MFA was to limit exports of textiles and apparel from

---

[4] Although research in industrialized countries has examined the possibility of using automation to replace workers in the apparel sector, thus far these plans have not yielded comprehensive results. Dickerson (1991, 120) points out that automation cannot handle "limp" fabrics.

[5] See Aggarwal (1985) for a full account of these arrangements.

[6] The MFA was renewed in 1977, 1981, 1985, and 1991 (Spinanger 1991, 545).

developing countries to industrialized nations. The MFA remained in force until its abrogation on January 1, 2005.

Parallel regional accords with the EC more directly shaped the external trade relations of the Mediterranean countries, notably Morocco and Tunisia. Although the EC signed on to the MFA, it established a special relationship with the North African countries through a series of Association Agreements ("Les Accords d'Association," May–June 1969, 9–12; White 2001).[7] Textile and apparel imports from the associated countries were exempt from MFA quota restrictions, enabling greater export access to EC markets. While imports from the East Asian countries were limited as long as the MFA remained intact, the countries of the southern Mediterranean had preferential access to Europe.

Signed in 1969, the first Association Agreements had little impact on Moroccan and Tunisian production because the bulk of Maghreb exports to Europe were primary products, which already faced low tariffs. Yet the accord had a profound effect on the North African political economies, particularly for Tunisia, by encouraging the newly independent countries to promote industrial development.[8] When the Association Agreements expired in 1974, the Maghreb countries pushed for another set of agreements with the EC, culminating in the bilateral Cooperation Accords of 1976 signed with Morocco, Tunisia, and Algeria. The accords guaranteed free access for Maghreb industrial goods to the EC but introduced restrictions on imports of textiles and apparel. The North African countries were increasingly unsatisfied with the arrangement on the grounds that it increased regional competition for access to European markets and compelled voluntary restraints on exports of certain products, even though some product categories had such high quotas that they were rarely fulfilled.

The Second Wave: 1980s

In the early 1980s, a global recession, coupled with the second oil shock and mounting inflation, fueled a second shift in global sourcing patterns. Many European apparel firms shifted their operations overseas,

---

[7] For a comprehensive review of Euro-Maghreb trade relations since the late 1950s, see White (2001).

[8] At the same time, the accord gave preferential access to the Maghreb markets for European goods not already produced in these countries. The arrangement effectively limited industrial development by undercutting the potential development of local industries in a variety of areas, such as textile manufacturing machinery (White 2001, 58).

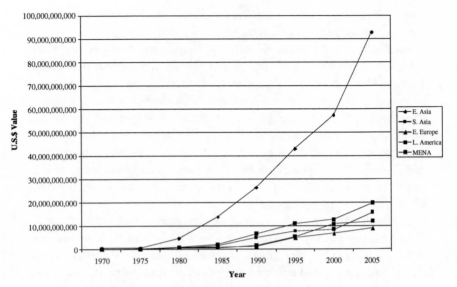

FIGURE 2.2. Apparel Exports from Developing and Postsocialist Countries, 1970–2005. *Source*: U.N. COMTRADE database, various years.

particularly to neighboring Mediterranean countries such as Tunisia and later Morocco (appendix A: I-42M). European Community production of textiles also stagnated, while East Asian countries, such as China, Hong Kong, South Korea, Japan, and Taiwan, accounted for the greatest increase in textile exports (Dickerson 1991, 114, 140).[9] Figure 2.2 depicts the rise in apparel exports from developing country regions from the 1970s onward.

As the data demonstrate, East Asia experienced the most dramatic rise in apparel exports, beginning in the 1970s, followed by the Middle East and South Asia in the mid-1980s, and, subsequently, Latin America and Eastern Europe.

Trade liberalization throughout the developing world increased the array of possible sites for overseas relocation of U.S. and European apparel firms. Many developing countries, including Morocco and Tunisia, undertook trade reforms for similar reasons: in response to mounting foreign debt, governments sought assistance from the International Monetary

[9] China grew at the fastest rate throughout the 1980s. Since China initiated economic reforms in 1978, it has become a significant manufacturer of textile and apparel products and with the elimination of the MFA seriously challenges most other producers of low- and medium-grade textiles and apparel.

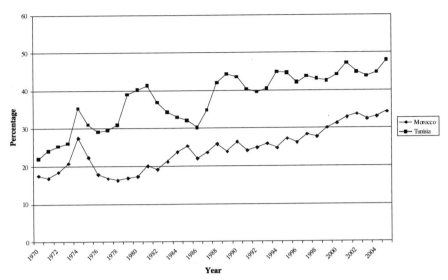

FIGURE 2.3. Exports and Imports as a Percentage of GDP in Tunisia and Morocco (1970–2005). *Source*: *World Development Indicators*, various years.

Fund (IMF) and World Bank, which in turn made debt rescheduling conditional on the adoption of a set of economic reforms designed to address key "imbalances" in the economy. The adoption of export-oriented industrialization strategies in the 1980s and early 1990s in Morocco, Tunisia, and many other developing countries occurred at a time when many major clothing retailers were forced to change their inventory patterns drastically to avoid bankruptcy.

Morocco and Tunisia initiated trade liberalization from different starting points. Tunisia since the early 1970s already had a major export program in place that established parallel yet separate domestic and export processing sectors. Morocco retained a more comprehensive protection of the domestic market until it began implementing trade liberalization in the 1980s. Figure 2.3 depicts Tunisia's greater integration into the global economy relative to Morocco from the 1970s onward.

In 1983, Morocco undertook a reform program with goals and policies that broadly resembled those implemented throughout the developing world in the same period. Liberalization began to affect the industrial sector in earnest in the late 1980s and early 1990s with a tangible impact on textiles. The state withdrew from direct investment in the sector and a number of textile products were partially liberalized. As part of the elimination of nontariff barriers, textile products were gradually transferred to "List A," the government-issued list of products that did not require import licenses (*La Vie Economique (LVE)*, August 25, 1989, 14–15; *LVE* April 30, 1993).

Regulatory reforms played a key role in encouraging private investment, particularly from new entrepreneurs. In January 1983, the administration enacted a new investment code to promote local and foreign private investment, including measures such as the elimination of import duties on certain inputs and capital equipment, exoneration of the corporate profits tax over a 10-year period, and free transfer of profits and goods for foreign investors.[10] These changes had a dramatic impact on the structure of the Moroccan economy, with manufactured goods rising from 13.2 percent in 1969 to 21.4 percent in 1987 (*LVE*, August 18, 1989, 10–11). Foreign investment also increased substantially, quadrupling from 1982 to 1991, with an average annual growth rate of 32.3 percent. The abrogation of the Moroccanization decrees in January 1990, which permitted the establishment of totally foreign-owned companies, liberalized trade and exchange rates, and streamlined investment procedures, was an important impetus for the growth of foreign investment, linking the local economy more directly with global markets.[11] The passage of the "Young Promoters" law, which enabled first-time investors to obtain bank credit at preferential lending rates for business projects, also encouraged the exponential growth of apparel factories in the mid-to-late 1980s. The increase in bank credit issued for textile and apparel projects attests to the rapid growth in these sectors. In 1984, long-term credit for these activities amounted to approximately $304 million (U.S.) (Royaume du Maroc, *Annuaire Statistique du Maroc*, 1989) and rose to $12 billion in 1994 (Royaume du Maroc, *Annuaire Statistique du Maroc*, 1994).

To profit from rising opportunities in global production circuits, local garment assembly subcontractors took advantage of a law permitting exporters to obtain inputs duty-free from global suppliers, provided that they reexport the goods in finished product form within six months (Royaume du Maroc, *Regimes*, September 1999, 7–12). Imports under this in-bond trade regime, known as *Admissions Temporaires* (AT),

---

[10] Under the new code, businesses were subject to a minimal corporate tax rate of 9 percent during their first five years of operation, followed by 18 percent after that period. By contrast, businesses targeting the local market paid approximately 40 percent in taxes, compelling most firms to avoid local market sales in the formal sector (appendix A: I-40M).

[11] Discussed in detail in chapter 5, the Moroccanization laws of 1973 stipulated that Moroccans must hold the highest-ranking administrative positions and own a majority of shares in firms located on Moroccan territory.

jumped from approximately $300,000 (9 percent of total imports) in 1983, to $1.9 million (25 percent of total imports) in 1991, to $3 million in 1995. The AT system had existed since the early 1970s, but regulatory reforms in 1985 streamlined its operation by eliminating the need for prior authorization through a licensing system (Bassani 1993, 113). Bank guarantees (*cautions bancaires*) or bonds issued jointly by two or more companies (*cautions mutuelles*) covered temporary imports (Royaume du Maroc, *Cautions*, September 1999).

In roughly the same period, Tunisia signed on to a similar package of economic reforms. The export sector, with a large apparel subcontracting component, was already well established thanks to partial trade liberalization in the early 1970s. In 1987, Tunisia launched a plan to deepen trade liberalization as part of a World Bank–led structural adjustment program.[12] The outlines of the agreement paralleled the Moroccan reforms, including a gradual reduction of tariffs, the progressive elimination of quantitative barriers, and exchange rate devaluation (Bassani 1993, 159). The plan aimed to remove all quantitative import restrictions and achieve lower and uniform rates of tariff protection by the end of 1991, with the goal of achieving a minimum tariff rate of 15 percent and a maximum rate of 35 percent by 1991 (Bassani 1993, 147–148; World Bank 1996, 29). As a result of these shifts, trade became more diversified and the economy opened to some degree: nonmineral exports as a share of GDP increased from 25 percent to 35 percent from the early 1980s to the early 1990s, and the manufacturing sector accounted for half of export earnings by 1996. Textiles, including apparel, were the fastest-growing sector, with 70–80 percent of textile exports originating from the off-shore sector (World Bank 1996, 30). Structural adjustment reforms began to affect the industrial sector most directly in 1990. The results fell far short of the goals, but the plan reduced some tariffs and the rate of tariff dispersion narrowed, while some import restrictions were removed.

The government was more reluctant to remove quantitative restrictions or quotas, which accounted for 25 percent of protection for domestic agriculture and manufacturing and constituted an important means of sheltering the local textile sector from foreign competition (Bassani 1993, 153; World Bank 1996, 29). As a result, the sharp drop in tariffs did not lower the effective level of protection significantly for most domestic activities and, in the case of some manufacturing industries, effective

---

[12] Tunisia signed a World Bank Industrial and Trade Policy Adjustment loan in 1986, disbursed from 1987 to 1989, and a structural adjustment loan in 1988 (Bassani 1993, 136).

protection actually increased (Bassani 1993, 156, 162). A key difference between Morocco and Tunisia in the progression of trade reform during the 1980s was that Morocco eliminated quotas and compressed tariff ranges simultaneously, while Tunisia emphasized tariff reduction rather than cutting quotas (Bassani 1993, 162–163).

Tunisia's liberalization program also entailed changes in investment laws. In 1987, a manufacturing investment law was introduced that abolished the need for prior government authorization for all projects that did not require investment incentives. The law provided generous benefits on a sectoral basis but, because most proposals sought incentives, the law had a muted impact (World Bank 1996, 32–33). In December 1993, the government passed the Unified Investment Code, which created across-the-board incentives, promoted exports, and aimed to expand the entrepreneurship base through the *Jeunes Entrepreneurs* law, which provided attractive credit terms to first-time investors. The Banque Tunisienne de Solidarité, a government lending institution that provides loans up to 5,000 Tunisian Dinars (TD) (in 2001, approximately US$ 3,800) for small projects and young entrepreneurs, also aimed to expand the capital base (appendix A: I-35T).

Under the 1993 investment code, foreign direct investment was virtually unrestricted in all activities except agriculture (World Bank 1996, 32), although foreign investment above 50 percent of total firm capital required approval by a national investment commission, the Commission Supérieure d'Investissements (Guésquiere et al. 1997, 20). The new code also attempted to narrow the gap between the on-shore and off-shore economies and reinforced incentives for off-shore operations (World Bank 1996, 33).[13] Off-shore companies benefited from numerous fiscal incentives, including a 10-year tax holiday followed by reduced tax rates, full exemption from all taxes on imported inputs and capital goods, and authorization to sell 20 percent of output on the local market unless their product competed with domestically produced goods. (In this case, firms could sell on the domestic market up to the equivalent of their local purchases of inputs.) Partial export firms received similar benefits in proportion to the share of exports in total production but did not benefit from special tax incentives and qualified only for refunds of import duties if no equivalent inputs and capital goods were available on the

---

[13] Because the law strengthened incentives for off-shore investment, important differences remained in the treatment of companies targeting local versus export sales, notably in access to the local market, tax treatment, and inefficient duty refund procedures for local companies (World Bank 1996, 33).

local market (Guésquiere et al. 1997, 21). Another important component of the reforms was the liberalization of the temporary admissions and duty drawback systems, which provided strong fiscal incentives to exporters. As a result of these policy reforms, Tunisian exports grew rapidly, rising from $1.6 billion in 1985 to $4.6 billion in 1994, and from 1980 to 1994 manufactures were the greatest source of export growth. Textiles and clothing have been the largest earner of foreign exchange in the industrial sector since the mid-1980s.

Despite a relatively long post–World War II experience with export promotion, Tunisian integration into the global economy was limited by the fact that the off-shore enclave engendered few backward linkages in the domestic economy (World Bank 1996, iv). Net exports of clothing increased from $250 million in 1980 to $1.5 billion in 1994, and net imports of textiles increased from about $200 million in 1980 to $900 million in 1994, reflecting the growth of temporary imports of textile inputs for garment assembly (World Bank 1996, 27). High tariffs and quotas sheltered the domestic market, while the off-shore economy accounted for the bulk of international trade and little foreign direct investment (FDI) flowed into the domestic economy.[14] The on-shore and off-shore economies were highly separate, and the domestic market remained protected (Guésquiere et al. 1997, 10).

The Third Wave: 1990s and Beyond

An economic downturn in the early 1990s put additional pressure on North American and European manufacturers and retailers, ushering in a third wave of relocation to lower-cost production sites in the developing world, especially for textile manufacturers, who, unlike apparel producers, had not yet transferred most of their operations to lower-cost production sites. The increasing decentralization of textile manufacturing added a new dimension to industrial development strategies. With the impending abrogation of the MFA, apparel producers in developing countries – particularly outside of China – increasingly emphasized full-package production and clustering to attract and maintain clients. Because these strategies require local access to high-quality textile cloth, thread, and other apparel inputs, competition among developing countries for FDI in the textile sector intensified.

The largest textile firms were still based in Western industrialized countries. But, in the 1990s, European and North American textile

---

[14] Eighty percent of FDI goes to the fuels sector (World Bank 1996, 7, 9).

TABLE 2.1. *Average Hourly Wage Rates*
for Apparel Assembly in Select
Countries, 1980 and 1990 (in US$)

Country	1980	1990
Germany	10.65	16.46
Italy	9.12	16.13
United States	6.37	10.02
Hong Kong	1.91	3.05
Taiwan	1.26	4.56
Tunisia	1.13	2.82
Turkey	0.95	1.82
Singapore	0.94	3.83
Morocco	0.85	1.28
South Korea	0.78	3.22
Thailand	0.33	0.92
China	n.a.	0.37

Source: *La Vie Economique*, October 2, 1992.

manufacturers began to transfer their operations overseas in increasing numbers, either by setting up their own factories or establishing joint ventures in low-wage countries or areas with significant emerging consumer bases.[15] An important impetus for overseas relocation of textile firms was also to move close to regions with strong apparel manufacturing industries, which would benefit from local access to internationally competitive textile inputs (appendix A: I-71M; I-50T; Kurt Salmon Associates, n.d. "Cross Border" and "Vision"). With mounting pressure to achieve quick-turnaround production, retailers increasingly source their products from countries with established upstream and downstream activities.

At the same time, competition intensified among developing countries for global market share in apparel manufacturing. Economic recession in the 1990s led to reduced consumer demand in Western Europe, a key consumer outlet, and as a result, prices on global markets dropped by an estimated 30 percent. In addition, many industrializing countries and transition economies in Eastern Europe and Asia promoted garment exports in the early 1990s, increasing the global pool of low-cost suppliers and further driving down prices (*Conjoncture* [Morocco], no. 774, October 1997, 21). Table 2.1 situates Tunisian and Moroccan average hourly wage

[15] In the Moroccan case, examples include Tavex, a Spanish denim fabric firm, which established Settavex in Settat, and Caulliez Frères, a French thread-spinning firm, which established a factory in Fès, Morocco (appendix A: I-63M; I-103M).

rates for apparel assembly in a larger set of countries. The data indicate the growing pressure from lower-cost East Asian suppliers between 1980 and 1990.

The adoption of microelectronics technology to cut production costs in high-wage industrialized countries deepened the competition, although this had a greater impact on workers in wealthy, industrialized countries rather than developing ones.[16] The 1997 Asian financial crisis exacerbated the challenges facing industries in the middle-income Asian countries, but at the same time, drastic currency devaluations enabled them to boost their exports at the expense of developing countries in other regions.

Regional tensions compounded the effects of mounting global competition for North African exporters. The 1990–1991 Gulf War was a major cause of the economic downturn throughout the Middle East and North Africa, and North African textile and clothing exports declined precipitously during and immediately after the war. Companies that worked exclusively with Iraqi and Middle Eastern clients were hit hardest, but overall European investment in the region declined. Some European clients, concerned about their investments, broke contracts with local suppliers when the war erupted.[17]

The thriving black market, particularly in Morocco, exacerbated the situation. Persistent political disputes between Morocco and Algeria led to the closure of the border near Oujda, a town in eastern Morocco that was a major outlet for black market manufactured exports. After the Lockerbie bombing in late 1988, Morocco suspended trade relations with Libya, another important export channel in the region, and some prominent families lost their fortunes in the bust.[18] The crisis worsened throughout

---

[16] Computerized manufacturing techniques have not supplanted manual assembly entirely but have succeeded in key areas in the pre- and postassembly phases such as design, cutting, handling, and merchandise control (Hoffman 1985; Mody and Wheeler 1987, 1278).

[17] Some firms closed, particularly those that worked extensively with the Gulf states or had outstanding debts from Iraqi clients. Tunisian economists estimated that local businesspeople earned about 150 million dollars annually through business with Iraqi clients, endangering about 200 companies dependent on exports to Iraq (*Réalités*, no. 285, February 3–14, 1991). Most firms affected by the crisis turned to the local market, but with little success (*Réalités*, no. 271, November 2–8, 1990, 21; *Réalités*, no. 284, February 1–7, 1991, 23–24).

[18] Trade relations between Morocco and Libya officially reopened in 1999 (*L'Economiste*, April 12, 1999, 10). Border shutdowns had a particularly detrimental effect on the production of denim jeans in Morocco. An estimated 50 percent of Moroccan jeans were produced in unregistered factories and then smuggled to Algeria and Libya. Illegal imports of inexpensive jeans manufactured in Asia further undercut local production, raising

the 1990s, when more and more factories throughout Morocco and Tunisia were forced to shut down or reduce work hours drastically (*Conjoncture* [Morocco], no. 774, October 1997, 12; *LVE*, December 22–29, 2000; *L'Economiste*, February 8, 2001).

In 1995, the decision by the World Trade Organization (WTO) to phase out the MFA presented a new looming threat to producers in North Africa and other developing regions. In theory, the treaty's elimination meant that imports from Asia would likely attain a large market share in Europe (appendix A: I-93M; Singleton 1997, 15–16). In practice, many loopholes remain that continue to block the full liberalization of the global apparel trade. During a transition period, the WTO permits temporary suspension of the process in the event of damage to the importing country. "Transitional safeguards" permit restrictions on imports from specific countries, provided that the importing country can demonstrate damage to its industry from a sharp increase of exports from a specific country. For example, as part of the EU-China Shanghai Accord of June 2005, China agreed to limit its textile exports to the EU until 2007 (Economist Intelligence Unit "Morocco," November 2005, 30). The Agreement on Textiles and Clothing (ATC) also allows special treatment for new market entrants, small suppliers, and the least developed countries (WTO, June 2, 2001). Still, the dismantling of the MFA is already damaging North African manufacturers by eliminating their privileged access to the EU market and putting them in direct competition with low-cost exporters from Asia (appendix A: I-71M; I-27T; I-62T; Economist Intelligence Unit, "Tunisia," October 2005; Economist Intelligence Unit, "Morocco," November 2005).[19]

These global and regional pressures induced new ways of thinking about industrial policy, opening up greater possibilities for collaboration among manufacturers in different sectors and with different trade orientations. First, policymakers and industrialists were increasingly convinced of the need to attract European foreign direct investment in textiles and apparel during the third wave of delocalization. Second, attracting

questions in the business community about how such a large volume of black market activity could evade customs officials (*LVE*, September 25, 1992, 23). By 1992, local production of denim jeans was severely damaged, and well-known factories such as Ticoma, which employed 300 workers, were forced to shut down (ibid.). The fate of the Sebti family is noteworthy because declaring bankruptcy is extremely rare in Morocco (appendix A: I-27M; I-31M).

19 A Moroccan textile manufacturer exclaimed, "All producers now have the same clients – the west, particularly western Europe. In the past, I was well received by European clients, but now they give me 'seven minutes.' I am forced to wait in line with Indians, Pakistanis, Chinese, Asians to show my wares. Then I am given seven minutes to present my line and that's it. Competition is fierce" (appendix A: I-72M).

investment from Asian – particularly Chinese – producers who want to capitalize on North Africa's proximity to Europe became an important goal (appendix A: I-102M; I-67T). Finally, trends in apparel production, which emphasized full-package production, led business groups and government officials to stress the importance of integration and clustering. These new approaches to industrial policy blurred the lines between the export and import-substitution sectors, creating the possibility for political alliances that would have been unthinkable in a previous period. The next section discusses the changing nature of global apparel manufacturing that set the context for shifting industrial development strategies.

TRENDS IN GLOBAL SUPPLY CHAIN MANAGEMENT

In the 1980s, in response to flagging sales, retailers sought ways to boost consumer interest. Creating multiple fashion "seasons" or "fashion change" was a prime strategy to maintain and attract customers in a sector characterized by relatively inelastic demand (Dicken 2003, 328). By the mid-1980s, the standard six-month season had fragmented into at least six fashion cycles, and many retailers began to offer about 12 distinct product lines annually.[20] To keep pace with new marketing practices, retailers had to maintain constant turnover, reduce costs, improve delivery reliability, and generate more accurate forecasts of stocking needs to reduce inventory risk. In a rapidly changing fashion environment, retailers strove to replenish fast-selling stock-keeping units (SKUs), or apparel categories, and phase out less popular items quickly (Kurt Salmon Associates, 2001, n.d. "Quick Response," n.d. "Vision").[21] The introduction of multiple fashion "seasons" compelled multinational retailers to seek manufacturers in low-wage countries who would fill smaller orders in minimal delivery times (Applebaum and Gereffi 1994, 49; Bonacich et al. 1994, 4). The change put pressure on manufacturers, who could no longer plan production well in advance and work according to predictable guidelines (appendix A: I-34M). The keys to success for garment subcontractors were now flexible production techniques that could respond to rapid changes in fashions and quick turnaround delivery.

New management practices emerged to meet challenges from changing demand patterns.[22] Low inventory holdings by retailers of an expanding

---

[20] The four basic seasons remain, but each receives multiple influxes of merchandise (appendix A: I-5O).

[21] Retailers rely heavily on in-house or external trend forecasting services (Gale and Kaur 2002, 136–139).

[22] See Abernathy et al. (1999, 2003), who refer to these new practices as "lean retailing."

array of goods have generated the need for rapid replenishment of orders and frequent but smaller shipments, shifting risks to manufacturers and subcontractors and pressuring them to speed up production and delivery. Coined in 1985, the quick response (QR) management system greatly accelerated the apparel supply chain by speeding up order fulfillment and enabling retailers to respond quickly to shifting consumer tastes through improved information and merchandise flows (Kurt Salmon Associates "Quick Response" n.d.; Hines 2001).[23] Implementing QR entails three steps. First, retailers adopt sales coding technologies such as the Universal Product Code (UPC), a computerized bar code for product identification; electronic point-of-sale technologies, which establish instantaneous communications between sales, reordering, and production units; the Uniform Commercial Code 128, a barcode for identifying shipping containers; and Electronic Data Interchange (EDI) or comparable computerized inventory and production management systems to exchange business documents with purchase orders and product specifications more easily.[24] Next, firms redesign internal processes by adopting standardized management techniques that facilitate faster turnaround of merchandise and few inventory holdings. Finally, retailers and manufacturers set up an integrated supply chain with joint product development planning and inventory forecasting. By now, most companies have implemented the first phase, but only a few larger multinationals have adopted the subsequent steps (Kurt Salmon Associates, "Quick Response" n.d.).

Technology plays a critical role in the practical implementation of QR. Although different buyers and therefore suppliers have different EDI software with varying protocols, the general processes of placing, receiving, and tracking orders and types of data transmitted are comparable from system to system.[25] Big retailers invest significant time and resources in bringing their suppliers up to speed on their designated procurement systems and training factory management to work with computer

---

[23] More recent management models aim to reduce the risk of excess inventory for suppliers: the "modular manufacturing" model, founded on a small, team-based approach to apparel assembly rather than a larger line of separate sewers, decreases turnaround time from order to delivery, enabling manufacturers to reduce holdings in the factory (Kurt Salmon Associates, "Modular Manufacturing," 2001).

[24] Electronic Data Interchange originated in the transportation industry in the 1970s and is a generic system of standardized business languages used to transmit information from business to business.

[25] This complicates the production process for factories with more than one client. Manufacturers must have sufficient know-how to be able to deal with different technological requirements for different customers (appendix A: I-5O).

technology and the Internet. Once they achieve an effective management system within a given factory, sourcing executives try to generalize the system over a number of supplier factories. Electronic Data Interchange demands tightly coupled planning, allocation, logistics, and inventory-tracking operations, as well as close relations between buyers and suppliers. With automated tracking systems, buyers can readily obtain information on the status of any order or shipment, facilitating more efficient inventory management (appendix A: I-3O). The contemporary security climate, particularly in the United States, has heightened the need for effective computerized supply chain management systems: U.S. customs regulations now require suppliers to provide precise details on shipment contents, container numbers, and shipping identification information 24 hours before loading merchandise on a boat (appendix A: I-4O).

Industry consultants and buyers constantly seek new ways to shorten the time between product development and delivery – that is, to shorten the supply chain. Longer import lead times make it more difficult for retailers to replenish merchandise, which forces them to lose potential sales and compels them to place larger orders, which creates excess inventories. Under the traditional "warehouse-ready" mode, suppliers were responsible for manufacturing and delivering the product to the buyer or retailer, who prepared the goods for store display by adding tickets, labels, and, where applicable, hangers. The new predominant merchandising approach, floor-ready merchandise (FRM), calls for cooperation between retailers and manufacturers on product development, inventory management, and related logistics. This approach shifts the display preparation from the retailer to the supplier, who now affixes price tags, UPC bar code tickets, hangers, and security tags, and presses and packages items for direct delivery to stores.[26] Retailers benefit by cutting inventory costs and transferring responsibility for in-store display to the supplier. The approach requires fundamental changes in both the information technology and physical layout of the factory, introducing logistical challenges. For example, different retailers use different labeling and packaging requirements, compelling American retailers to propose the adoption of national voluntary standards for these areas. In addition, suppliers must redesign their information systems to track each product from the time of

---

[26] Floor-ready merchandising achieves full-package production par excellence. Ultimately, retailers want to "send a sketch and a check" to suppliers and receive floor-ready merchandise at individual stores (appendix A: I-5O; Todaro 2003). FRM can be complex, with different store locations requiring different combinations of merchandise (appendix A: I-3O; Hines 2001, 37; Kurt Salmon Associates n.d., "Vision").

manufacturing to arrival at the storefront and interface with buyer EDI systems (appendix A: I-34M; Kurt Salmon Associates, 1997). Multinational buyers and retailers often work with key suppliers to support the adoption of new technologies and management techniques.

Accelerated apparel production cycles and the need for rapid turnaround from order to delivery changed the prerequisites for competitiveness in some apparel categories. As retail markets further segment into "fashion" and "commodity" products, cost is no longer the primary basis for boosting market share for certain items. Fashion items, based on current trends, account for between 20 percent and 40 percent of SKUs in Western Europe, the United States, and Japan. Fashion items are highly time-sensitive, so cost plays a lesser consideration in order fulfillment. The remaining 60 percent to 80 percent of apparel items are commodity-like and hence are more price-sensitive. Sourcing decisions in these different categories involve trade-offs between geographic proximity, which reduces the time elapsed from order to market, and low-wage overseas production sites, which reduce labor costs. In a consumer-driven environment, availability at the right moment is more critical than price for some items. Nonfinancial costs may also compel retailers to seek local or geographically proximate suppliers. Time, effort, and money spent sourcing items from afar and monitoring overseas production, as well as the opportunity cost of lost sales from late or incomplete delivery, favor relationships with reliable, nearby manufacturers (Dicken 2003, 330–331; Hines 2001, 32–35).

South and East Asian countries had a decided advantage in garment assembly, thanks to low labor costs and local availability of raw materials for textile inputs, enabling them to dominate production of low-value-added, simple apparel, such as T-shirts. The acceleration of fashion seasons, however, provided niche markets in the quick restocking of products with medium to high value-added in which producers in the southern Mediterranean could excel (appendix A: I-63M; I-65M; I-70M; I-93M; I-45T; I-50T; I-90T). While shortened fashion seasons made production forecasting more complicated, North African firms were well positioned to adjust to the new supply cycles in global apparel markets. The small and medium-sized firms dominating Moroccan and Tunisian apparel exports were better suited to producing limited collections than many Asian and Eastern European suppliers, who tended to operate from large factories. To maintain a no-stock policy, which entailed low inventory and "just-in-time" production strategies, European clients chose to source from their southern neighbors, giving rise to a new apparel export sector in

Morocco and fueling the expansion of the sector in Tunisia. Production for retailer restocking was a fundamental source of growth for Moroccan apparel exporters. In the 1970s, there was no production for restocking; in the 1980s, it constituted only about 5 percent of total production; and in 1999, it accounted for about 60 percent of apparel manufacturing in Morocco (appendix A: I-34M). Local producers offered quick turnaround times, delivering orders within three weeks, and accepted small orders, usually with a minimum of 2,000 pieces. This allowed European retailers to try out different products, assess sales volumes, incorporate necessary modifications, and change collections quickly. Meanwhile, many Asian suppliers demanded full payment in advance, larger order sizes – often 40,000–50,000 pieces – and delivery on much longer lead times.

Throughout the late 1980s and early 1990s, Morocco and Tunisia were still competitive in international apparel markets, in part because they were only beginning to feel the effects of competition from lower-wage East Asian countries (see Table 2.1). Furthermore, because of their geographic proximity to the EU, the world's largest apparel importer, the Mediterranean countries were ideally placed to refill orders on short notice and to work on a just-in-time basis (appendix A: I-33M; I-34M; I-35M; I-41M; I-31T). By the late 1980s, Moroccan industrialists were "overwhelmed" with orders (*Conjoncture* [Morocco], no. 774, October 1997, 20–21).

Shifts in the global supply chain are beginning to alter local power dynamics in apparel production sites by promoting capital concentration. In the past, low barriers to entry invited investment by relatively small capital holders. The increasingly technical and computerized nature of the production process, as well as the larger warehouses needed to fulfill the demands of FRM, favors suppliers with greater capital and skills. Dominant retailers increasingly seek out large factories that can produce an entire fashion line. As in the modular production model of the consumer electronics industry (Sturgeon 2002), apparel manufacturing is more concentrated both at the retail and supply stages – at least on the initial tier of subcontractors (appendix I-27T; I-5O; Kurt Salmon Associates, 1997; Schmitz and Nadvi 1999, 1505).[27] Large retailers increasingly assume the tasks of fashion forecasting and marketing and are more involved in direct

---

[27] See also Hoffman and Rush (1984) and Mody and Wheeler (1987). Accelerated supply cycles have also encouraged manufacturers to adopt more flexible capital equipment. In certain apparel categories, notably jeans and men's underwear, machines are standardized and therefore cannot convert easily to other uses. For many apparel products, however, manufacturers must adjust their production processes rapidly, allowing small firms that

contracting (appendix A: I-34M; Applebaum and Gereffi 1994, 125–126; Bonacich et al. 1994, 4; Toyne et al. 1984, 19).

The trend toward overseas relocation potentially supports the efforts of producers and policymakers in developing countries to boost local production capabilities across the supply chain by promoting industrial clusters. Countries with significant apparel assembly sectors now compete to attract foreign direct investment from European, North American, and Asian thread and cloth firms (appendix A: I-54M; I-72M; I-74M). In the contemporary global production context, the overseas relocation strategies of textile firms as well as the goals of firms and governments in developing countries are encouraging the construction of locally integrated production sites.

East Asian manufacturers have excelled at full-package production, which compels large retailers to source more and more production from China and other Asian countries at the expense of manufacturers in other developing regions (appendix A: I-4O). Indeed, the combination of full-package production and low wages has made China virtually unbeatable in world apparel markets (Gough 2004; Kahn 2004). For most U.S. and European distributors, East Asia is geographically inconvenient when compared with production in Latin America, North Africa, or Eastern Europe. But East Asian dominance in the global apparel industry is also due to the perception that workers in countries such as Hong Kong, Taiwan, and China, as well as more recent entrants to the industry such as Vietnam, Cambodia, and Indonesia, are highly skilled. Similarly, managers from Hong Kong, Taiwan, and neighboring countries have a reputation among buyers in industrialized countries for boosting factory productivity and easily adapting to new technological systems, whether their factories are located in Chinese-speaking countries or overseas.[28] The combination of high-skilled production, relative technological savvy, and low wages means that the full dismantling of the MFA will ultimately lead to further concentration of global apparel production in East Asia, and in China in particular (Todaro 2003). Under the new regime, in which buyers are no longer compelled by the quota system to source in diverse

use flexible production techniques and specialize in small orders to remain competitive (appendix A: I-85M; Gherzi Organisation 1999, 42–43; Mody and Wheeler 1987).

[28] Some industry executives claim that Mexican factories are far less productive, a fact that they ascribe to inferior management practices and an alleged difficulty in mastering the technological requirements of full-package production. For these reasons, many U.S. apparel retailers prefer to source in East Asia (appendix A: I-60; I-70).

countries, it may be more cost-effective to ship some time-sensitive items by air freight from Asia rather than to source locally.[29] At the same time, East Asian producers and trading companies are establishing operations in countries closer to the North American and Western European markets, and geographic proximity may remain important, particularly for rapid replenishment (appendix A: I-3O).[30]

INDUSTRIAL DEVELOPMENT STRATEGY IN THE CONTEMPORARY
GLOBAL ECONOMY: CLUSTERS IN GLOBAL VALUE CHAINS

Industrial clusters (Porter 1990) have a long lineage in economic geography and related disciplines. A diverse literature on the local and regional roots of industrial development stresses the importance of context-specific assets in shaping prospects for success in global production.[31] The globalization of markets has not swept away the importance of regions, which remain integral sites of interaction and knowledge exchange in a global economy (Scott 1998, 4, 11, 21, 68). Regions possess "untraded interdependencies," or location-specific factors such as conventions, informal rules, and habits, that affect production processes by coordinating individuals under conditions of uncertainty. Globalization will not wipe out

[29] Industry executives emphasize that not all kinds of trade barriers may disappear with the elimination of quota restrictions, and the true nature of the trade regime to replace the MFA is unclear. U.S. retailers will undoubtedly stop buying apparel from some countries where the availability of production quota allotments largely justified sourcing decisions, but antidumping challenges may restrict some imports from East Asian countries (appendix A: I-3O; I-5O). Preliminary evidence suggests that such factors have already prevented a massive shift to Chinese suppliers by multinational buyers (Rozhon 2005).

[30] Li & Fung, the premier supply chain management and trading firm in the apparel industry, notes: "While cost considerations have resulted in the concentration of manufacturing activities in Asia, recent years have seen an expansion of Li & Fung's quick-response capabilities in areas like the Mediterranean, Eastern Europe, and Central America that are closer to customers in Europe and the U.S." (Li & Fung, 2003).

[31] Studies of regional production dynamics often build upon or respond to the notion of the "industrial district," which is based on the work of Alfred Marshall on nineteenth-century England. The notion embodies both a vertical division of labor among firms as well as an "atmosphere" supporting interaction and collaboration (Asheim 2000, 418; Storper 1997, 5). Piore and Sabel's (1984) "flexible specialization," in which the rapid redeployment of labor and machinery enables production of a changing array of specialized, high-quality goods, builds on the concept. On the differences between flexible specialization and Marshallian industrial districts, see Amin (2000). See also Donaghu and Barff (1990) on "nodes and networks" models and Sturgeon (2002) on the rise of "modular production networks."

"economies of proximity" because the region is a critical locus for learning and innovation (Scott and Storper 1986, 11–12; Storper 1997, 5, 22).[32]

The idea of industrial "clusters" is grounded in a similar logic. Proponents claim that localized growth poles such as clusters are the most effective way to compete in global markets because they enhance national or local competitiveness. Competitive relations among geographically proximate firms can drive knowledge generation, making local groupings of firms in distinct parts of the supply chain a key source of competitive advantage.[33]

The industrial clusters approach has specific policy implications, compelling business and government to create conditions fostering innovative growth. But is it possible to *construct* clusters? Porter admits that creating clusters may not be viable or useful in developing countries, which often lack the resources to support knowledge-based innovation. He maintains that clusters in places with more sophisticated kinds of competition and the "concomitant rise in knowledge and innovation intensity" will be more effective (i.e., drive more innovation and productivity) (Porter 2000, 23).

Two sets of factors call for caution in endorsing clusters as an industrial development strategy. First, politics and the sociology of power are conspicuously absent in Porter's approach to industrial clusters. Regimes have varied kinds of linkages to the business community (Chibber 2005; Evans 1995), which can be essential to enlist support for and gain input into proposed reforms. Alternatively, political repression can deter the rise of symmetrical business–government relations, which permit the exchange of information that is so central to the process of constructing clusters (Cammett 2006). Localities are not blank slates upon which healthy competition and cooperation between firms can be constructed. Political connections, privileged social networks, wealth and capital holdings, and other immaterial resources, such as preexisting stocks of knowledge and technical know-how, shape the incentives that firm owners face when making choices about production and upgrading strategies.[34]

Second, the distribution of power in the global economy affects the feasibility of pursuing cluster-based industrial development. Porter's

---

[32] How knowledge exchange occurs and promotes innovation is relatively underexplored (Feldman 2000, 389). For one interpretation, see Saxenian (1994).

[33] Porter stresses competition, but interfirm *cooperation* may be more conducive to innovation (Hotz-Hart 2000, 436).

[34] Smith, too, claims that cluster models neglect power, but provides few concrete suggestions about how to address this lacuna (Smith 2003, 17–40).

framework overlooks the constraints that position in global value chains often places on the ability to construct or foster clusters in developing countries.[35] The concept of the global commodity chain developed by Gereffi and his collaborators (Bair and Gereffi 2001; Gereffi 1994; Gereffi 1999) depicts the global apparel industry as a geographically dispersed, globally extended production system that encompasses households, firms, and states operating across national boundaries.[36] Because technological and organizational advances have facilitated a vast expansion of production and sourcing on a global scale, multinational corporations have dispersed their operations across an unprecedented number of countries (Gereffi 1994).

In its early renditions, the global commodity chain framework drew a sharp distinction between "core" and "peripheral" regions in the supply chain.[37] Core nodes, usually located in advanced, industrialized countries, reap disproportionate shares of the profits and differentiate themselves through innovation breakthroughs in design, marketing, and sourcing. Any part of the production process that requires computerized technology or specialized skills and training inevitably is located in advanced, industrialized countries. Nodes in the periphery, concentrated in developing countries, carry out the lower-value-added components of the manufacturing process and operate in a more cutthroat atmosphere, where low wages are the primary basis of competitiveness. Because multinational corporations have the flexibility to shift sourcing patterns easily in the buyer-driven commodity chain, manufacturers and subcontractors in low-wage countries are essentially "price-takers," and "merchants," or the executives who coordinate sourcing, exercise significant power (appendix A: I-36T; I-84T; Bonacich et al. 1994; Gereffi 1994; Gherzi Organisation 1999; Hoffman 1985; Mody and Wheeler 1987).

Later elaborations of the global commodity chain approach show how organizational learning through participation in certain trade networks can enable firms in developing countries to advance up the supply chain by

---

[35] Porter cautions that few places (particularly in the developing world) can actually construct successful clusters; however, the major reason behind this caveat has to do with local institutional endowments rather than constraints imposed by power dynamics in the global production context.

[36] For a useful summary and critique of the GCC approach, see Henderson et al. (2002, 440–442).

[37] In this respect, Gereffi's work traces its intellectual roots to dependency theory and the new international division of labor approach (Henderson et al. 2002, 440).

adopting full-package production (Bair and Gereffi 2001; Gereffi 1999). But full-package production is at best a fleeting advantage when neighboring countries can adopt similar strategies (Schrank 2004).

An emerging synthesis in the literature on global manufacturing stresses the importance of integrating key insights from the global value chain approach into studies of how national or subnational institutions, policies, and strategies affect industrial upgrading (Amin and Thrift 1992; Henderson et al. 2002). For most producers in developing countries, the development of internationally competitive production has occurred as part of integration in global production networks.[38] This has been particularly true for the last two decades, with the increasing globalization of production in many industries (Held et al. 1999). Buyers and large retailers exert tremendous pressure on suppliers, notably in setting the terms of sales but also on how and what contractors and subcontractors produce. A synthetic approach integrating insights from the value chain and cluster perspectives usefully identifies the power dynamics embedded in global value chains, which shape local choices about what, when, and how to produce (Henderson, et al. 2002, 439; Humphrey and Schmitz 2002, 1018).

A cluster-based approach, then, tends to overlook the realities of global manufacturing in developing countries by suggesting unrealistic possibilities for upgrading given the "right" institutional mix in specific localities. Regional assets such as local concentrations of knowledge, skills, and expertise, as well as cooperative institutional relationships that foster collaborative interfirm relationships and exchange of information, are only assets insofar as they fit the needs of global production chains. The dynamics of national and subnational regional development therefore are shaped as much by global factors as by local conditions (Coe et al. 2003, 12–13, 17).[39]

In general terms, clusters in industrialized and developing countries fit into global production chains in very different ways. While developed country clusters often contain global leading firms and dominate design

---

[38] Humphrey and Schmitz (2002) affirm that integration in global value chains can foster supplier upgrading but emphasize that such improvements are confined to more limited types of upgrading, which focus on improving production efficiency and introducing superior technology, rather than more advanced forms of upgrading, which entail the production of more sophisticated goods or an increased skills context in the production process.

[39] Of course, global production networks alone do not determine the ability to upgrade (Coe et al. 2003, 13).

and innovation, developing country clusters "tend to work to specifications that come from outside" (Schmitz 2004, 4). Lead firms have a
vested interest in maintaining tight control over chain governance, or
the "coordination of economic activities through non-market relationships" (Humphrey and Schmitz 2002, 1018; see also Humphrey and
Schmitz 2004, 97). With the heavy emphasis on branding, design, and
product differentiation in apparel and other consumer industries, retailers must ensure that their exact specifications are met. The risk of supplier
failure is particularly high when retailers differentiate themselves on non–
price-related factors such as quality, safety, and other standards; production and delivery speed and reliability; and rapid turnover of merchandise
(Schmitz 2004, 6). Even in areas where price-based competition prevails,
the need for chain governance rather than market-based relations remains
strong. In the current retail environment, in which speed to market and
reliability are critical, the quest for new, lower-cost suppliers may entail
greater risk of supplier failure and therefore call for vigilant control of
the supply chain (Humphrey and Schmitz 2004, 106–107).

The pursuit of full-package production and industrial clusters by producers and governments in developing countries may be driving greater
capital concentration in supplier countries. Because multinational retailers and their agents demand suppliers who can meet strict quality-control
criteria and tight production and delivery deadlines, their supplier base
has narrowed and will likely continue to narrow, at least on the first tier
of contractors (but not necessarily on the level of prime and secondary
subcontractors). Local firms with sufficient production capabilities and
scale, as well as positive working relationships and experience with multinational firms and their agents, have a decided advantage and may exercise considerable authority in choosing suppliers or subcontractors for
their local operations. Furthermore, large local firms that establish tight
linkages to global buyers either as relational or increasingly turnkey suppliers (Sturgeon 2002; Gereffi et al. 2005, 9) undoubtedly seek to limit the
number of local firms that can attain this status. Given the relatively high
barriers to entry in terms of minimum capital endowments and economies
of scale needed to attain local lead firm status, it is not difficult for dominant firms to protect their close relationships with multinational buyers.
In addition, as Humphrey and Schmitz (2002, 1020) argue, the relatively
"benign" view of local upgrading in some conceptualizations of global
commodity chains (Gereffi 1999) neglects the fact that buyers have an
incentive to prevent any upgrading that competes with their core compe-
tencies.

Constructing industrial clusters has become a popular industrial development strategy in the contemporary period, although it is difficult to implement and is certainly no panacea (Schmitz and Nadvi 1999; UNIDO 2001;
UNESCWA 2002). Increasing global competition in the apparel industry
and the corresponding push by multinational companies (MNCs) for full-
package sourcing has only reinforced the trend. The creation of the export
sector in Morocco and the deepening of export incentives in Tunisia in the
1980s and early 1990s initially enabled the two countries to take advantage of contracts with multinational retailers for simple apparel assembly.
But as competition intensified in global markets, the combination of low
production costs and geographic proximity was no longer sufficient. As a
result, a clustering strategy became increasingly attractive to Tunisian and
Moroccan policymakers, business associations, and manufacturers.[40]

[40] Chapter 7 discusses the implications of business responses to economic opening, discussed
in chapters 5 and 6, for implementing cluster-based industrial development initiatives.

PART II

THE INSTITUTIONAL CONTEXT

3

Business and the State in Tunisia

Statist Development, Capital Dispersion, and Preemptive Integration in World Markets

Formal independence from France brought the recognition that industrialization was a crucial factor for national development, and both the Tunisian and Moroccan *industrial* bourgeoisies trace their origins to the 1960s. But despite these and other commonalities, the Tunisian and Moroccan postindependence industrial classes developed in distinct ways. The varied historical development of business–government relations and class structure is critical to explaining divergent patterns of business mobilization in the two countries in the 1990s. These divergent trajectories can best be explained by two factors that shaped policies regarding business after independence: the distinct social bases of the Tunisian and Moroccan independence movements, later reflected in state economic policies, and the size of their domestic markets, which affected the perceived feasibility of adopting protectionist trade measures.

STATE-BUILDING AND ECONOMIC ELITES IN TUNISIA

The Tunisian industrial class, for the most part, emerged after independence in 1956.[1] The transition from colony to independent state constituted a sharp demarcation in the history of Tunisian business. Following independence, a new economic elite emerged that was only minimally rooted in the previous era. This new class owed its good fortune, if not its very existence, to the state. These parameters shaped business interests as well as the means by which business expressed its demands.

---

[1] Bellin (2002) also makes this point.

From Colonial Administration to State-Building:
The Rise of the Single-Party State

The French occupation of Tunisia was designed to facilitate economic domination. The Résidence Général, the administrative authority in colonial Tunisia, had tight links to large French companies, which obtained concessions to build the economic infrastructure of the colony (Dougui 1992).[2] To pursue their economic goals, French bureaucrats instituted an indirect form of control over the colony, extending the precolonial administrative apparatus and allowing some Tunisian ministers and council representatives to retain their roles. Tunisian public officials, cooperating with the colonial power, remained ostensibly involved in the governing process, but French bureaucrats took control over key ministries and government posts (Anderson 1986, 141, 225).[3] Alongside agencies headed by Tunisians, the French created new ministries that handled much of the business of running the colony and ensured that colonial officials held top positions. On the exterior, the bey – the Ottoman ruler who governed Tunisia – and his ministers retained the appearance of running the state and local concerns. In reality, a dualistic set of administrative structures arose, enabling the French to administer the affairs of the growing French settler community without interference (Ben Salem 1976, 10–11; Duvignaud 1969, 194).

A major effect of French rule was to bolster state centralization (which was already extensive) by drastically reducing the number of *qaids* and sheikhs representing local districts and reassigning them as government officials with stakes in the administration. French reorganization of the army and tax administration also reinforced the administrative strength of the state. With increasing bureaucratization, kinship ties to the state and connections to elite families became less important, while interactions with the administration became crucial. New political roles, and intermediaries such as lawyers and business owners who had the ability to understand the technical aspects of the administration, were elevated

---

[2] Describing a backlash against the monopolization of economic opportunities by big French companies and the consequent negative effects on the Protectorate budget, Dougui (1992, 13–18) emphasizes that relations between the Résidence and French business were not consistently cozy.

[3] Preliminary historiography on the French Protectorate in Tunisia demonstrates that local officials largely cooperated with the French, although discussions with Tunisian and French historians highlighted that research has not thoroughly explored the position of the beys during this period and thus has not fully problematized the question of beylical collaboration with the French (appendix A: I-93T).

in importance, and the influence of tribal leaders and the precolonial elite declined (Anderson 1986, 142, 148–150; Lârif-Béatrix 1988, 115).[4]

Tunisian collaboration with the French colonial power had the effect of distancing the population from its own officials, fueling nationalist demands to end both colonial rule *and* the beylical regime. Association with the French delegitimized the Tunisian ruling elite enormously – and, by extension, the economically privileged class – rendering them incapable of leading the movement for national liberation.[5] Many of the leaders of the independence movement, who subsequently became the leaders of postcolonial Tunisia, came from the Sahel, a fertile central-eastern coastal region that was relatively uninhabited by French settlers. Although only 11.5 percent of Tunisia's total population lived in the Sahel, about 25 percent of government ministers from the 1960s through 1980s came from the region (Lârif-Béatrix 1988, 195; Tessler et al. 1995, 423). These agitators, many of whom were the French-educated sons of minor civil servants from the provinces, were the backbone of the movement that ultimately became the Neo-Destour Party and led the victory to an independent state.

Founded in 1934, the Neo-Destour Party was an offshoot of the Destour Party, a party opposing the French occupation that was active in the 1920s.[6] Habib Bourguiba, a French-trained lawyer from a modest family in Monastir, a town in the Sahel, headed the party and was president of Tunisia until his overthrow in 1987. Bourguiba's main bases of support were the petit bourgeoisie landowners and merchants of the Sahel as well as members of the labor movement. The heads of the Neo-Destour Party were as concerned with economic inequality as with the need for political rights for Tunisians, and they eschewed the legalistic, gradualist approach of their predecessors. This concern with social inequality resonated with the broader Tunisian population, which suffered under French occupation, and enabled the party to develop a national following while isolating potential rivals, such as the Communist Party (Anderson 1986, 167–168, 173; Angrist 2006; Moore 1965, 82–83; Sethom 1992, 114–115). Furthermore, the Neo-Destour derived their support from a distinct social base,

---

[4] Asma Lârif-Béatrix (1988) argues that French colonization only superficially bureaucratized the Tunisian administrative system and did not lead to the institutionalization of a "rational" bureaucratic state. Instead, she argues, the Bourguiba regime was founded on neopatrimonialism.

[5] Angrist (2000, 3) cites archival evidence that documents the responses of the nationalist movement to Tunisian collaborators.

[6] See Anderson (1986, ch. 8) for a thorough overview of the various phases in the nationalist movement.

alienating the urban bourgeois backers of the Destour while promoting its petit bourgeois supporters from the hinterland. The Neo-Destour capitalized on clientelist networks that arose around the Protectorate and the commercial economy as well as the Destour's already established organizational infrastructure, extending it by building on particularistic ties at the local level (Anderson 1986, 229). The party's successful construction of an organizational infrastructure, founded upon local cells well before independence, demonstrates that state-building actually began prior to 1956.[7] The ready-made availability of the network greatly facilitated the party's continuing state-building efforts after independence.

Tunisia is a one-party state. From the beginning, power was centralized and the party was virtually synonymous with the state.[8] When the French departed, Neo-Destour cadres took over vacant positions in the state bureaucracy. Laws passed shortly after independence authorized prosecution of accused Tunisian collaborators with the French. Based on ambiguous definitions of "collaborator," the Law of Ill-Gotten Gains, passed in August 1957, and the Law of National Indignity, passed in November 1957, gave broad power to the government to confiscate property and issue harsh prison sentences to collaborators (Moore 1965, 88–90, cited in Angrist 2006). With an electoral law favoring Bourguiba's supporters, the National Assembly deposed the bey and elected Bourguiba president in mid-1957 (Anderson 1986, 235; *Réalités*, July 25–31, 1997, 41). The electoral system, instituted in January 1956, ensured the dominance of the Neo-Destour by forbidding split ballots, which would permit voters to elect candidates from different parties. As a result, corporatist institutions representing societal interests, such as the Union Générale des Travailleurs Tunisiens (UGTT), the national labor union, and the Union Tunisienne de l'Artisanat et du Commerce (UTAC), the peak-level business association, were compelled to form a single front in the elections (Lârif-Béatrix 1988, 155).

The responsibilities of and procedures for appointing the Governing Council also demonstrated the tight links between the party and the state. The Governing Council, which was the president's chief advisory

---

[7] Ben Salem (1999, 339) makes this point in her rejection of the traditional periodization of Tunisian history, which establishes a sharp break between the nationalist struggle and nation-building. In an earlier work, Ben Salem (1976, 14) describes the Neo-Destour's construction of an extensive political infrastructure throughout Tunisia during the 1930s and 1940s.

[8] For an overview of Tunisian postindependence political history, see Tessler et al. (1995). Angrist (2006) traces the reasons for the formation of a one-party state in Tunisia.

body, was composed of 30 members nominated by local party cadres and appointed by decree of the Ministry of the Interior. All Governing Council members simultaneously served on the Regional Coordination Committee, which acted as an intermediary between the party base and leadership (Lârif-Béatrix 1988, 167). A 1963 law formally merged the Neo-Destour and the state, stipulating that the president of Tunisia must be the president of the party, that all cabinet members and provincial governors were required to be members of the party's central committee, and that provincial governors would simultaneously preside over the Neo-Destour regional offices (Angrist 2006).

Other institutional features also ensured the dominance of the party and, particularly, Bourguiba's control over the administration: Article 43 of the constitution granted him the power to pass legal decrees, authorize laws, and make appointments to high-level civil and military posts; and Article 46 named him the supreme commander of the armed forces. No supreme court was created to act as a judicial check on legislative and executive authority. The chief advisors and supporters of the president were the secretaries of state, who headed various administrative departments and owed their positions to the president. In practice, the structure of the administration, which deviated somewhat from the classic model of a presidential system of government, granted the president vast powers.

A decree instituted in July 1957 created the office of the Secretary of State of the Presidency, which reported directly to the president and oversaw all regulatory actions undertaken by other state administrative offices. All government decrees required approval from the Secretary of State of the Presidency, which coordinated and directed all state affairs. The office, however, threatened the influence of the Secretary of the Economy and Planning, which also retained vast power in government affairs. Lârif-Béatrix (1988, 157–158) speculates that the rivalry between these two positions enabled Bourguiba to further his power by playing them against each other. The transformation of the Secretary of State of the Presidency into the Prime Ministry in 1969 did not, in reality, provide a more effective check on presidential control, and the new office answered entirely to the president.[9] Furthermore, the division of administrative capacities among more offices, notably with the dissolution of the Ministry of the

---

[9] Lârif-Béatrix (1988, 163) argues that Bourguiba created the prime ministry in order to deflect personal responsibility for the failures of the collectivization experiment of the 1960s, which is discussed later in this chapter.

Economy and Planning and its conversion into distinct departments covering finance, agriculture, and industry and commerce, reinforced presidential power in the administration. The administrative structure of the government, extending into the hinterlands, also furthered state centralization. A hierarchy of regional governors and subregional delegates were named by the executive-appointed Council of Ministers and were closely supervised by the Ministry of the Interior (Angrist 2006; Lârif-Béatrix 1988, 158–160, 165).

On November 7, 1987, Zine el-Abidine Ben Ali succeeded Bourguiba in a bloodless coup. In his efforts to outwardly democratize the country, Ben Ali promoted an existing but largely ineffective consultative body, the Economic and Social Council, by requiring the government to consult with this body on any matter concerning economic or social affairs. Consisting of representatives from unions, public enterprises, professional organizations, and civic groups, as well as delegates from regional governorates and state-appointed advisors, the Economic and Social Council is arguably more representative than parliament. However, the organization's decisions are nonbinding and, given the stakes of expressing dissent (discussed in chapter 5), its recommendations rarely deviate from the party line (Angrist 1999, 99–100).

The National Constitutive Assembly, the main legislative body, provides little check on executive powers. It does not appoint or approve cabinet members and cannot initiate legislation. When the legislature is out of session, the president can issue laws by decree. Angrist (1999, 98–99) points out that the structure of the Assembly ensures its subordination to the executive office. Seven permanent commissions – each devoted to a specific policy area – examine, debate, and propose modifications to draft laws. The main ruling party, which was renamed the Rassemblement Constitutionel Démocratique (RCD), or Constitutional Democratic Rally, in 1988, effectively chooses the members of the individual bodies, selecting 13 or 14 individuals for each 15-member commission.[10] Deliberation sessions are closed, and the proceedings are not publicly available. Adopting decisions by consensus, the commissions largely approve legislation already drafted by the ministries (Lârif-Béatrix 1988, 159).

Opposition parties have limited followings and little maneuvering room, and have not acted as effective channels for popular discontent

---

[10] In 1964, during a period of *étatisme*, the Neo-Destour was renamed the Parti Socialiste Destourian, or the Socialist Destourian Party. Ben Ali thus renamed the party for a second time (Angrist 1999, 8).

with state policies.[11] The best-known opposition party, the Mouvement des Démocrates Socialistes (MDS), founded in 1978 by Ahmed Mestiri, emerged out of a dissident wing of the Neo-Destour. Linked to old bourgeois families from Tunis, the leaders of the MDS focused their demands on legality, public liberties, and democratization, and were supported by urban elites linked to the original Destour Party. Other supporters of the party have included intellectuals, members of the liberal professions, and some elements of the business community. In 1989, Mestiri resigned from the MDS to protest the RCD's continued monopolization of politics; his successor, Mohamed Mouadda, openly confronted Ben Ali in 1995 over the president's failure to implement real pluralism. In response, the state closed MDS headquarters, seized party property and documents, and arrested Mouadda (Angrist 1999, 96; Lârif-Béatrix 1988, 281–282; Ruf 1984, 112).

The rise of so-called opposition parties in Tunisia took place more in name than in deed. The November 1988 National Pact, a pro-democratic statement of principles on Tunisian politics and society cosigned by President Ben Ali, various political parties, and civic organizations, declared a new trend toward political liberalization, including the active participation of opposition parties in political life (Gasiorowski 1992, 88). For several reasons, nominal multipartyism did not pose a real challenge to the RCD in 1988. First, the state harasses and closely monitors members of the opposition through legal manipulations and even physical force. Second, the electoral system prevents the rise of a significant opposition party. For many years, the system was based on a majority rule system. A modification in 1994 reserving a certain number of seats for non-RCD candidates did little to change the system. The RCD won the vast majority of seats, which were still allotted according to majoritarian rules. Finally, the opposition parties themselves have remained weak, in part because harassment from the regime has deterred party leaders from mobilizing a mass base and because the state has co-opted many opposition figures. The

---

[11] See Angrist (1999) on the lack of pluralism in contemporary Tunisian society. Benedict (1997, 35–36) also discusses Tunisian authoritarianism under Ben Ali, touching upon the failure of the 1988 National Pact to create real multipartyism. Opposition parties include the Parti de l'Unité Populaire, Union Démocratique Unioniste, Mouvement des Démocrates Socialistes, Mouvement Ettajdid, Parti Social Libéral, and Rassemblement Socialiste Progressiste (Angrist 1999, 10). In the early 1970s, Entelis (1974) described popular discontent with the Bourguibist vision, basing his evidence on survey research conducted among Tunisian university students in Paris and Tunis. The survey demonstrated that the bulk of the sample favored the formation of a multiparty system (Entelis 1974, 560–562).

state's decision to outlaw the main Islamist party, Al-Nahda, which had a significant following in the early 1990s, undercut an important channel of dissent. Opposition parties have not been able to sustain publications, an important propaganda tool, largely because direct and indirect pressure from the state has deterred advertisers from listing in opposition journals, and the state maintains tight controls on the media. Public financial support for political parties, introduced in a 1997 law, also undercut the opposition. Each opposition party is entitled to an annual sum of 60,000 Tunisian Dinars, or about $45,000, provided that it reveals sources of private contributions. Not surprisingly, the law dried up most financial support for the opposition (Anderson 1995, 171; Angrist 1999, 92, 95; Bellin 1995, 134–135; Gasiorowski 1992, 85, 89, 92; Moore 1993, 51–52).

Ben Ali's takeover initially appeared to herald a new era of political freedom. Within a year of his ascension to power, the new president released most political prisoners, introduced greater freedom of the press, and permitted new political parties to form (Anderson 1990, 145; Gasiorowski 1992, 86–87). By the early 1990s, however, it became clear that the new regime was not committed to political liberalism. Instead, Ben Ali strengthened the grip of the RCD on civic life, increasing the number of party cells throughout the country and boosting membership.[12] At the same time, new programs to inculcate local leaders in official party discourse bolstered party discipline. An impressive security network, supported by informants throughout Tunisian society, as well as selective access to employment, educational scholarship, and legal protection reinforced party control over civil society (Angrist 1999, 94; Angrist 2006; Khiari and Lamloum 1998, 394–395).

WHO MADE THE RULES? THE NEW ADMINISTRATIVE ELITE

The postindependence state did not actively co-opt elite urban commercial interests and discredited beylical aristocracy in the state-building process. Precolonial and colonial ruling elites played a marginal role in the struggle for national liberation and therefore had little influence on the character and goals of the new state (Dimassi 1983, 1). The preindependence ruling aristocracy, composed of large-scale property holders who were by and large the vestiges of the precolonial beylical class, lost significant holdings to the French administration and settlers, yet remained highly

---

[12] Moore (1993, 53) shows that RCD membership jumped by 50 percent during Ben Ali's first year in office.

dependent on the colonial authority, often collaborating openly with the French. With its tendency to maintain existing holdings without seeking increased capital accumulation, the economic power of this group was limited. The alleged decision to collaborate with the French on the part of Tunisian elites shaped the fortunes of these social groups in independent Tunisia. Both the ruling beys and urban commercial interests were effectively excluded from the state-building process (Ben Romdhane 1986, 40, 42–43; Denieuil and B'chir 1996, 191; Dimassi 1983, 8).

Participation in colonial governing institutions discredited the beylical aristocracy, branding them as collaborators with the French. As part of the French design to penetrate Tunisia economically, a major colonial innovation was to promote the expression of bourgeois interests through the *Grand Conseil*, or the Grand Council, and the municipalities. Created in 1922 by the French, the Grand Council was a consultative body that mainly advised the Protectorate authorities on the budget but also transmitted policy demands to the French authorities.[13] Although it largely represented the interests of French colonists, the Grand Council set aside seats for Tunisian members, whose representation increased steadily until the mid-1930s. The Tunisian contingency included a few merchants but was dominated by large agricultural interests and property owners. In reality, French officials closely controlled the candidate lists, ensuring that only compliant locals participated in the organization (Angrist 2006; Ben Hamida 1992, 130).

Association with the French delegitimized the Tunisian ruling elite enormously – and, by extension, the economically privileged class – rendering them incapable of leading the movement for national liberation (Angrist 2000, 3). Laws passed shortly after independence authorized prosecution of accused Tunisian collaborators. Based on ambiguous definitions of "collaborator," the Law of Ill-Gotten Gains, passed in August 1957, and the Law of National Indignity, passed in November 1957, gave broad power to the commission to confiscate property and issue harsh prison sentences to collaborators (Moore 1965, 88–90, cited in Angrist 2006). The state sold much of the land it expropriated to provincial elites, who were the main supporters of the party. As a result, the old beylical families were destroyed or severely undercut at independence, and a new class arose around the administration (appendix A: I-38T; Anderson 1986, 149;

---

[13] The Grand Council replaced the Conférence Consultative, which had been established in 1907 and included a section composed of 16 Tunisians appointed by the Résident Général, or colonial administrator in Tunisia (Ben Hamida 1992, 130).

White 2001, 82). In part due to its small numbers, as well as to colonial limitations on its development during the French occupation, the local merchant class was also a minor force in the struggle for liberation, particularly when compared with its Moroccan counterpart (Ruf 1984, 101).

The key figures in the Neo-Destour, the national party that played a crucial role in the struggle for liberation, were mostly professionals such as lawyers, teachers, and doctors, who had little connection to the former aristocracy and wealthy merchants. To be sure, the party had some linkages to the traditional bourgeoisie, but only the petit bourgeoisie (whose power was institutionalized in the Neo-Destour and the UGTT) were able to take power at independence (Ben Romdhane 1986, 97, 114–118; Dimassi 1983, 1). The Neo-Destour was linked mainly to urban workers and medium landowners and peasants rather than to wealthy merchants or landholders.

Comparatively low levels of corruption in business–government relations – an important feature of the Tunisian system until recently – further deterred the former economic elite from gaining undue influence in the system and prevented business from receiving a disproportionate share of the spoils in the Tunisian postindependence political economy (Bellin 1991; Bellin 1994, 432–430).[14] Furthermore, the system did not operate according to the rules of patron–client relations – at least not for the purpose of gaining access to economic opportunities.[15] Moore (1977, 258–259) critically assesses the concept of patronage, demonstrating that it does not adequately capture postindependence Tunisian politics during the first decades of Bourguiba's rule. The clientelist paradigm presumes a direct relationship between patron and client, and in its earlier conceptualizations allowed little room for change and flexibility in patronage networks. Moore's close examination of internal Tunisian politics in the first two decades after independence demonstrates that the party, which effectively was and remains the state, was well implanted throughout society and that the favorite candidates of top officials were not assured choice spots in the government.[16]

---

[14] Bellin (1991, 94) defines corruption as the "misuse of public office (or access to public goods) for the sake of private enrichment."

[15] I want to emphasize this point because Moroccan rural notables, many of whom collaborated with the French during the Protectorate and therefore were widely discredited at the end of the colonial period, nonetheless played a central role in postindependence politics as a result of the monarchy's reliance on their support (Leveau 1985). See chapter 4.

[16] Moore (1977) links government spending and declining patronage. When government spending rises, he argues, opportunities for patronage diminish as the state takes over the distribution of resources from personal networks. This logic, however, presumes that

In the early 1960s, the profile of the average Tunisian government official, including ministers, governors, high-level civil servants, and deputies, reflected the traditional demographic support base of the Neo-Destour.[17] The majority came from middle-class backgrounds, mostly from the agricultural sector and liberal professions, and only a few came from elite merchant or industrialist families. Further, most ministers were provincial elites who came from either the Sahel or Tunis and had been members of the party since before independence. In terms of professional origins, most ministers were high-level government officials before acquiring their posts, and often were trained as lawyers or university professors. Some subsequently became the directors of large state-owned or parastatal enterprises (Anderson 1986, 159; Lârif-Béatrix 1988, 208–209).[18] In short, the most successful and coveted career trajectory in Tunisia centered on the public sector.

The political priorities of the new state, conveyed through government policies, reflected the social origins and traditional support bases of the Neo-Destour leaders as well as the party's efforts to incorporate Tunisian society writ large.[19] State policies in the decades after independence promoted social mobility, particularly through heavy investment in education. As a result, Tunisia distinguished itself in the Arab world by its substantial middle class and constructed a more equitable society than many other Middle Eastern and North African states, including Morocco (Bras 1996, 176, 180–181).

STATE POLICIES AND CLASS FORMATION: THE DEVELOPMENT
OF A TUNISIAN INDUSTRIAL CLASS

In postindependence Tunisia, the new private sector developed in fits and starts largely because of disjunctures in state policies toward private

---

social groups do not try to capture pieces of the state and use its resources toward their own goals. See Heydemann (2004).

[17] See Ben Salem (1968; 1976) for analyses of the social backgrounds of high-level government officials in Tunisia.

[18] The third part of Asma Lârif-Béatrix's (1988) study of the postindependence Tunisian administration provides useful descriptive statistics on the demographic origins of high-level state officials.

[19] White (2001, 99–100) correctly asserts, "The state has not been a vehicle for class domination by the disparate class of property-owning traders, artisans, and small establishment owners," citing the fact that many of these elements did not support economic opening in the 1970s. Furthermore, social policies, and the general emphasis on social mobility through education, demonstrate that the state implemented policies that transcended the interests of the petit bourgeoisie.

investment in the transition from colony to independent state. During the first decade after independence, the alternate marginalization and promotion of private economic interests in state policies resulted in a discontinuous course of private-sector development. Although some of the same families maintained private holdings throughout various development phases, official ambivalence toward the private sector prevented them from transforming themselves into "big capital," as in the Moroccan *groupes*, until the 1990s.[20] Capital was partially reconstituted with each new political phase.[21]

The Early Years of Independence: A Gradualist Approach

Economic development and the creation of a basic national infrastructure were priorities for the newly independent Tunisian state, particularly given the vacuum created by departing French business interests. The formation of a national market, which remained largely fragmented under French occupation, was the task of the new independent state (Ben Marzouka 1996, 28; Sethom 1992, 141; Signoles et al. 1980, 25–26). Despite factional differences within the Neo-Destour on certain issues, notably between elements favoring a greater role for private capital in national development and those advocating a *dirigiste* (statist) approach, the government adopted a practical stance toward private ownership. State policy favored a gradual adjustment to the loss of European investment and skills and to the exodus of the local Jewish community, which had significant economic holdings (Sethom 1992, 115). Monetary and fiscal policies were relatively conservative, while the state concentrated on creating a monetary system independent of the French franc and forging a new customs code to replace the customs union with France (Bassani 1993, 58–60; *Maghreb-Machrek*, March–April 1964, 40; Micaud 1964, 172–173).

The party leadership adopted a liberal view on capital but tempered its approach with attention to social policy (Dimassi 1983, 49, 52–53;

---

[20] As discussed in chapter 5, big business lacked substantial influence until the 1990s.
[21] There is substantial literature written by both local and foreign scholars tracing the distinct development phases in postindependence Tunisian development, with virtual unanimity on the periodization of major policy shifts. See, for example, Anderson (1986); Bassani (1993); Bellin (1991); Ben Romdhane (1986); Ben Romdhane and Signoles (1982); Dimassi (1983); Dlala (1989; 1993); Guelmami (1996); Labouz (1981); Mahjoub (1978); Murphy (1999); Poncet (1980); Sethom (1992); Trabelsi (1985); and White (2001). The following account draws upon a selection of these works in addition to data gathered in interviews.

Sethom 1992, 116). With 19 percent of government spending in 1955–1956 allocated to education and to the construction and distribution of health and medical services, the state explicitly aimed to boost the middle-class foundations of Tunisian society (Findlay 1984, 221–222; Poncet 1970, 94).

In the initial years after independence, the reformist wing of the party prevailed, pushing for a development strategy that would encourage local private capital to invest in the national economy while the state developed a local transport and communications infrastructure. Bourguiba placed particular emphasis on attaining self-sufficiency in basic areas such as food and clothing. Toward this goal, the government helped a handful of merchants and weavers to launch textile factories of their own. These nascent industrialists portrayed themselves not only as business executives in a technical trade but also as pioneers in the nationalist struggle to industrialize the country. Support for local private interests included indirect measures, such as liquidating beylical land tenure institutions and suppressing real wages, as well as direct measures, such as instituting tax breaks for businesses and protective trade barriers on certain locally produced goods (Ben Romdhane 1986, 170–188; Dimassi 1983, 110, 126–130).

By the early 1960s, however, investment levels had remained low. Local private interests were reluctant to undertake industrial ventures, and average investment levels declined by 5.2 percent during 1956–1965 compared with the period 1950–1955. Rampant tax evasion by the commercial bourgeoisie further impeded capital accumulation. Despite the explicit goal of the new state to encourage the local private sector to actively engage in national development, half of all investment during the first five years of independence was publicly financed (Dimassi 1983, 135, 139, 209).

The 1960s: *Dirigisme,* ISI, and the "Socialist" Experiment

Recognizing the failures of the economic policies implemented during the first years of independence, reformists and *dirigistes* struck a compromise, resulting in a more explicitly state-led development plan. The main political goals of the program were economic decolonization, improving living standards, boosting productivity, and promoting self-sufficiency (Ruf 1984, 106). An interventionist state also served an important political goal: by taking charge of social advancement and transformation, the state promoted social cohesion and undercut the strength of potential challengers who represented otherwise dispossessed social groups (Guelmami 1996, 143).

Ahmed Ben Salah, who was appointed minister of the economy and planning in 1961, was given license to pursue his statist vision for national economic development.[22] By the mid-1960s, the ruling elite concluded that direct control of the surplus in the commercial and agricultural spheres was the only way to spur development, giving rise to the "cooperative movement," the notorious Tunisian collectivization experiment of the 1960s (Dimassi 1983, 97, 209; Harik 1992). For the radical wing, a state-led restructuring of the economy was the only way to achieve "the promotion of a society that was balanced, homogeneous and free of class struggle" (Union Nationale de la Coopération 1969, cited in Poncet 1970, 101). During the triennial plan of 1962–1964, the state collectivized agricultural land throughout the country, created service cooperatives, and called for the return of all foreign-owned lands on Tunisian soil to the public domain. The program reclaimed 400,000–500,000 hectares of the most productive land in Tunisia from foreign landholders (Poncet 1970, 101). During this period, the state played a leading role in creating basic industries in a wide variety of sectors, ranging from mining to manufacturing, and it established a number of institutions to coordinate consumer imports and distribution channels.[23] This massive state-led development effort resulted in enormous growth in public investment, which was over two times greater than private investment during the period 1962–1970 and accounted for almost 70 percent of total investment (Ben Romdhane 1986, 291).

At the same time, the collectivization drive largely destroyed what was left of the preindependence big landowning families and hindered further private industrial development by scaring off existing and potential investors (appendix A: I-38T; I-40T). To ensure official compliance by the business community, Bourguiba replaced the head of the national producers association, Ferdjani bel Hadj 'Ammar, with a member of the party faithful, Ezzedine Ben Achour. State leverage over private holders through economic policies, particularly withholding access to credit and import licenses, also compelled business submission, at least in the short term (Angrist 2006).

Even at the height of the so-called socialist experiment, the state supported private capital. As Bellin (1991, 49) points out, statism was designed more to "centralize economic decision making in the hands of

---

[22] In 1964, Ben Salah acquired more extensive responsibilities when he also became Secretary of the Economy and Finance (Poncet 1970, 100).

[23] Restructuring wholesale commerce and bulk imports began in 1962, and the system was extended to retail commerce between 1964 and 1967 (Asselain 1969, 120–123).

state bureaucrats than to realize socialism in Tunisia." State policy toward the textile sector is indicative of this ambivalent strategy (Brugnes Romieu 1968, 150–151). By 1958, state officials had begun contemplating ways to promote a local textile sector and sent Tunisian students to France to study textile engineering. Some of Tunisia's most prominent *textiliens* benefited from this opportunity. Two years later, the administration created the Office National des Textiles, which was responsible for coordinating production and imports of textile products, creating over eight state-owned textile firms and unifying prices across all stages of production and distribution. The new agency drew up plans to create the Société Générale du Coton, or Sogicot, a state-owned textile complex. Established in 1963, Sogicot had subsidiary firms in all branches and stages of thread and cloth manufacturing as well as a clothing unit. The formation of Sogicot, subsequently renamed the Société Générale du Textile, or Sogitex, resulted from a fusion of several state-owned thread, cloth, cloth-finishing, and apparel factories founded in the early 1960s, including Sogilaine, Tissmok, Somotex, and Siter.[24] Headed by Bechir Saidane, Sogitex had a full-time French consultant on staff, a consulting committee of a handful of local textile manufacturers, and several technical directors overseeing the various factories. In 1976, the state again decided to split Sogitex into separate factories according to subsectoral activity, but all retained the same central administration and management structure based in the Sahelian town of Ksar Hellal, which had a long tradition of artisanal and industrial textile manufacturing. The factories included a thread factory in Sousse, weaving facilities in Moknine, Ksar Hellal, and elsewhere in the Sahel, and a cloth-finishing unit in Bir Ksaa. Clothing production took place in a plant in Menzel Bourguiba. These factories operated with reasonable success until the early 1980s, when most either shut down or were slated for privatization (appendix A: I-49T; I-60T; I-74T; I-82T; Asselain 1969, 120).[25]

---

[24] Now dismantled and largely privatized, Sogitex encompassed a number of textile firms, including thread, woven cloth, and cloth-finishing factories. The Société Industrielle des Textiles (SITEX), which primarily manufactured denim cloth, was the first of the group to be privatized. In the late 1980s, Swift, an American textile company with offices in Ohio and Canada, purchased part of the group's shares. Subsequently, the International Finance Corporation of the World Bank Group, a Tunisian bank, and several Tunisian and Kuwaiti private investors acquired the rest of the capital (appendix A: I-40T; I-74T; I-85T; Harik 1992, 218–219). SITEX has no direct clients in Tunisia but instead works with local subcontractors who produce for European or American brands (appendix A: I-6T; I-74T; I-82T).

[25] In his analysis of privatization in Tunisia, Harik (1992, 214) cites several reasons for the failure of public enterprises, including underestimation of investment that led to high debt

Many future owners of private textile factories launched their careers in the Office National des Textiles and the constituent factories of Sogitex, acquiring knowledge and experience that enabled them to launch their own firms from the 1970s onward (appendix A: I-49T; I-60T; I-82T). The owners of major textile factories founded in the 1970s, including such well-known figures as Mohamed Ali Darghouth, Hachemi Kooli, Abdelaziz Dahmani, and Mohsen Ben Abdallah, acquired crucial experience in the state-owned enterprise. Beyond the textile sector, the majority of company owners and high-level managers launched their careers in the bureaucracy or state-owned enterprises (Harik 1992, 211). This career trajectory also reflected the reluctance of private capital to invest in capital-intensive activities, leaving the state to handle big projects, while local businesspeople gravitated toward smaller-scale, quick-return opportunities (Poncet 1970, 101).

Tunisian government policy during the 1960s played a crucial role in creating the foundations for a local industrial bourgeoisie; collectivization was never designed to displace the "profitable" private sector (Ruf 1984, 106).[26] State policies, consisting of import tariffs sheltering the local market from foreign competition, as well as fiscal incentives for businesses, laid the foundations for the growth of an indigenous industrial bourgeoisie. In the first years of independence, for example, 16 products were protected by quantitative restrictions on competitive imports, while by the mid-1960s, over 80 categories of industrial imports were subject either to restrictions or total prohibition. Fiscal incentives reinforced these pro-business measures, including state guarantees for loans incurred to establish new companies, exemptions on many taxes for the first 5 to 10 years of operation, and tax rate stability over a 15-year period, as well as guaranteed state contracts for 5 years and state limitations on competitive imports.

Protected by customs duties and other measures implemented after independence, Tunisian industrialists had no incentive to develop internationally competitive operations, and they created virtually no local thread-spinning or cloth-weaving capacity for export. As a result, private textile firms were almost entirely domestically oriented. Local cloth producers

---

levels, state-imposed price caps, and excess employment. For a more general treatment, see Waterbury (1994).

[26] A Tunisian industrialist contended, "We are products of the socialist period. When the country turned toward more liberalism [in the 1970s], there was at least a small industrial base in place thanks to the previous era's policies. This fact must be acknowledged" (appendix A: I-54T).

tried repeatedly to establish contracts with multinational apparel firms operating in Tunisia, such as Levi's or Gap, but their overtures were consistently rejected on the grounds that their products did not meet minimum quality standards (appendix A: I-6T; I-67T; I-84T). The most poorly developed branch of the domestic textile sector was the cloth-finishing industry, inhibiting overall sectoral development. Manufacturers contended that state domination of the finishing industry through Siter, the cloth-finishing unit in the Sogitex group, discouraged private investors from developing adequate cloth-finishing capabilities, while Siter did not compensate for the lack of private investment (appendix A: I-82T). As in Morocco and many other developing countries, the modern textile sector in Tunisia emerged in the context of protective import-substitution industrialization policies. Local apparel manufacturers imported cheaper and higher-quality cloth and thread from overseas or received these inputs from international clients for assembly and reexport as part of subcontracting arrangements.

Throughout the 1960s, the administration consolidated and expanded fiscal concessions, culminating in a unified investment code in 1969 (Bassani 1993, 62; Dimassi 1983, 501–504, 509–510).[27] The code, which required prior government approval for all investments, provided the same fiscal incentives for all sectors but allowed the government to grant additional advantages for large-scale projects, including monopoly position and protection from import competition (appendix A: I-82T). Although contrary to the ostensible goals of collectivization, allowing private monopoly holdings in certain sectors was designed to promote the growth of private business holdings (Dimassi 1983, 514; Guésquiere et al. 1997, 20). Ben Salah himself pointed to the growth of the local private sector during the 1960s:

There is much private investment in industry, which didn't exist before. Go see the industrial zone of Sfax and ask. When and by whom was this line-up of factories on I-don't-know-how-many kilometers created? By Sfaxiens, which shows that we were not at all against national capital. We pushed them by providing encouragement through all sorts of very favorable measures. (cited in Ben Romdhane and Signoles 1982, 271)

[27] For a detailed discussion of state efforts to lay the foundations for the rise of a local industrial bourgeoisie, see Ben Romdhane (1986, 250–256). Among the extensive incentives to private-sector development was a stipulation allowing monopoly holdings in certain sectors that was designed to allow consolidation of important private business holdings (Dimassi 1983, 514).

State policies of the 1960s had important long-term ramifications for Tunisian class formation. Although collectivization threatened local private interests, it was a crucial step in the process of building a local industrial base.

The collectivization experiment soon ran its course. By 1968, resource mobilization and production stagnated and even declined, while the state increasingly relied on domestic and foreign borrowing. Importantly, the *dirigiste* elite encroached upon the interests of the Neo-Destour's main constituents, culminating in tensions between the "state bourgeoisie" and local private interests, particularly small and medium landholders in the Sahel (Anderson 1986, 239; Dimassi 1983, 296; Findlay 1984, 223; Poncet 1970, 102, 105; Ruf 1984, 107). When the state announced plans to generalize the cooperative movement to all agricultural lands, open conflict erupted between the *dirigistes* and private capital holders (Asselain 1969, 141; Poncet 1970, 102). With the economic crisis deepening and political struggles within the party multiplying, Hédi Nouira, known for his liberal economic views, replaced Ben Salah, who was ousted in 1970, and the cooperative experiment came to an end. Private investment did not meet expectations, contributing to the administration's decision to adopt a radically different approach to national development in the 1970s.

A CRITICAL JUNCTURE: EARLY INTEGRATION IN GLOBAL MARKETS AND THE EMERGENCE OF THE DUAL MARKET

During the 1970s, economic policy changed course and the state increasingly implemented fiscal and trade policies favoring industrial development, particularly in the export sector. The new policies, which explicitly promoted the local private sector, and encouraged integration in the global economy through the export sector, constituted a critical juncture, establishing durable patterns of business–government relations in the Tunisian political economy.[28] The turn toward *infitah* (economic opening) was a product of both exogenous and endogenous factors. External economic constraints, which were particularly acute for small countries such as Tunisia, made economic opening a logical choice for a country with a small domestic market (Katzenstein 1985; White 2001, 96–98). Internal political struggles, culminating in the triumph of a liberal faction with

---

[28] On the critical junctures framework, see Collier and Collier (1991) and, for a modification, Mahoney (2002).

the support of key social constituencies who were frustrated with collectivization policies, also propelled the shift.

In this period, the government created several bodies designed to promote industrial development, notably the 1973 Agence pour la Promotion de l'Industrie, or the Industrial Promotion Agency, which provided technical and research-related support to investors, and the Fond pour la Promotion et Décentralisation Industrielle (Fund for Industrial Promotion and Decentralization), also set up in 1973, which provided loans at favorable rates for the creation of new enterprises (Dimassi 1983, 714–718). These institutions encouraged the growth of the local private sector (appendix A: I-45T; I-50T; Findlay 1984, 223, 227–228).

The most significant measure adopted by the state in the 1970s was the "1972 Law," enacted on April 27, 1972, which promoted exports and foreign direct investment by creating a vast set of incentives for totally export-oriented companies, both foreign and local.[29] Most incentives embodied in the law were fiscal, stipulating exemptions from taxes and duties such as the company patent tax for a 10-year period; the company earnings tax, also for a 10-year period; and customs duties levied on imports of equipment and primary materials used in the production process, for a 20-year period. Foreign companies benefited from unrestricted capital transfer in hard currency. A second important law, Law 74–74, adopted in August 1974, modified the 1969 Investment Code, provided additional tax breaks for Tunisian-owned manufacturing firms, and offered bonus incentives for firms generating high employment and those located in less developed regions of the country. Most significantly, Law 74–74 gave additional tax breaks to Tunisian firms that exported at least 10 percent of their annual revenues.[30] A third important law adopted in 1981 granted incentives to multinational firms that invested in services such as banking, warehousing, and distribution.

For many private businesspeople, the Nouira period was the golden age of business in Tunisia (appendix A: I-4T; I-38T; Harik 1992, 212). The manufacturing sector grew significantly during this period, as seen in figure 3.1.

In the 1970s, the field was wide open for investors who produced consumer goods for the domestic market, and increasingly protectionist trade

[29] To have "resident" or local status, 34 percent or more of the firm's capital must be in the hands of residents, while "non-resident" status entails having 66 percent or more of the firm's capital in foreign hands (Ben Romdhane 1986, 372).
[30] These companies came to be known as "1974 Law companies" (Centre National d'Etudes Industrielles 1981, 2).

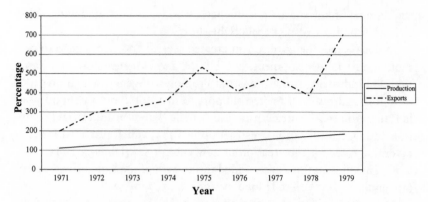

FIGURE 3.1. Percentage Growth in Industrial Production and Exports of Manufactures in Tunisia, 1971–1979 (Base: 1970). *Sources*: République Tunisienne, *Annuaire Statistique de la Tunisie*, Ministère du Plan, Institut National de la Statistique, 1976; République Tunisienne, *Annuaire Statistique de la Tunisie*, Ministère du Plan, Institut National de la Statistique, 1981.

policies for local market activities fostered private investment.[31] To protect local industry and increase state revenues, the government introduced a system of high and variable customs duties as well as a range of nontariff barriers, which ultimately constituted the primary means of protecting local producers. When economic problems emerged in the early 1980s, the state responded by further increasing import taxes and tariffs, which ranged from 5 percent to 236 percent, and tightening import controls. High effective rates of protection induced a spike in production for the local market. Trade and fiscal policies also introduced structural change in the national economy, with the share of industry rising from 21 percent to 32 percent from 1971 to 1981 and a concomitant decline in the share of agriculture (Bassani 1993, 64–65, 68, 75–76). Private investment soared in the textile, clothing, and leather sectors. Indeed, 87 percent of employment and 54 percent of investment created by the 1972 Law was in the textile, clothing, and leather industries, creating an imbalanced pattern of industrial development (Findlay 1984, 229). Within the textile sector, investment was also imbalanced (see figure 3.2). Few local investors in

---

[31] Still, the vitality of the Tunisian private sector during this period should not be exaggerated. Chedly Ayari, a former minister of the economy and a close associate of Nouira, noted, "The private sector...did not explode during the 1970s: we should not have illusions" (*Réalités*, February 12–13, 1993, 15). Furthermore, as Ben Romdhane and Signoles (1982) observe, the growth of private investment was greatly imbalanced both sectorally and spatially.

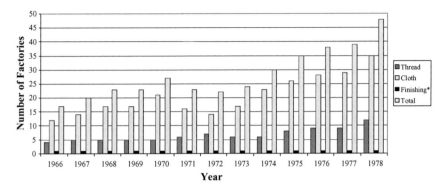

FIGURE 3.2. Factories in Tunisian Textile Sector by Branch (1966–1978). The Sogitex group had a cloth-finishing firm that processed almost all domestically finished cloth. *Sources*: République Tunisienne, *Annuaire Statistique de la Tunisie*, 1972; République Tunisienne, *Annuaire Statistique de la Tunisie*, 1976; République Tunisienne, *Annuaire Statistique de la Tunisie*, 1981.

textiles contemplated thread manufacturing, preferring to import rather than invest in such a capital-intensive industry (appendix A: I-82T).[32]

Whatever thread production existed in Tunisia was integrated in knitwear factories, which manufactured thread for use in their finished products and sold only small quantities on the local market (appendix A: I-36T; I-40T; I-60T). The most poorly developed branch of the Tunisian textile sector was the cloth-finishing industry, which inhibited overall sectoral development and stalled proposals to promote Tunisian apparel production on world markets through a clustering strategy. Without adequate cloth printing and dyeing facilities, the local cloth industry was inherently disadvantaged vis-à-vis competitor countries, and efforts to integrate the local textile and apparel sectors were stymied.

Rising imports, rapid fashion changes, and technological improvements in competitor countries also compelled the state-owned finishing factory to cut production dramatically.[33] While in the 1970s the company

---

[32] Thread production grew during the 1970s, with 7 firms operating in 1972 and 14 spinning facilities by 1980, but was never the most important branch of the textile sector. The Centre National d'Etudes Industrielles (1976, 1–2), a research group affiliated with the API, listed about 20 factories in 1976, but some were publicly owned, while others were branches of the same firm. More investors chose the cloth industry. From 1972 to 1989, the number of cloth-weaving factories increased from 14 to 46 (Centre National d'Etudes Industrielles 1976, 3–4; Trabelsi 1985, 137, 141).

[33] Many rumors circulated about the fate of Siter and its prospects for privatization. A French investor, Gérard Bittan, working with a Tunisian investor, Zouheir Ayadi, bought

processed 33 million square meters of cloth per year, by the late 1990s the company treated only four million square meters of cloth per year (appendix A: I-82T). At the same time, the small size of the domestic market and rapid changes in global fashion markets deterred Tunisian finishing companies from keeping pace with shifts in global textile markets. As a result, local production of cloth for apparel and fashion items suffered, limiting overall growth in the Tunisian textile sector (appendix A: I-85T).

Because the local apparel sector operated almost exclusively in the off-shore economy, Tunisian garment manufacturers were largely unscathed by trade reform and even welcomed the process. The initial phase of liberalization reinforced the strict separation between the on-shore textile sector and off-shore apparel industries as the declining costs of textile inputs on international markets further compelled many garment manufacturers to import intermediate goods rather than source them locally (World Bank 1996, 29).

The high percentage of foreign investment in the apparel sector meant that another significant component of producers based on Tunisian soil favored economic reform and were not concerned about the local ramifications of trade liberalization. Many foreign garment producers and buyers operating in Tunisia's off-shore zone had little or no contact with Tunisian-owned firms and minimal linkages to the domestic economy. For example, Levi's, which sources 75 percent of its supply for European markets in Tunisia, works with nine subcontractors in Tunisia, of which only one is fully Tunisian owned. European companies with factories operating in the Tunisian off-shore economy own the eight remaining firms (appendix A: I-84T). Foreign manufacturers implanted in Tunisia would obviously benefit from economic opening by gaining even greater access to imported inputs. Locally oriented producers had few institutionalized channels through which to convey their grievances and minimal collective influence in the political sphere.

Most wealthy families and big private interests in the Tunisian economy started out on a limited scale in the 1970s (appendix A: I-54T; I-87T). In this period, the government encouraged entrepreneurship in the middle classes through an array of technical and financial support instruments (appendix A: I-66T; *La Presse*, February 19, 1998). State-sponsored credit programs played a key role in helping small entrepreneurs to launch

both Siter and Tissmok in 2000 (appendix A: I-85T; "La Privatisation en Tunisie," www.tunisieinfo.com/privatisation/bilan-detaille.html, accessed February 3, 2006).

businesses. The Fond pour la Promotion du Developpement Industriel (FOPRODI), created in 1973, was the primary source of credit. Some of the wealthiest and most prominent businesspeople who emerged after independence came from decidedly modest origins and launched their activities with FOPRODI support. Tunisia's most legendary success story came from a modest family. Ben Ayed, the head of the Poulina group, which has extensive holdings in sectors such as food processing, furniture, supermarkets, restaurants, and retail stores, initiated his business ventures in the 1960s by raising and marketing chickens (appendix A: I-44T).[34] Nonetheless, the vast majority of FOPRODI beneficiaries in both the on-shore and off-shore sectors were small-scale producers (appendix A: I-56T). Government incentives and programs instituted after independence ensured that the distribution of capital was relatively equitable in Tunisia. As a result, a large-scale economic elite that dominated national politics did not develop.

Profiting from the newly implemented incentives for business, some local entrepreneurs established partnerships with multinational firms to assemble and market consumer products in Tunisia. The Zghal family, for example, founded one of the first consumer electronics firms, Telestar, which assembled televisions. A German firm, Telefunken, supplied all components and spare parts for local assembly. Along with another family-owned consumer electronics assembly firm, affiliated with Thompson International, Telestar enjoyed a virtual monopoly in the television industry until the late 1980s (appendix A: I-39T; I-55T; I-59T). The handful of industrialists who embarked on these ventures made fortunes at this time, when demand vastly exceeded supply and almost no competition existed on the domestic market.

Until 1988, official regulations prohibited the establishment of holding companies, with investments in multiple sectors of the economy. Unlike in Morocco, where the big *groupes* had stakes throughout the economy, Tunisian business owners tended to confine their holdings to a single sector, focusing either on manufacturing, banking, or mining, for example. A Tunisian economist noted, "Access to capital was always democratic. Most private actors came from small-scale origins, and usually they were bureaucrats, technicians, or engineers. They did not come from 'big'

---

[34] Azzedine Hentati, the founder of a company that manufactures oil filters for American, Japanese, and European cars, was another prominent business executive who came from a modest background. Having minimal resources of his own, Hentati started his business with funds from FOPRODI (appendix A: I-44T).

families, but rather mostly from modest families" (appendix A: I-52T). A local journalist and longtime observer of Tunisian politics concurred, emphasizing that Tunisia boasted many truly "self-made men" (appendix A: I-87T). It was not until the 1980s and 1990s, after economic reforms were introduced, that prominent families – usually those with close connections to Ben Ali and his family – expanded their holdings significantly across diverse sectors (appendix A: I-35T; I-40T; I-55T).

Most importantly, the 1970s witnessed the institutionalization of parallel domestic and export sectors. The 1972 Law gave rise to a class of exporters with extensive linkages to overseas markets and clients at a time when most other developing countries were still pursuing some form of import-substitution industrialization that served to consolidate the position of elites targeting the local market (Ben Romdhane and Signoles 1982, 84–87). The rise of the apparel sector is indebted to Nouira's policies. Many apparel assembly and manufacturing plants, both Tunisian and European, were founded in the 1970s. With its quick returns and limited capital investment, garment assembly was an attractive option. Subcontractors had a limited relationship with the local market, often receiving their inputs with the orders and reexporting them in finished form (Ben Hammouda 1995, 191; Dammak 1980, 92).

The 1972 Law also encouraged foreign investment in the off-shore sector, creating a significant presence of foreign firms who had little stake in local politics (Sethom 1992, 354–356). From 1971 through the early 1980s, foreign investment rose steadily, from 6.75 percent in 1971 to 9.2 percent in 1980 (Ben Marzouka 1996, 29). By 1986, it had dropped to about 3 percent of the gross industrial product.

Characteristic of semiopen economies, the turn toward export-oriented industrialization in the 1970s should not suggest that Tunisia abandoned protectionist trade policies. Production targeting the local market remained sheltered from foreign competition, establishing, in effect, a dual market in the Tunisian economy comprised of on-shore and off-shore activities with little interaction across the two spheres and minimal integration within sectors (appendix A: I-47T; Ben Romdhane and Signoles 1982, 90). The lack of integration was particularly acute in the textile sector, where underdeveloped cloth-finishing capabilities restricted the development of a competitive local cloth industry (Centre National des Etudes Industrielles 1984, 7). The implementation of an export-oriented development strategy alongside the small, protected domestic market created two distinct and largely separate elements of the industrial bourgeoisie. The dual market structure, and its attendant creation of a bifurcated local and export-oriented business class structure, set the stage for intensified trade liberalization in the late 1980s and early 1990s.

The rise of an authoritarian, single-party state undeniably shaped the political fortunes of all major social groups in Tunisian society. An extensive security apparatus quashed actual and potential sources of "instability." But state repression does not entirely explain political apathy in the industrial class. Rather, because they owed their fortunes to generous state programs, industrialists were largely satisfied with state policies. Tunisia's brand of an authoritarian, "developmental" state (Amsden 1989; Johnson 1982; Woo-Cumings 1999) emerged out of nationalist struggles in which existing political and economic elites were marginalized and therefore wielded little influence on postindependence economic policymaking. Instead, state officials largely created a new industrial class after independence. Thanks to supportive administrative measures implemented in the 1960s and 1970s, such as licensing, price controls, and protective tariff barriers, business interests were beholden to the state. Beginning in the 1970s, a dual market structure arose, composed of parallel export and domestic sectors dominated by small and medium holders, and each flourished in its own sphere. Exporters and local industrialists coexisted peaceably thanks to regulations ensuring the strict separation of the on-shore and off-shore economies. Economic liberalization, detailed in chapter 2, merely reinforced this separation. The resultant patterns of postindependence business–government relations and the bifurcated business class structure, which was dispersed across a protected domestic sphere and an export sector created preemptively in the early 1970s, help to explain business political quiescence in the 1990s.

4

Business and the State in Morocco

Business Penetration of the State and the Genesis of the "Fat Cat"

The structure of the industrial bourgeoisie and pattern of business–government relations that emerged in Morocco's postindependence era influenced how later industrialists would respond to economic opportunities and constraints in the reform period. Many analytical treatments of the private sector, particularly in literature on North African politics, present "business" as a homogeneous class. This study, in contrast, emphasizes the variegated nature of the business class and, more specifically, divisions within the *industrial* bourgeoisie. In the postindependence era, the rise of a well-connected protectionist elite, organized in multisectoral groups or holding companies, emerged out of two factors: first, their importance in the anticolonial struggle, which enabled them to penetrate the independent state and shape economic policy; and second, the perceived capacity of the domestic market to sustain ISI, at least in the short to medium term. The existence of this privileged elite shaped the institutional and political context within which different business factions maneuvered, spurring reactive mobilization by emergent exporters in the 1990s, almost five decades after independence.

BUSINESS–GOVERNMENT RELATIONS
IN POSTINDEPENDENCE MOROCCO

The postindependence structure of the Moroccan industrial bourgeoisie and forms of business–government relations emerged as a result of several factors, including French administration policies during the colonial period, the relationship of economic elites to the colonial administration, and, most importantly, interactions between the monarchy and existing business classes after independence.

The Political System: The Palace, Parties, and Parliament

When the French occupied Morocco and subsequently established the Protectorate in 1912, they implemented a two-track pattern of administration. One track safeguarded the institutions of the *makhzen*, the seat of central authority dating back several centuries and embodied in the sultanate and local power structures; the other gave control over day-to-day affairs to the colonial administration.[1] The French explicitly aimed to consolidate the influence of many rural local leaders (*qaids*), thereby reinforcing and reshaping indigenous institutions rather than supplanting them. The new system reduced the autonomy of tribal areas (*bled al-siba*) – the "land of dissidence" – by centralizing control over Moroccan territory.[2] By replacing a more fluid set of power relations in which local religious leaders (*marabouts*) were influential, colonial rule under Resident-General Louis Hubert Gonzalve Lyautey and his successors enabled the sultan – and, more to the point, the French Residency – to gain extensive control over previously "dissident" areas through rural elite proxies (Sluglett and Farouk-Sluglett 1984, 56–57; Tessler 1982, 43). Because rural power configurations differed, the new administrative structure imposed by the French did not conform to a single national model but varied considerably across regions. In this way, the French nominally "preserved" indigenous institutions yet radically altered their nature (Hammoudi 1999, 165).

---

[1] The *makhzen* is the term developed in French colonial historiography for the precolonial Moroccan central authority. Traditionally, the *bled al-makhzen*, or the "land of government," was juxtaposed to the *bled al-siba*, or the "land of dissidence," populated by tribes and other local power bases that largely refused to pay taxes to the Moroccan sultan. Despite critiques of this dichotomous depiction of precolonial Moroccan society and significant modifications to the concept (Ayache 1997; Laroui 1993), some analysts continue to rely on this binary framework. See Pennell (1993) for a discussion of the origins and evolution of the *makhzen* and *siba* concepts, Claisse (1987) on their continued conceptual relevance in postindependence Morocco, and Ben Ali (1987, 118–123) for an overview of diverse uses of the term *makhzen* and its historical roots. Hammoudi (1999, 129–130) stresses that the notion of the *makhzen* is contested.

[2] Bendourou (1996, 109) observes that the *ulema*, or religious scholars, were the historical arbiters of sovereignty because they had the power to depose a sultan who did not fulfill his duties. With the establishment of the Protectorate, the French undercut the *ulema* by granting the power of sovereignty to the sultan to boost their ability to rule through his office.

The monarchy, which was and remained a national institution, gained importance in national politics, facilitating its role as a key player in the nationalist struggle and contributing to its secure grip on power at independence.[3]

The political system in postindependence Morocco is ostensibly a constitutional monarchy. Like its successors, the first constitution, which was adopted in 1962, established the primacy of the monarchy in national politics but created legislative and judicial bodies that formally shared in national governance.[4] Until 1997, when a second legislative chamber was introduced, the Assembly was the sole legislative body, with two-thirds of its members elected through universal suffrage and the remaining third elected by interest groups. A 1997 constitutional amendment altered electoral procedures and parliamentary structure by creating the Chamber of Counselors (composed of representatives of local councils, professional associations, and trade unions) and stipulating that members of the Assembly, renamed the House of Representatives, would be elected by direct popular vote. On paper, the parliament plays a significant role in national politics because it passes all laws, including the annual budgetary law. Relative to many other countries in the Middle East and North Africa, Morocco enjoys substantial freedom of the press and freedom of speech, yet the unspoken rules of political life forbid criticism of the king (Bendourou 1996, 110–111; Layachi 1998, 98).[5]

In reality, the palace remains the ultimate seat of power.[6] Parliament and political parties wield little influence, and elections are generally rigged (Munson 1999, 259, 274; Waltz 1999, 283, 296). Each constitution, designed by the king and officially ratified by popular vote, subordinated all other political institutions to the monarchy. The king commands the army, appoints and dismisses the prime minister and other high-level

---

[3] Hammoudi (1999, 165) argues, "[R]ather than eliciting the democratic potential of the so-called traditional Moroccan institutions, the colonial system made other choices; it tapped the autocratic potential of these institutions within a new integration of forms and categories." See Hermassi (1972, 59–74) for a concise discussion of the distinct styles of French rule in the North African colonies and the implications for postindependence political development. Sluglett and Farouk-Sluglett (1984, 51–59) describe the imposition of French rule over Morocco and the institutional choices of the colonial administrators.

[4] Subsequent constitutions were adopted in 1970, 1972, and 1992.

[5] Until recently, all dailies, whether pro-government or publications of the opposition, received state subsidies (Bendourou 1996, 114–115).

[6] Waterbury (1970, 399) observes, "[T]he real politics of the country became concentrated in the competition for patronage among various ministers and their protégés. This kind of competition was and is far easier for the King to manage than that of political organizations and political ideology."

government officials, promulgates laws, and, on several occasions, has even dissolved the parliament and suspended the constitution. In effect, for much of Morocco's postindependence history, the constitution was meaningless, and the government merely executed rather than deliberated over policies devised by the king and his close advisors. In addition to clientelism, which established a system of selective access to economic opportunities, force and repression have played an important role in maintaining the king's power, as the treatment of opposition figures and the spotty human rights record of King Hassan's Morocco attest (Munson 1993, 140; Perrault 1990; Tessler 1982, 48, 63–64; Zartman 1987, 25–27).[7]

To prevent the rise of a single influential body that could capture mass allegiance, after independence the palace encouraged the creation and proliferation of multiple political parties (Zartman 1990, 223–230). Pro-government, conservative parties included the Mouvement Populaire (MP), which was established in 1958 and has a significant Berber base; the Parti National Démocratique (PND), established in 1981 by splinters of the Rassemblement National des Indépendants (RNI) (founded in 1978); and the Union Constitutionnelle (UC), created in 1983. The latter two parties, known as the "administration parties," were created by the regime. Together, the MP, PND, and UC formed a pro-government bloc in 1993, known as the Entente Nationale. Two other pro-government parties, the RNI and the Mouvement National Populaire (MNP) (created in 1991 as an offshoot of the MP), opted not to participate in the bloc. The main constituents of the RNI and MNP tend to come from rural areas, where conservative parties cultivated extensive linkages to the local populations.

Opposition parties alternately participated in the government and boycotted elections. From 1997 to 2003, they controlled the government, thanks to the former king's appointment of longtime opposition figure Abderrahman Youssoufi as prime minister. The principal parties of the opposition include the Istiqlal, the Union Socialistes des Forces Populaires (USFP), the Parti du Progrés et du Socialisme (PPS), and the

---

7 Munson (1993) takes issue with many anthropological studies of Morocco, such as those of Combs-Schilling (1989) and Geertz (1968), which center on religious legitimacy in explaining the popular appeal of King Hassan II's rule. Holiness does not explain the endurance of the Moroccan monarchy, as Munson suggests through anecdotal evidence on popular apathy toward the king during moments of crisis in poor urban districts in Morocco. Munson's argument would also oppose Hammoudi's (1997) explanation for the endurance of Moroccan authoritarianism, which is founded on the pervasiveness of the master–disciple "cultural schema" in the minds of the population.

Organisation de l'Action Démocratique et Populaire (OADP). The Istiqlal, the nationalist party founded in 1943, enjoyed great legitimacy because its founders led the struggle for independence and helped to reinstall the king after his exile by the French colonial authorities. Many families of the traditional bourgeoisie from Fès and other historic Moroccan cities, as well as some elements of the intelligentsia, were heavily involved in the party.[8] The USFP, founded in 1959, is the main party of the Left and has a substantial base in public administration and parastatal enterprises. The PPS, a Marxist party and successor to the former Communist Party that was founded in 1974, has a small following, particularly among university professors. The OADP was founded in 1983 by former members of the USFP. In 1992, after a rapprochement between the Istiqlal and the USFP, the opposition parties formed the Democratic Bloc, or Kutla Democratiyya (Azam and Morrison 1994, 85–87; Bendourou 1996, 112; Claisse 1987, 45; Tessler 1982, 51–55). In addition, a moderate Islamist opposition party, the Party of Justice and Development (PJD), recently gained legal recognition but remains closely watched.

In short, an extensive set of formal political institutions developed in postindependence Morocco but were not the most effective means of channeling societal interests. For elites in particular, personal and kinship connections to palace officials and the king's close advisors were a much more valuable means of transmitting preferences and obtaining specific requests. Indeed, even for nonelites, personal ties were an important way of interacting with the bureaucracy (Sabah 1987).

The Roots of the Economic Elite: Commercial Families and Social Ties

Some of Morocco's Fassi urban elite had already developed extensive local, regional, and international commercial interests before independence and even prior to the Protectorate.[9] At independence, according to John Waterbury (1970, 98), there were three general types of Fassis: (1) the commercial families, some of which had trade links with the interior of Morocco, sub-Saharan Africa, the Maghrib, the Middle East, and Europe

---

[8] For example, Catusse (1999b, 17) cites the El Fassi, Balafrej, Bennani, Sebti, Berrada, and Tazi families. Lamrhili (1978, 34, 37) argues that the main motive of the Fassi bourgeoisie for launching the nationalist movement was their desire to take over the lucrative economic activities of the French. See Ashford (1961) for a detailed account of the formation and rise of the Istiqlal.

[9] *Fassi* originally referred to the *grandes familles* of the imperial city of Fès, but here the term connotes privileged older elites from any major urban area.

dating back hundreds of years; (2) the *makhzen* families, who were not necessarily wealthy in their own right but acquired influence through their close association with the state; and (3) the *sharifian* families, whose primary asset was religious legitimacy. There is a long tradition of close ties between the state and the urban elite. For example, in exchange for paying taxes to the state fisc, the Fassis enjoyed state protection from invading tribes. While some of these elite families were marginalized economically during the Protectorate and following independence, others enjoyed massive growth during these periods, having invested in new economic activities, such as transportation and agro-industry. The Fassis cemented their privileges and holdings by sending their sons to select schools. They also intermarried to gain access to business opportunities and to consolidate their holdings within the family, or at least within an elite group. Indeed, many of the largest business groups arose as a result of marriage-based alliances between important trading families (Benhaddou 1997, 27–35; Waterbury 1970, 95–104).[10]

When the French departed in 1956, the Fassis, who had independent financial bases, constituted the embryo of a cohesive indigenous industrial bourgeoisie. In postindependence Morocco, the power of the urban bourgeoisie was institutionalized directly in the public sphere as members of prominent families obtained key positions in the administration, national banks, parastatal organizations, and producer organizations (appendix A: I-52M; I-54M; I-69M).[11] A common career trajectory for members of prominent Fassi families began with a ministerial position, followed by a high-ranking post in a national bank. As Ben Ali remarked (1991a, 56), because "access to state favors became a necessary condition for success in business and contributed to the consolidation of a hold on the economy," prominent families quickly realized the advantages of establishing a firm foothold in the new system.[12] Indeed, some of Morocco's most prominent families expanded their fortunes considerably by benefiting

---

[10] Waterbury (1970, 95–103) notes that the dense family networks that arose as a result of intermarriage and business alliances proved useful in mobilizing nationalist sentiment when the French made political organizing increasingly difficult. Interestingly, an industrialist from a prominent family of Fassi origin advised me to read Benhaddou's (1997) book, claiming that it presents an accurate picture of the Moroccan elite – albeit from a negative viewpoint (appendix A: I-79M).

[11] Waterbury (1970, 107) provides a table listing major government and banking posts that demonstrates the extensive representation of the urban bourgeoisie in these spheres.

[12] Similarly, Berrada (1992, 89) claims that "the aptitude for penetrating public decision-making spheres determined and still determines the construction of the fortunes of a good number of active elements in the dominant private sector."

from their control over key posts in the administration.[13] Elite families cultivated close links with the king's advisors and often developed patronage relationships with specific royal counselors (appendix A: I-6M; I-11M; I-14M; Saâdi 1989).[14] In this way, dense networks between public officials and private interests arose, blurring the lines between business and government and enabling a privileged few to benefit from protective trade policies.

Through these connections, elites gained access to preferential economic opportunities (lucrative government contracts, in particular) and obtained exclusive import licenses, thereby increasing their chances of financial gain.[15] A well-known family name also facilitated access to bank credit, which was virtually unavailable to small entrepreneurs (appendix A: I-31M, I-60M; Ben Ali 1991b, 57). Only a theoretical boundary between "public" and "private" exists in the Moroccan political economy, prompting a longtime observer to dub the system "cozy capitalism" (appendix A: I-22M).

A small number of capital holders controlled diverse activities through family-based business groups.[16] Rarely confined to a single area of activity, large-scale private interests often had business concerns spanning the industrial, agricultural, and financial sectors. The largest conglomerate, the Omnium Nord Africain (ONA), was controlled by the royal family, which had diversified its holdings from land into industry and finance by the 1980s (Belghazi 1997, 82–86; Zartman 1987, 29). The ONA comprises at least 40 companies engaged in mining, agro-industry, automobile assembly, transportation, real estate, and manufacturing. In

---

[13] In fall 1999, the Youssoufi administration proposed a law that would explicitly forbid government officials from owning and managing private companies while holding office. In practice, however, the law would be hard to enforce and easily evaded by temporarily placing family members in top management positions of companies.

[14] In the early 1990s, when a member of the Royal Council died, the families under his patronage were compelled to establish a similar relationship with another Counselor in order to secure their interests. Until they firmly established a new contact, family members were uncertain about their economic future and social stature (appendix A: I-4M).

[15] Adopting a state-centric approach, Ben Ali (1987) argues that the *makhzen* used the public sector as a means of controlling social reproduction and effecting class formation, particularly by distributing access to economic opportunities and appointing high-level technocrats.

[16] See Waterbury (1970, 85–86, 93) and Benhaddou (1997) for sociological discussions of marriage and business linkages between elite private-sector elements. Common educational backgrounds also enhanced the cohesion of the urban elite. Many friendships dated back to school days, and the colleges of Moulay Idriss in Fès and Moulay Youssef in Rabat were populated by the children of the urban commercial bourgeoisie (Hermassi 1972, 102).

1982, the ONA merged with two other holding companies, COGESPAR and SIHAM.[17] The conglomerate adopted an aggressive acquisition strategy in both the pre- and postindependence periods. SIHAM was a Danish holding company operating in Morocco, with extensive interests in the agro-food sector. In the 1960s, Prince Moulay Ali founded COGESPAR, which bought several other companies, including SIHAM (Saâdi 1989). Together, the ONA and another major holding company, the Société Nationale d'Investissement, controlled about 9 percent of GDP. In conjunction with four other multisectoral conglomerates, these companies controlled about 30 percent of GDP (appendix A: I-16M).[18] Overlapping ownership structures in these organizations consolidated shared interests and reinforced social ties among elites, including the royal family.

Many of the families heading major holding companies started out in the textile sector, or at least acquired holdings in the industry as they expanded their operations. Prior to independence from France in 1956, virtually no indigenous industry had developed in Morocco. In 1939 and 1940, French investors established the first semimodern cloth factories in Morocco, notably SAFT and the Comptoir Francais, which later became Orbonor and Etablissements Foucherot, respectively. Some locally owned industrial ventures were launched during World War II, when the colonial economies were essentially cut off from European and world

---

[17] French and Dutch banks founded the original ONA conglomerate in 1919 to consolidate their interests in Morocco, establishing in 1943 an auxiliary transport company called ONA.

[18] The precise number of companies that "control" the Moroccan economy is a subject of debate and greatly depends on subjective definitions of "control." For example, a Moroccan journalist contended that as many as 10 holding companies reign over the national economy (appendix A: I-20M). Saâdi estimated that 28 families and conglomerates controlled 15.3 percent of capital in the processing industries in 1980. In a subsequent publication, Saâdi claimed that four groups alone – the Larakis, the Lamranis, the Kettanis, and the ONA – controlled 7.5 percent of industrial capital and 14.7 percent of total private capital in Morocco, while the top 10 families control 11.3 percent of industrial capital and 22.2 percent of total private capital (Saâdi 1992, 8). These debates echo the literature on the Moroccan political economy in the immediate postindependence period, which produced conflicting claims about the number of families who reigned over national economic activities and wielded substantial political influence. While some set the figure at 300 (Saâdi 1983, 116), others argued that as many as 500 families controlled the Moroccan economy. Lamrhili (1978, 36–37) supports the former estimate but claims that a mere 30 families constitute the real "big business" class. Tessler (1982, 37–38) depicts "concentric circles" around the monarchy, with varying numbers of families and individuals composing each ring. Despite these distinct images, informants uniformly agreed that a tight clique of insiders who head a handful of multisectoral holding companies dominate the economy. The secondary source literature roundly confirms these contentions.

markets. After the war, French investors quickly boosted their holdings in North Africa, and much of Morocco's basic industrial structure developed between 1949 and 1955 (Avonde 1922, 335–336; Ayache 1997, 37; Gallisot 1990, 23–24; Sluglett and Farouk-Sluglett 1984, 68).[19] A new wave of textile mills were created, and thread and dyeing facilities were established, including Icoma, Mafaco, Sefita, Filroc, and Manufacture de Fès. At the same time, several French-owned clothing and knitwear factories were founded, such as SCIM, Masurel, Nehera, Rolny, CIB, IBOMA, SINAC, SOGEB, and IMC. Whatever local, nonagricultural private interests existed prior to independence were almost exclusively engaged in commercial activities, while French business interests established industrial firms in the northern coastal cities of Casablanca, Mohammedia, and Kenitra. By 1956, approximately 150 local and foreign textile firms were operating in Morocco, employing 12,000 workers (Bégot 1969, 83–86; Fejjal 1987, 31–32; Geissman 1999; Khatibi 1968, 88).[20]

Independence and French capital flight brought the recognition that industrialization was important for national development. In the relatively capital-intensive textile sector, the state took the lead in launching textile mills, while many Moroccan investors were hesitant to undertake such "high-tech" ventures. Still, some families took over textile factories from departing French industrialists, and a few even launched their own firms. Almost entirely export-oriented, the apparel industry did not develop until later, initially in response to trade agreements signed with Europe in the 1970s. The industry boomed in the 1980s and early 1990s as a result of trade liberalization policies and growing opportunities on global markets. Until this time, a traditional clothing industry had long existed in Morocco but was not organized as a modern, mass-production industry (appendix A: I-74M; Ben Ali 1993, 3; Cairoli 1998, 30–31; Fejjal 1987, 58–59; LVE, May 14, 1976, 44).

The Moroccan industrial bourgeoisie traces its origins to the 1960s, when the textile industry began to develop in earnest, but it grew out of urban, commercial families. Prominent families gravitated toward several sectors supplying the domestic market, notably food processing, textiles, and construction. Built-in consumer demand as well as state incentives were major reasons for investment in these industries, and private capital

[19] The Alami, Sebti, and Bennani families profited extensively during this period (Hermassi 1972, 183).
[20] See Bégot (1969) for an overview of the rise of the modern textile sector in Casablanca, where the bulk of industrial activity was concentrated under the Protectorate and beyond.

dominated in light industry (Saâdi 1992, 13). But it would be misleading to argue that the state created the industrial bourgeoisie, as in Tunisia, because the Fassi elites leveraged their importance in the nationalist movement to penetrate the state and influence economic policy.

Thread and cloth manufacturing was also a logical choice for the traditional urban bourgeoisie because many had long experience in the textile trade and had built up extensive commercial networks stretching from West Africa to the United Kingdom. During the Protectorate, a number of merchant families from Fès immigrated to Senegal and Ivory Coast as well as to Europe, where they set up textile trading firms. Many of these traders imported cloth, particularly from England and Egypt, to sell in West and North African countries (appendix A: I-72M; I-74M; I-79M; Lamrhili 1978, 32). When they returned to Morocco, many remained in the cloth business, setting up wholesale and retail storefronts in the Casablanca neighborhood of Derb Omar and even founding cloth factories.[21] During the 1950s and 1960s, textile industrialists amassed substantial fortunes and, until the mid-1980s, almost all based their operations near their homes. Subsequent generations either shut down their family businesses and shifted into other activities or moved the factories to newly constructed industrial zones in the outlying regions of Casablanca and Ain Sebaa (appendix A: I-54M; I-61M; Fejjal 1987, 60–61).[22]

Of all industrial activities, Moroccan investors most successfully penetrated the textile and food-processing sectors in the first decade after independence. Some prominent families had amassed sufficient capital to take over textile and garment factories established by European investors during the Protectorate (appendix A: I-34M; I-35M; I-71M; Berrada 1991, 968).

THE INSTITUTIONALIZATION OF THE PROTECTED ECONOMY

Elite control over vast spheres of the economy did not emerge spontaneously. For its part, the state, influenced by officials with ties to elite

---

[21] In general, the commercial bourgeoisie was hesitant to invest in long-term industrial projects and, therefore, the rise of a true industrial sector occurred gradually (Adam 1970, 228).

[22] Many textile factory owners whose fathers switched from commercial activities to manufacturing in the early years after independence complained that the older generation lacked the "industrial spirit." The second generation was often educated in France, where they obtained degrees in textile engineering and business management, and therefore they considered themselves to be more astute businessmen than their forebears (Adam 1970, 227; appendix A: I-54M).

families, instituted a series of policies that consistently favored private economic interests. Thanks to state intervention, elite families were able to further their economic interests considerably.[23]

The Early Years of Independence

During the struggle for independence, the urban commercial bourgeoisie strongly supported the sultan through the Istiqlal and was greatly responsible for the survival of the monarchy during the Protectorate (Joffé 1988; Leveau 1993, 250–251).[24] In return, Istiqlal leaders expected the newly independent state to favor its interests. Instead, a political struggle erupted in 1956–1960 between the Istiqlal, which openly favored the establishment of a British-style constitutional monarchy with a nominal role for the king, and the palace, which sought to undercut the strength of any potential political rivals.[25] In part to counterbalance the influence of urban elites, King Mohamed V cultivated close linkages to rural notables and concentrated national investment in agriculture after regaining the throne. This tactic was a continuation of French colonial policy, which manipulated and favored rural tribal leaders as a means of weakening urban nationalists. As a result, agrarian elites remained intact and constituted an important social stratum in the postindependence political scene (Charrad 2001, 149). The rural notables, composed mainly of local *qaids*, were traditional rivals of the urban commercial bourgeoisie, and the failure of the Istiqlal to mobilize the countryside was a major impediment to the party's aspirations for national political power. Several Istiqlal leaders openly sought to undercut the tribal structure of Moroccan society,

[23] Berrada (1992, 86–87) observes, "The post-colonial state, in effacing itself, by not affirming its existence, in other words by keeping its distance, by letting be, by adopting a low profile, rendered a great service to certain categories of local and foreign private holders. Evidently, the absence of intervention meant intervention."

[24] Of course, the motives for bourgeois participation in the independence movement are not necessarily so noble. In an article misleadingly titled "Origins of the Moroccan Bourgeosies" – misleading because it focuses more on the role of the bourgeoisie in the national movement than on its origins – Kamal ed-Din Mourad (1997) argues that urban elite participation in the movement for national liberation merely served its own interests while ignoring those of the masses, who constituted the base of the Istiqlal Party. The alliance between capital and labor consequently broke down at independence in 1956. For Mourad, Moroccan nationalism was "no more than the march of the bourgeoisie to power" (Mourad 1997, 98).

[25] The limited social base of the party greatly facilitated this task for the monarchy. The intricacies of these political struggles are well documented elsewhere. For example, see Waterbury (1970, 48–49, 194–195), Hermassi (1972, 172–176), El-Mossadeq (1987), Zartman (1987, 3–6), and Ben Ali (1991a, 52, 55).

automatically pitting themselves against rural elites (Charrad 2001, 154–155; Hermassi 1972, 103, 111; Joffé 1988).

Support for agrarian elites manifested itself in the monarchy's avoidance of real land reform, allowing rural notables to retain control over two-thirds of irrigated land.[26] Large farmers also received a disproportionate share of land from departing French landowners in state redistribution programs, while state policies ensured a vast pool of inexpensive peasant labor for big agrarian capital. In macroeconomic terms, state investment focused more heavily on agriculture than on the industrial and commercial sectors, the purview of many Istiqlal supporters. As a result, the gap between small and large farmers widened, and big landholders were increasingly linked to international markets and involved in commercial agriculture. In this respect, Moroccan policies differed markedly from those of many other newly independent countries, including Tunisia, which focused its development efforts on building up industry at the expense of the "traditional" agricultural sector (Azam and Morrison 1994, 87–88, 90; Ben Ali 1991a, 52–56; Bendourou 1996, 109; Doumou 1990, 65–66, 73; Findlay 1984, 193, 201; Hermassi 1972, 181–183; Leveau 1985, 238).

Still, the palace did not totally marginalize the urban elites, its erstwhile supporters. During the Protectorate, France established a customs union with Morocco, enabling free trade between the two countries. Consequently, Morocco had virtually no trade or exchange rate barriers when it gained independence. To the delight of many commercial interests, the palace maintained the overall economic policies of the Protectorate until the early 1970s (Ben Ali 1993, 12; Sluglett and Farouk-Sluglett 1984, 83–84).[27]

To further consolidate elite bases of support across all sectors of the political economy, the monarchy gradually instituted a protectionist trade regime and promoted the expansion of local private enterprise. In the late 1950s and particularly in the 1960s, the newly independent Moroccan

---

[26] At the same time, the threat of land reform constituted a "Sword of Damocles," ensuring the allegiance of rural notables who lived in fear that the state would actually implement the policy (Ben Ali 1991a, 59).

[27] Writing in the early 1980s, Sluglett and Farouk-Sluglett (1984, 84) observe, "In very general terms, the social and economic policies promoted by almost all post-independence governments have tended to operate primarily in the interests of the old loyalist strata in Moroccan society, particularly merchants, landowners and manufacturers, which like those of the monarchy itself, lay in the maintenance and perpetuation of the economic and social structures inherited from the protectorate."

state implemented a series of measures designed to promote the development of local industry. Investment codes played an important role in promoting industrial growth in the context of broader economic development plans. The 1958 and 1960 codes encouraged the creation of local firms through fiscal incentives, exempted investors from certain local taxes, and provided capital transfer guarantees for foreign investors. Despite liberal foreign investment terms, particularly in the 1960 code, the new legal frameworks did not give rise to significant foreign capital inflows (Houssel 1966, 78; Jaidi 1979, 39–40; *Maghreb-Machrek*, July–August 1964, 41, 44).[28] Some local private economic interests, however, benefited from the advantageous terms to establish industrial firms. Bolstering the investment incentives, in 1957 the government modified the terms of the Act of Algéciras, a treaty signed with France in 1906 that established a liberal trade regime in Morocco, by instituting protective national trade barriers. While primary goods and equipment for industrial and agricultural activities were taxed minimally, semifinished products faced duties of 5–20 percent and finished products were taxed at a rate of 15–35 percent.

Henceforth, customs duty levels increased progressively until trade liberalization, first implemented in the 1980s as part of a World Bank–led SAP, began to dismantle the protective trade regime (Ben Ali 1993, 14–15; Royaume du Maroc, *Tarif Douanier*, 1964; 1968; 1981).[29] Fiscal and budgetary policies in the 1960s and 1970s also suggested a bias in favor of private capital and the wealthier segments of the population. Regressive tax structures promoted wealth concentration, while public transfers to private business in the form of tax exemptions, incentives, and subsidies exceeded public expenditures on social programs (Berrada 1979, 100, 110).[30]

---

[28] Hamdouch (1978, 88, 98–106) observes that the 1958 code aimed more at national economic *liberation*, or economic independence, while subsequent codes introduced during the 1960s took an explicit turn toward economic liberalism. Prime Minister Abdallah Ibrahim, in power from 1958 to 1960, adopted a decidedly statist approach in his economic and social policies (El Aoufi 1999, 39–42).

[29] For a brief overview of the various development plans adopted in the 1960s, see Ben Ali (1993, 14–16). Akesbi (1986) provides a comprehensive overview of Morocco's various industrial investment codes implemented from the late 1950s through the early 1970s, arguing that all produced disappointing results and exacerbated regional wealth disparities. See also Belal (1964) for a discussion of economic policy in the first decade after independence and Morocco's continued economic dependence on the West.

[30] Berrada (1986) argues that the state consistently ensured that salaries remained low in the public sector and even in private activities through its policies on the *Salaire Minimum Industriel Guaranti* and the *Salaire Minimum Agriculturel Guaranti*, as well as through other instruments. In part, Berrada argues that import-substitution industrialization

The initial rise of the local textile industry in the postindependence era was intimately related to the adoption of import-substitution industrialization (ISI) policies initiated in the first five-year plan, which was implemented from 1960 to 1964. The institution of protectionist policies encouraged cloth merchants and traders to transform their activities into industrial ventures (appendix A: I-61M). Considered the industry with the greatest prospects for success in such a development strategy, textiles held a privileged place under the plan.[31] Investment codes also played an important role in promoting the industry in the context of broader economic development plans. In 1961, duties were increased, and in 1962, under pressure from major textile producers, tariffs on textile products were further augmented (Jaidi 1979, 40–41; *LVE*, May 24, 1991, 18). Not surprisingly, high taxes on imports served the interests of both the state, for which the duties constituted an important revenue source, and local textile manufacturers, who profited immensely from the barriers to outside competition. The local textile industry, then, began to develop in earnest during the early 1960s. At this time, about 60 factories, most of which integrated spinning, weaving, and cloth-finishing activities, were established. Within five years, these local firms were able to cover almost 50 percent of national textile needs. During the late 1960s, the textile industries continued to grow at a rapid pace, while additional subsectors began to develop, notably knitwear, garment assembly, and embroidery (*Textile Info*, March 1998, 4).

A series of trade agreements with the European Union during the 1960s and 1970s also encouraged industrialization, particularly in labor-intensive activities such as garment assembly (Joekes 1982). In March 1969, the EC signed association agreements with Morocco and Tunisia, providing free access for industrial products to European markets. In practice, the arrangements had a minimal impact on the Moroccan economy, which largely exported primary products that already faced low tariffs.

---

policies fostered this state of affairs. He claims, "In this framework, salaries are not a cost and a creator of internal demand at the same time, but on the contrary only a cost" (Berrada 1986, 22). But his argument is ambiguous because ISI, which presumes a significant domestic market, would indeed require a labor force with enough purchasing power to sustain a domestically based development strategy (Cardoso and Faletto 1979).

[31] Jaidi (1979, 36–37) argues, however, that innate inconsistencies in ISI policies ultimately sent mixed signals to industrialists, inhibiting the development of a solid local textile industry. Furthermore, subsequent national economic plans, notably the three-year plan of 1965–1967 and the five-year plan of 1968–1972, placed greater emphasis on tourism and agriculture, relegating the industrial sector to the back burner in development priorities.

In the longer term, however, the accord provided a window of opportunity. Aiming to intensify trade with Europe, Morocco signed a cooperation accord with the EC in March 1976. The accord provided open access for Moroccan industrial goods (with restrictions or "voluntary restraints" on some textiles and garments), limited access for agricultural products, established financial and technical cooperation schemes, and guaranteed nondiscrimination for Maghrib labor residing in the EC. With massive wage discrepancies between Europe and its southern neighbors, European manufacturers increasingly sought subcontracting relationships with North African producers. Because of Moroccan economic dependence on Europe, the agreements effectively spurred industrial development, critically reshaping the domestic political economy (*LVE*, May 14, 1976, 12–17; Royaume du Maroc, *Tarif Douanier*, 1981, 21; White 2001, 56–64).[32]

A "Critical Juncture": Moroccanization and Class Consolidation in the 1970s

Protectionism in Morocco was consolidated in the 1970s, when the state adopted policies designed to promote the local private sector. Classic measures such as the requirement to obtain licenses for most imports, overvaluation of the dirham, and the imposition of import duties were key instruments. By the end of the 1970s, taxes and duties protecting the local market varied between 50 percent and 200 percent for consumer goods and reached as high as 300 percent or greater for certain industries (Ben Ali 1993, 19; Berrada 1991, 965, 969). The policies had profound implications for the subsequent development of private business interests, which penetrated the industrial sector in earnest in the 1970s.

Moroccanization was by far the most significant policy adopted during this period.[33] French investors retained extensive interests in Morocco long after independence in 1956. In order to at least nominally transfer majority ownership of French-owned companies to local private interests, the Moroccan government passed a series of laws in the early 1970s known as the "Moroccanization" laws, most notably the *dahir*, or decree

---

[32] One factory owner estimated that Moroccan wages ranged from $.10–.20 per hour, while European wages ranged from $2–5 per hour during the 1960s and 1970s. As a result, he claimed, Moroccan manufacturers were "slaves to the European garment industry for the thirty years following World War II" (appendix A: I-85M).

[33] Ben Ali (1991a, 60) refers to Moroccanization as "a fundamental measure in the definition of a new social pact."

enacting law 1-73-210 of March 2, 1973, and a new investment code passed in August 1973 (Berrada 1988, 29–68; Berrada 1991, 966; El Aoufi 1990, 13–14; Saâdi 1989). The laws stipulated majority owner-ship by Moroccan nationals of companies based on Moroccan soil in the secondary and tertiary sectors, which meant that locals were required to hold at least 50 percent of capital and managerial positions for any given commercial, financial, or industrial firm. Executive positions were reserved solely for Moroccans. The government emphasized that the new policy did not amount to nationalization but, rather, retained the tradi-tional liberal business environment while enabling Moroccans to share in the country's wealth (*Maghreb-Machrek*, July–August 1973, 24–25; *Maghreb-Machrek*, May–June 1974, 17–18).

Ostensibly aimed at returning Moroccan assets to Moroccan hands, the laws enabled the economic elite to consolidate its holdings while encour-aging the formation of important large business groups. A lively literature among Moroccan scholars debates the origins and effects of the policies (Berrada 1988; Berrada and Ben Abdellah 1980; El Aoufi 1979; El Aoufi 1990; El Malki 1980; Hamdouch 1978; Saâdi 1983; Saâdi 1989). A study by Saâdi (1989) based on a survey of 102 industrial firms largely owned by prominent families is the most authoritative source and constitutes the empirical foundation of most analyses of the effects of Moroccanization. The crux of Saâdi's argument holds that the law reduced the influence of foreign capital in the local economy to a limited degree, facilitated access to the economic spoils for the "techno-bureaucracy," or high-level govern-ment officials, and, above all, enriched large private Moroccan capital. Profiting from the law, prominent families initiated a far-reaching pro-cess of financial concentration, often in conjunction with foreign business interests.[34] A prime mover in the Moroccan political economy and the key unit of analysis in Saâdi's study was the *groupe*, a cluster of companies linked by financial and personal relations as well as their relationships to the same decision-making center. Personal connections and family name played a crucial role in the influence of the group, which was often identi-fied with a particular member of the family controlling the organization. Ethnic or regional ties, however, were not essential for the coherence of the group, which often transcended these types of bonds (Fejjal 1987, 65; Saâdi 1983, 119–120; Saâdi 1989, 28, 158–160).

Bowing to pressure from the political opposition, the king initially limited the beneficiaries of Moroccanization to public agencies and

---

[34] For a summary of the argument, see Saâdi (1983).

institutions. When it was revised two months after adoption, the law permitted private entities to benefit as well. Opposition figures claimed that pressure from members of wealthy Fassi families who were "in permanent residence in the antechamber of the King" successfully lobbied for the amendment. Even at the time of the law's passage, some claimed that the new policy amounted to the "Lamranisation" and "Larakisation" of the domestic economy, so named after two elite families (*Maghreb-Machrek*, July–August 1973, 24–26). Indeed, the high collateral required to obtain a bank credit to purchase a Moroccanized company, as well as the fact that the main beneficiaries of Moroccanization also held substantial stakes in banks, granting them easy access to loans, automatically favored large capital holders from prominent families (Berrada 1988, 71). Despite the government's declared intention of bolstering the nascent middle class, the laws primarily allowed the preexisting economic elite to cement its holdings and integrated the upper-level government bureaucracy, particularly ministers, high government officials, and heads of parastatals, into the ranks of the economically privileged.[35] Henceforth, the local private sector was sharply demarcated between dominant big capital, composed of foreign companies and a handful of Moroccan families, and a much more numerous group of locally owned small and medium enterprises (Berrada 1991, 90; El Aoufi 1990, 12, 125).

Shoring up urban elite support for the monarchy, which had recently suffered several failed coup attempts, was a not-so-coincidental byproduct of Moroccanization.[36] The failed coups, spearheaded by military officials from rural elite origins, compelled King Hassan II to strengthen his ties to urban bourgeois families, who had been marginalized vis-à-vis rural notables in the first decade after independence. After the coup attempts, land distribution accelerated, with as much land reallocated in 1972 as in the 16 years after independence (Ben Ali 1991a, 199; Leveau 1993; Zartman 1987, 6–8). Broader economic conditions also compelled the policies. Population growth and increasing urban migration introduced new pressures, prompting the state to expand the public sector

---

[35] Ben Ali (1991b, 202) cites the cases of the Société Nationale des Produits Pétroliers, Zellidja, and Lessieur.

[36] Waterbury (1972) provides a detailed discussion of the coup attempt in Skhirat in 1971. Joffé (1988) briefly discusses the motives for the event, including anger at mounting corruption and inequality in Moroccan society, fear among Berber officers that their traditional domination of the military was threatened, and the conviction that King Hassan II lacked the charisma of his father, Mohamed V, and therefore was an ineffective ruler. See Coram (1972a; 1972b), who dismisses the notion that ethnicity – specifically, the Berber identity – explains the motives for the attempted coup.

substantially and undertake a new wave of land distribution from departing French settlers. A boom in phosphate prices in 1974 greatly facilitated the expansion of the public sector and enabled Morocco, a net oil importer, to shield itself from the severe effects of the 1973 oil crisis (Azam and Morrison 1994, 91–92).

The promotion of domestic industry embodied in the Moroccanization process spurred continued growth in the textile and clothing industries. During the 1970s, a number of policy measures – not least of which was the new industrial investment code encouraging Moroccan ownership – fueled the textile boom. Additional protective tariffs and restrictions on textile and clothing imports, which virtually banned cloth and thread imports, as well as the creation of the Office du Developpement Industriel, a parastatal organization that identified and helped to finance investments in the industrial sector, also promoted the expansion of domestic textile production. Industrie Cottonière du Oued Zem, an integrated cotton-processing, spinning, and weaving plant, was a high-profile project receiving Office du Developpement Industriel support (*LVE*, May 14, 1976, 44). As a result, investment boomed in the textile sector and the nascent nontraditional clothing and knitwear industries, although industrialists in the two distinct sectors did not seek to integrate their activities (*LVE*, May 19, 1978, 1415; *LVE*, May 18, 1979, 4). These measures enabled a handful of local industrialists to reap huge fortunes in the textile sector (appendix A: I-34M; I-41M). Prior to the adoption of a SAP in 1983, customs duties on textile products reached as high as 300 percent, virtually prohibiting thread and cloth imports and deterring the development of local high-quality production.

At the same time, the passage of the Export Code, including a temporary import regime, and the establishment of the Centre Marocain pour la Promotion des Exportations (CMPE) encouraged local investors to export their goods. Although exports did not constitute an important component of apparel production until the late 1980s, the new regulations had enabled some Moroccan industrialists to acquire experience in world markets as far back as the 1970s (*LVE*, January 5, 1990, 18). On paper, Morocco's foreign investment laws in the export sector were also liberalized. Firms were exempted from taxes on exports for the first 10 years of production, enjoyed full rights to retransfer profits, and benefited from 50 percent exemptions on taxes for local sales for the first 5 years of production, among other guarantees. A major limitation on the effectiveness of these incentives, however, was the near total lack of foreign currency available to compensate foreign companies for their dividends (appendix A: I-31M). Although few foreign firms chose to locate their operations on Moroccan soil, a handful of local investors in apparel assembly profited from subcontracting opportunities with European companies as early as the 1970s. Until this time, thread and cloth production had developed more extensively than the clothing industry. The search for low-cost suppliers by European firms was a critical impetus for the growth of a Moroccan apparel industry (appendix A: I-42M; I-48M).

Moroccanization molded local class formation by reinforcing the position of traditional elites and expanding their ranks. The results deviated from the declared intentions. Although the Moroccanization process aimed to encourage Moroccans to take over businesses from foreigners, many locals benefiting from the reforms established partnerships with foreign interests, in effect allowing foreign capital to retain a significant stake and even increase its holdings in the Moroccan economy. Yet even if foreign investors continued to profit from opportunities in Morocco, domestic producers benefited significantly and rising trade barriers favored local interests. The increasingly protectionist trade regime sheltered local producers from the effects of foreign competition, protecting the holdings of industrialists who had benefited from Moroccanization. Thus, the Moroccan economy was only partially integrated into the world economy, specifically through exposure to global price fluctuations in commodity exports, such as phosphates, and international debt markets. Furthermore, the ostensible emphasis on Moroccan ownership of locally based companies deterred foreign direct investment, putting a check on the role of foreign capital in the local political economy.

Moroccanization and protectionist trade policies increased the holdings of a privileged group of elites, largely members of prominent families who had already established significant economic holdings, while incorporating newer elements outside of the traditional Fassi elite, including some Berber families. Elites deepened their stakes within their existing holdings, particularly in the textile and food-processing industries, and the wealthiest families diversified their interests across numerous sectors, branching out into consumer electronics, pharmaceuticals, chemicals, rubber, plastic, cement, and other manufactures (Berrada 1991, 971, 976).[37] Moroccanization and the new trade regime reinforced, if not created, a powerful group of interests with vast stakes in the local market. The new generation of export-oriented manufacturers that had emerged in the 1980s viewed

---

[37] Identifying the families that most diversified their holdings in the 1970s, Berrada (1991, 976) cites the Kettani, Lamrani, Alami Tazi, Abdelaziz Alami, Prince Moulay Ali, Agouzal, Hakam, Bargach, Ben Salah, Benjelloun, Zniber, Bouftas, Abaakil, and Oukrid groups. In general, Fassis retained more extensive economic holdings than businessmen from the Soussi Berber region.

this as a disastrous chapter in national development that cemented the influence of an archaic, rent-seeking elite (appendix A: I-65M).

Trade Liberalization and Class Formation

The emergence of new export-oriented manufacturers and the trade regime that facilitated their endeavors effectively established two separate markets operating on Moroccan soil by the late 1980s and early 1990s.[38] One set of producers remained oriented toward the domestic market in sectors such as textiles. These interests continued to enjoy high levels of protection through trade barriers, albeit significantly reduced since the early 1980s. A second and, for the most part, newer component of the private sector sought its fortunes on global markets, largely through subcontracting relationships, and was relatively delinked from the local economy.

Domestic economic reforms coincided with propitious external events to fuel the rise of the new export class. Growing global consumer demand and the trend toward relocation to low-cost production sites by European manufacturers propelled Moroccan investors to launch apparel garment assembly plants. Many informants claimed that perceived opportunities in global markets played the greatest role in compelling them to found their businesses as European clothing producers established extensive subcontracting relationships with Moroccan manufacturers.

From 1986 to 1991, apparel exports boomed. In 1983, the Moroccan apparel sector had 264 firms and 16,397 formal employees. By 1997, the number of firms had nearly tripled, with 738 registered firms, and employment boomed, rising to 116,923 formal sector jobs. Figure 4.1 further attests to the rapid growth of the sector during the 1980s and 1990s.

At this time, newcomers made huge fortunes in the business, while many small-scale, domestically oriented garment producers were forced to shut down (appendix A: I-36M; *Conjoncture* [Morocco], no. 774, October 1997, 11).

Working through the *Admissions Temporaires* (AT) regime, or the in-bond, temporary import regime for export-oriented production, subcontractors and exporters maintained minimal connections to the domestic market and cultivated extensive interests in the global economy. Through the AT system, local export manufacturers could divorce themselves almost entirely from the national market by dealing exclusively with foreign textile suppliers for inputs. Overseas clients and multinationals

---

[38] See chapter 2 on trade liberalization in this period.

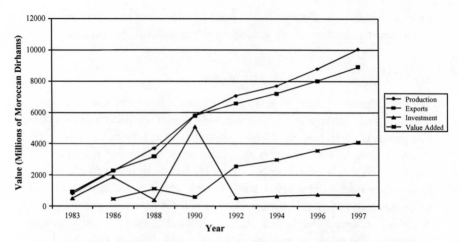

FIGURE 4.1. Development of Apparel Manufacturing in Morocco, 1983–1997. *Sources*: Kingdom of Morocco, *Annuaire Statistique du Maroc*, 1986; Kingdom of Morocco, *Annuaire Statistique du Maroc*, 1989; Ministry of Commerce and Industry, *Les Industries de Transformation.*

often supplied all inputs, including cloth, thread, zippers, buttons, and other accessories. As a result, backward linkages were virtually nonexistent and local value-added was minimal.

Linkages between local suppliers and European clients developed in a number of ways. Personal initiative was a key element of success for new business interests. Attending trade shows in Morocco and abroad was an obvious strategy for establishing connections with European garment sourcers. Because participation in these events was costly and usually required presentation of a complete collection, this approach was not accessible to many local producers. Most Moroccan apparel firms worked on a subcontracting basis, precluding them from developing their own collections, while small operating budgets prevented big outlays for these events.

Contacts with locally based liaison offices for multinational clothing companies constituted a second means of connecting to global markets. Some international chains, such as Gap and Decathlon, set up local offices that coordinated relations with local subcontractors but did not invest directly in production units (*Conjoncture* [Morocco], no. 774, October 1997, 23).[39] More recently, a number of enterprising Moroccans have

---

[39] Some multinational garment retailers, such as the British chain Marks & Spencer, invested directly in the factories of their suppliers, while others established their own factories.

created local offices that represent multiple foreign companies, selecting subcontractors and handling supplier relations on behalf of multinational sourcers. These liaison offices establish direct linkages between
Moroccan and European companies without government intermedia-
tion (appendix A: I-34M).[40] Working through these channels, a new
class of "entrepreneurs" arose that was less invested in the fate of the
national market than traditional elites and less beholden to the state for its
fortunes.

By and large, local textile manufacturers and apparel exporters came
from distinct social origins. The vast majority of apparel exporters came
from comparatively modest origins and only a handful hailed from prominent, wealthy families. Many had a small nest egg to invest and, given
the relatively low barriers to entry in garment assembly, chose this sector. Often, middle-class professionals such as bankers, lawyers, pharma-
cists, or doctors who had amassed a small amount of capital launched
apparel factories in the 1980s. Others had spent significant time working
in Europe and returned home to invest their savings locally in small-scale
projects. A manager and part owner of a medium-sized apparel export
firm described his social trajectory as "typical" in the sector. The informant, who came from a modest, non-elite family, completed an advanced
degree in textile engineering in France financed by his parents' meager
savings and odd jobs held throughout his studies. When he returned to
Morocco, he gained some experience by working as a manager in a local
garment firm owned by a wealthy Moroccan he had met while studying
in France. He then established another firm in partnership with his boss
(appendix A: I-71M).[41]

---

[40] Individually, producers relied on a number of additional strategies for establishing
contacts with overseas buyers. Exporters obtained lists of potential clients from local
banks, the newsletter of the textile and garment producers' association, government
ministries, foreign consulates and embassies, international trade magazines, and referrals from European input suppliers and transport companies. Above all, personal contacts, often cultivated while studying in Europe, were the most important means of
setting up contracts. Furthermore, many apparel manufacturers traveled frequently to
initiate relationships with potential overseas clients (appendix A: I-40M; I-66M; I-67M).
Both textile and apparel manufacturers almost unanimously emphasized that landing an
important contract with a big multinational firm did not require connections with state
agencies.

[41] Others launched their own firms after acquiring significant hands-on experience in the
sector. One apparel exporter worked as a textile sector analyst at a large public development bank and then obtained a position as the technical director for a knitwear firm.
In 1996, he established a small factory with 30 workers, expanding to 200 employees
within three years (appendix A: I-91M).

To be sure, few entrepreneurs came from genuinely poor or even lower-middle-class families. Although much less capital-intensive than textiles, garment assembly also required an initial capital investment that was beyond the means of the vast majority of Moroccans. Furthermore, obtaining credit was nearly impossible without substantial collateral (appendix A: I-59M). The minimum down payment required by local banks to establish a company was about $10,000, backed by $50,000 in assets (appendix A: I-40M; I-67M). Nonetheless, garment assembly offered a space for small capital holders outside of the traditional, well-connected elite to improve their social status and even amass large amounts of capital. Many residents of new, posh neighborhoods such as Hay Riad in Rabat and Anfa in Casablanca allegedly made their fortunes through these activities (appendix A: I-54). Some apparel manufacturers operated illegally either by failing to register their factories, thereby avoiding taxes, minimum wage regulations, and social security payments, or by violating the AT system by selling part of their production on the local market. Many even worked as subcontractors for legal firms supplying overseas clients. This nondeclared and therefore untaxed production generated enormous liquidity (appendix A: I-54M).[42]

To understand why Moroccan industrialists became politicized around the issue of trade liberalization in the 1990s requires a picture of the historical constitution of business class structure and the relationships between different segments of industrial capital and the state. Morocco has a long urban bourgeois elite or Fassi tradition predating the French Protectorate, and postindependence policies reinforced the position of local elites. The Moroccanization laws of the early 1970s along with an increasingly protectionist trade regime bolstered and slightly expanded the ranks of a powerful group of interests that had vast stakes in the local market and close linkages to the palace. The existence of a close-knit, well-connected set of elites who controlled vast segments of the national economy shaped the nature of industrialist struggles over trade liberalization in the 1990s. New private capital holders, who emerged in the 1980s and 1990s as a result of trade liberalization and the changes in

[42] It was widely known that the authorities tolerated and even participated in such practices. Local officials such as prefecture governors wield significant influence in the political system, and it would be virtually impossible to conduct these activities without their complicity. Indeed, some contended that Driss Basri, the all-powerful former minister of interior, benefited from illegal production of textiles and apparel (appendix A: I-54M).

global production patterns described in chapter 2, came into direct conflict with older elites who were firmly rooted in the national market. Lured by opportunities in global markets and excluded from many lucrative investment prospects in the domestic sphere, the nascent class of export-oriented subcontractors pinned their fortunes on manufacturing for world markets.

PART III

GLOBALIZATION AND INSTITUTIONAL CHANGE

5

Business as Usual

State-Sponsored Industrialization and Business Collective Inaction in Tunisia

Although by some accounts trade liberalization threatened to bankrupt one-third to one-half of all local industrial firms, Tunisian industrialists did not formulate coherent interests and mobilize politically to confront this threat; relations between industrialists and the state did not change noticeably with trade reform. The progressive institutionalization of a single-party, authoritarian state has undoubtedly enabled it to retain control over potential sources of disruption and challenges from social groups. But a purely state-centric explanation for the relative absence of business mobilization in Tunisia begs the question of how the state was able to control and manipulate the private sector and dominate economic policymaking so thoroughly. Literature on the Tunisian political economy tends to treat business and labor as undifferentiated wholes, yielding only partial accounts of how groups respond to economic change. By downplaying important variables such as the relatively fragmented structure of social groups and the nature of exchanges between the state and business, analysts give too much credit to state repression and, more broadly, regime type in explaining societal quiescence.

PREFERENCES AND LOBBYING: INTENTIONS VERSUS ACTION

The political behavior of Tunisian manufacturers revealed a disjuncture between their policy preferences, articulated in interviews, and their interests, defined as politically expressed goals. This section compares the preferences and actual behavior of Tunisian textile and apparel industrialists, demonstrating that manufacturers took little, if any, concrete action to pursue their declared policy preferences.

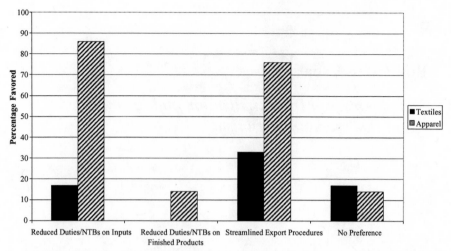

FIGURE 5.1. Trade Policy Preferences of Textile and Apparel Manufacturers in Tunisia.

Intentions: Policy Preferences

Interviews conducted as a part of this study show that textile and apparel factory owners and managers have divergent and mutually exclusive policy preferences (see figure 5.1).[1] The results seem to confirm the predictions of rational-choice models of political reactions to trade reform. In response to a series of questions designed to assess attitudes toward trade reforms, textile manufacturers overwhelmingly opposed reduced tariffs and nontariff barriers on thread and cloth imports. The same sample of respondents expressed no opinion on the prospect of reduced duties on apparel imports, while only a minority voiced their support for streamlined export procedures. Conversely, over 75 percent of apparel exporters in the sample expressed support for reduced customs duties and trade barriers on textile inputs and favored further streamlining of trade regulations.

Interviews with Tunisian manufacturers confirmed these findings. In Sfax, an industrial city in southern Tunisia, a garment manufacturer who targets the domestic market claimed that the EU Association Agreement

---

[1] Appendix B lists the interviews with Tunisian textile and apparel manufacturers whose responses provided the data for figure 5.1. The sample could not yield generalizable findings because political obstacles prevented access to a wider range of informants. Information from interviews with other informants, however, overwhelmingly confirmed the findings.

was an "absolute catastrophe" for local producers, especially in the thread and cloth industries but also in the locally oriented apparel sector (appendix A: I-17T).[2] Meanwhile, exporters expressed minimal concerns and fears about the liberalization process. The director of several off-shore garment firms claimed, "My firm was not affected by recent economic reforms in Tunisia because it is all export-oriented and was founded to produce for and compete on the European market to begin with" (appendix A: I-90T). On the contrary, many exporters welcomed the streamlining of administrative procedures, as well as reduced customs duties on textile goods, that accompanied liberalization. The director of a knitwear export firm strongly supported the liberalization process:

As an exporter, I am pleased with the agreement with Europe because this will boost export activities. Exporters are already prepared for total liberalization because they are already open to the world market. Their products are already in European markets, so they know that they can compete with European producers.... Furthermore, the customs authority has improved recently. It now works faster and more efficiently, notably with respect to its inspection and customs processing procedures. The customs authority has held many meetings with industrialists. At least four important meetings per year take place to discuss ways to improve customs procedures. (appendix A: I-56T)

For apparel manufacturers, support for trade liberalization centered on the prospect of increased access to cheaper textiles on world markets. Exporters emphasized that thread produced in Tunisia was 25 percent more expensive than thread from India or China, largely due to labor cost differentials and greater economies of scale among Asian suppliers (appendix A: I-18T). A few apparel exporters, however, voiced reservations about reliance on imported inputs. Repeated delivery delays of imported merchandise prevented exporters from meeting contract schedules and hindered business planning. Furthermore, assuring quality standards was more difficult with imported goods. For these reasons, the manager of a knitwear firm noted, "We are often obliged to get ourselves out of a bind to meet our contracts on time" (appendix A: I-18T). Despite the ease of access to duty-free goods, complete reliance on imports was not perceived to be a viable option (appendix A: I-18T).

The perspectives of local textile manufacturers and apparel exporters did not contradict the predictions of rational-choice theories of local

[2] More reticent than apparel exporters, textile manufacturers largely declined to elaborate on their opposition to trade reform. Such reluctance undoubtedly stemmed from a desire to conform to official rhetoric, which emphasized Tunisia's eagerness to integrate into the global economy.

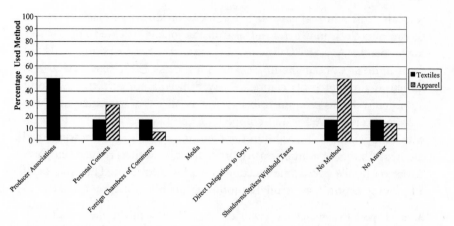

FIGURE 5.2. Lobbying Methods of Textile and Apparel Manufacturers in Tunisia.

responses to trade liberalization: namely, that local manufacturers will oppose trade liberalization, while exporters will favor economic opening. Yet the findings present an interesting paradox: the policy preferences of Tunisian industrialists paralleled those of their Moroccan counterparts described in the next chapter, while the political behavior of manufacturers in the two countries diverged. The next section describes the actual responses of Tunisian producers to economic change.

Actions: Political Behavior

Although textile and apparel industrialists articulated clear policy preferences, neither developed a set of coherent demands nor organized politically in pursuit of their goals. In standardized interviews, informants described the methods they used to convey policy interests to the government, including lobbying through formal producer associations, relying on personal contacts, joining and vocalizing interests through foreign chambers of commerce based in Tunisia, voicing demands through the media, participating in direct delegations to government ministries and agencies, and even resorting to extreme measures such as staging factory shutdowns, participating in producer strikes, and withholding taxes to the state. Figure 5.2 compares the responses of textile and apparel manufacturers regarding their lobbying methods.

The findings reveal that industrialists in the sample exerted little pressure to pursue policy goals. Indeed, producers completely avoided the most public and potentially confrontational tactics, notably conveying demands through the media, participating in direct delegations to the government, and staging aggressive actions such as strikes and factory shutdowns. Apparel exporters reportedly employed almost no collective lobbying tactics, and half of the sample declared that they do not attempt to convey demands to the state at all. Textile manufacturers were slightly more prone to lobby for their demands, primarily through business associations, but the ineffectiveness of these organizations, discussed in detail later in this chapter, undercuts the utility of this approach. Juxtaposed to the Moroccan case, the behavior of Tunisian businesspeople is all the more puzzling. While Moroccan apparel manufacturers launched an all-out offensive in support of their demands, their counterparts in Tunisia adopted a business-as-usual attitude. Likewise, Moroccan thread and cloth producers openly opposed trade reform and clashed with proliberalization exporters, yet Tunisian textile producers seemed largely complacent in the face of impending bankruptcy.

Interest group pressure in response to trade reform was virtually nonexistent in Tunisia, and whatever lobbying occurred took place outside of the public sphere. In interviews with businesspeople, respondents consistently attested that the local business community never engaged in organized lobbying activities.[3] A prominent industrialist claimed:

Lobbying is not a common activity in Tunisia. There are different lobbying organizations, such as CEPEX [Centre pour la Promotion des Exportations] and UTICA [Union Tunisienne de l'Industrie, du Commerce et de l'Artisinat], but this is not real lobbying.... Of course, businessmen talk to ministers and convey their perspectives, but this is really only after a decision is made. There is no real lobbying to affect decision-making. Only a few people close to the president have direct access to power. (appendix A: I-15T)

Even in the face of profound economic reform, businesspeople shied away from collaborative business initiatives. The marketing director of a large industrial firm emphasized, "In Tunisia, it is every man for himself. There is no organized or cooperative strategy in response to liberalization" (appendix A: I-64T). Contending that manufacturers lack a "cooperative spirit," the marketing director of a major textile firm claimed that he tried to organize vertical and horizontal integration efforts among textile firms

---

[3] For example, a prominent businessman with holdings in multiple sectors of the economy claimed, "There is no such thing as a local lobby in Tunisia. Businessmen in Tunisia are not good lobbyists" (appendix A: I-9T). Other respondents described the private sector as a "policy taker" rather than "policymaker," commenting, "The private sector does not tell the state what to do – it asks what state policy is" (appendix A: I-4T) and "The [lobbying] mentality does not exist here" (appendix A: I-15T).

to boost their collective competitiveness but "Nobody else wanted to get involved.... When we speak of mergers between two textile companies, they laugh" (appendix A: I-27T).

The political behavior of industrialists leading up to and in response to the signing of the EUAA in 1996 demonstrated the extent of private-sector docility in Tunisia. Industrialists neither pushed for the agreement nor attempted to block or delay it. The director of a local consulting firm summarized business responses to the agreement: "The debate over liberalization in Tunisia is not really a debate. It's not about who is in favor of it, but rather who is ready to deal with it." A Chamber of Commerce official suggested that business passivity is really an acceptance of the inevitable: "Companies have not tried to block or slow down economic opening because they are powerless to do so. They cannot block globalization."

Government "consultation" with the private sector on the signing of the agreement with Europe came after the fact, when officials informed the business community of the agreement's stipulations. A prominent manufacturer targeting both local and export markets claimed, "Yes, my opinions were consulted and state officials made an effort to consult with businessmen. But, in the end, the reforms were already adopted so it was not a matter of discussing whether the changes should be adopted but how companies can adapt themselves to the situation."[4] Local manufacturers did not view lobbying – either to delay or modify the reforms – as a viable solution.

A sense of powerlessness vis-à-vis the administration pervaded descriptions of business–government relations and business passivity. Respondents consistently described a Kafkaesque situation in which a maze of bureaucracy and shifting responsibility prevented interest transmission and the organized pursuit of policy goals. The director of a textile firm declared, "Nobody takes responsibility for the sector. In order to make any kind of decision, you must go all the way to the minister of industry who, in turn, tells industrialists that they should be more active in promoting their interests." Lack of access to information on economic policies compounded the situation. Rumors, rather than published or publicly announced decisions, were a primary source of information on policies and business transactions.

---

[4] Some owners of large firms boasted that they had more access to decision makers and, therefore, to information on economic policy. But even big capital holders did not claim to influence the policymaking process (appendix A: I-15; I-19T).

In the absence of organized business lobbying, individual capital holders opted for "exit" rather than "voice" strategies of participation in the political system (Hirschman 1970). Indeed, when pressed on the question of how the business community conveyed its demands to policymakers, an apparel manufacturer in Sfax suggested that shutting down rather than pushing for policy demands was the primary response of manufacturers to economic crisis; but the challenges of launching new business activities limited the option to divest. "If I could," she declared, "I would leave this business immediately" (appendix A: I-17T). When possible, industrialists closed their factories and took up commercial activities, such as the importation and distribution of consumer goods. A Tunisian economist maintained that many local industrialists resorted to *rentier* behavior in response to poor business prospects. "They persist in asking for state aid.... Some even asked the state to pay for their airline tickets abroad for trips to seek new markets for their products!"

The relative complacency of Tunisian manufacturers in the face of economic reform should not suggest that they did not express any policy goals and preferences. Tunisian industrialists articulated their perspectives on specific issues, such as fiscal and trade reforms, at state-sponsored meetings between business and government representatives as well as in private venues. For example, after the signing of the EU Agreement, manufacturers voiced their concerns about the competitiveness of Tunisian manufacturing at meetings between UTICA and Ministry of Industry officials. Businesspeople cited issues such as the lack of qualified workers, the alleged inflexibility of the Labor Code, the high cost of bank credit, and the need for current account convertibility (*Réalités*, June 16–22, 1995, 23; *Réalités*, May 23–29, 1997, 20; *Réalités*, March 23–29, 2000, 20). Outspoken individuals, such as Mohamed Ali Darghouth, the director of one of Tunisia's oldest and most prominent textile firms, repeatedly articulated his apprehensions about the ramifications of trade liberalization for the future of the local textile sector (*Réalités*, May 12–18, 1995, 18; *Réalités*, May 26–June 1, 1995, 15; *Réalités*, June 2–8, 1995, 23). Yet the business community did not express its dissatisfaction with existing policies in a unified, organized fashion. Instead, individuals raised issues sporadically and made no effort to develop a comprehensive set of demands or to pursue them systematically.

Tunisian private-sector complacency was all the more puzzling because industrialists believed that the contemporary global production context called for integration across firms in the diverse branches of the textile and apparel sectors. Sectoral studies of the Tunisian industrial sector repeatedly advised both the state and the business community to upgrade local textile capabilities and encouraged manufacturers to purchase inputs domestically from high-quality firms located in Tunisia. In 1997, Gherzi Organisation, a European consulting bureau specializing in textiles and apparel manufacturing, released a comprehensive assessment commissioned by the Tunisian Ministry of Industry of the local textile and apparel sectors. The study stressed the urgency of developing the local textile sector as part of a broader development strategy and concluded that Tunisian textile production, particularly thread spinning, was not internationally competitive, while the export-oriented woven and knitwear apparel industries faced brighter prospects in a tight economic climate. The Gherzi report became the prime reference for both industrialists and government officials in their prescriptions for the local textile and apparel sectors (Gherzi Organisation 1999).

Official evaluations of the industrial sector echoed the recommendations of the document, including a white paper published by the Ministry of Industry, which outlined various ways to boost private investment (appendix A: I-90T; République Tunisienne, "Livre Blanc," 1999). Pronouncements at business group meetings also called for greater sectoral integration. At the Third Annual Forum of the Mediterranean Textile and Clothing Sector, organized by the Institut Arabe des Chef d'Entreprise (IACE), an exclusive association grouping together big business interests, participants discussed the idea of a "Mediterranean" textile and garment sector. The formation of a free trade zone, in which the textile and apparel industries of Europe and North Africa would form an integrated sector based on each region's specializations, constituted the foundation of the proposal. At the 1999 Annual Quality Textile Tour, attended by industrialists as well as by representatives from the Ministry of Industry, Union Tunisienne de l'Industrie, du Commerce et de l'Artisanat (UTICA), and the Fédération Nationale du Textile (FENATEX), much talk focused on the need for total integration of the Tunisian textile and clothing sectors.

Industrialists recognize the importance of pursuing sectoral integration. Textile producers who participated in the study repeatedly expressed interest in promoting sectoral integration, and apparel manufacturers often rued the lack of access to locally produced high-quality cloth (appendix A: I-49T). A French apparel manufacturer and longtime resident of Tunisia declared:

If Tunisia does not develop its textile industry, the local export-oriented clothing industry will disappear. Foreign companies operating under the 1972 Law will leave to produce elsewhere where local textile capacity is more developed. I have stressed the importance of developing a local textile industry for the last twenty years, and only now the government and operators in the sector are starting to take this argument seriously. (appendix A: I-90T)

In Tunisia, as in Morocco and many other developing countries, both local and foreign investors in textile and apparel manufacturing supported sectoral integration – at least in principle.

Unlike their Moroccan counterparts, Tunisian industrialists did not take concrete action to pursue the widely recommended integration strategy. Neither the compelling arguments of the Gherzi study and other reports nor the appeals of individual manufacturers incited organized lobbying in pursuit of this common goal. Industrialists remained politically fragmented, hesitant to adopt collaborative political or economic tactics, while competitive dynamics prevented cooperation among firms (appendix A: I-49T; I-60T; *Réalités*, June 22–28, 2000, 38).

The case of Siter, a state-owned cloth-finishing factory that was sold to private investors after a lengthy privatization process, exhibited the reluctance of manufacturers to adopt a sectoral integration strategy. Local businesspeople repeatedly considered a proposition to acquire the company jointly. The idea received no support, despite the fact that a functional cloth-finishing factory would have widespread benefits for both the textile and apparel sectors. The director of a textile firm who firmly supported the proposal expressed her frustration over the unwillingness of manufacturers to work together:

With liberalization, there has not been a move toward more cooperation among industrialists. Instead of grouping together and forming partnerships, they are even more separated and spread out than before. For example, at a recent CETTEX [Centre Technique du Textile] seminar, Monsieur Ali Darghouth [a prominent textile producer] suggested that some firms cooperate together to buy Siter and he asked all those in favor to raise their hands. Nobody raised his hand. Individualism is the ruling mode. Everybody thinks he is the exception and will escape the harsh effects of liberalization, or at least manage to prevail in the end. Obviously this is not true. (appendix A: I-26T)

State officials also bemoaned the reluctance of local industries to pursue sectoral integration. A government official claimed, "The Ministry of Industry has organized seminars on numerous occasions to bring textile and clothing producers together with the aim of promoting sectoral integration but so far these efforts have not been fruitful. These producers from different branches of the sector have entirely different mentalities. They are not taking initiatives."

Local manufacturers overwhelmingly opted for short-term profits rather than medium- to long-term political and economic strategies that would save the national textile industry and guarantee future profits. Fueling a trend toward deindustrialization, manufacturers increasingly shifted toward import activities and distribution of foreign brands. A local consultant observed, "The question is whether on-shore sector companies are organized enough to respond effectively to the challenge posed by economic reform. Instead, many companies are becoming dealers rather than producers. The big ones are opening branches of foreign companies in Tunisia" (appendix A: I-61T). If the trend continues, textile manufacturing will survive on Tunisian soil only through the relocation of European firms to low-cost production sites. But even this would require lobbying: local apparel manufacturers, who would gain most directly from access to high-quality textiles, would have to push for wage freezes and more flexible labor laws in order to entice multinationals.

Collaboration and, more specifically, integration strategies among firms, can enhance the competitiveness of a national industry in global markets. But pursuing cooperation requires political will and a readiness on the part of local investors to work collectively toward long-term goals. Although Tunisian manufacturers acknowledged the value of sectoral integration schemes, they did not actively push for collaborative strategies. While investors in competitor countries implemented the prescriptions of foreign consultants, Tunisian industrialists took no action to promote the mutual benefits of developing local capabilities in both textile and apparel production.

STATE REPRESSION, ORGANIZATIONAL WEAKNESS, OR PREEMPTIVE INCENTIVES? COMPETING ACCOUNTS OF TUNISIAN BUSINESS COMPLACENCY

What explains the passivity of Tunisian industrialists facing both the reality and the prospect of massive economic upheaval? Students of North African politics, Tunisian government officials, and local industrialists offer a variety of answers to this question. Area specialists point to state repression and the weakness of civil society, which deter societal dissent and prevent the formation of effective lobbying and pressure tactics. State officials and consultants for international financial institutions, on the other hand, stress that activism is unnecessary given the extensive battery of government programs that ostensibly aid local firms in their adjustment to globalization. Both of these divergent explanations focus on the state as the key determinant of the political behavior of Tunisian manufacturers but highlight distinct tools for ensuring societal complacency. The former approach points to the "stick" of government repression, which forces manufacturers to endure economic challenges without protest. The latter account emphasizes "carrots," or incentives, distributed to industrialists, which perhaps eased the reform process, or at least bought their silence. The stick and carrot perspectives provide important components of an explanation for Tunisian business passivity but do not sufficiently explore how these factors – especially state sponsorship of industrialization – shaped internal business politics. The political behavior of Tunisian businesspeople is also a product of the absence of conflict among domestic and export factions of the industrial class.

Sticks: State Repression and Societal Submission

During the reform process, the Tunisian state wielded significant power over the private sector through the arbitrary enforcement of business laws and regulations. On occasion, tactics also entailed outright harassment and threatening phone calls to targeted individuals and their family members and, in extreme cases, framed plots involving alleged sex- or drug-related scandals (appendix A: I-72T; I-75T).

The Looming Threat of Fiscal Blackmail. Selective tax auditing is the most commonplace means of state control over business dissent. In a context where most businesses routinely ignore tax laws and environmental regulations, the looming threat of an official audit is an important instrument of social control. Political dissent or mobilization can invite the state to "enforce" these laws, which would ruin a business (appendix A: I-1T). The Brigades Economiques, the tax auditing wing of the Ministry of Finance, visits targeted companies, taking over their offices for a few days while it reviews their books. A foreign diplomat claimed, "These groups act at the behest of the state and target stubborn businesspeople who refuse to play the game." To avoid this, businesspeople acknowledge certain tacit rules. For example, when the state solicits donations for its coveted poverty alleviation and income generation funds, businesspeople contribute generously to avoid trouble with tax officials.

The Fonds National de Solidarité, or the "2626 Fund," and the Banque Tunisienne de Solidarité are state programs that were ostensibly created to help needy elements of Tunisian society.[5] Promoted extensively by the president, the funds operate separately from the standard tax system. The

---

[5] See Hibou (1999, 18–22).

2626 Fund, created in 1993, targets poverty in the "shadow zones" of Tunisia, or poor rural areas of the country, by providing direct financial assistance to low-income families (*Réalités*, November 2–8, 2000, 26). Businesses keep a special bank account in which they deposit their contributions to the fund. The Banque Tunisienne de Solidarité provides capital for small investors who do not qualify for bank loans and particularly targets educated youths who need financing to launch their own businesses (appendix A: I-42T).[6]

The resources for these funds come from "donations" from businessmen and citizens. In effect, contributions are obligatory and constitute a critical element in the politics of business–government relations in Tunisia. A local business executive noted, "People use [these funds] to avoid tax audits. I contributed to the fund because I had to, but I consider it lost or wasted money. If you have a problem [with the state], all you have to do is contribute to these social funds. In principle, the funds are positive institutions for Tunisian society as a whole, but nobody is sure where the money goes" (appendix A: I-42T). More than vehicles to promote equitable national income distribution, the funds are an important tool of social control for the state.

Selective Law Enforcement. At times, the state also uses selective crackdowns to ensure business quiescence. A high-profile scandal exemplified the arbitrary nature of law enforcement under Ben Ali and its dampening impact on business politics in Tunisia. In 1997, Mohsen Ben Abdallah, the head of Bacosport, a major business group concentrated in the textile and garment sectors, was sentenced to seven years in prison and had to pay a massive fine for fiscal "irregularities."[7] Ben Abdallah, among the most prominent businesspeople in Tunisia, was both president of the FENATEX, the organization for textile and apparel manufacturers, and a high-level official in the UTICA, the peak-level business association, for

---

[6] During its first year of operation, official statistics claimed that the fund issued 11,708 loans, which allegedly facilitated the creation of nearly 18,000 jobs (*Réalités*, June 17–23, 1999, 28). Of these projects, 73 percent involved commercial activities (*Réalités*, August 5–18, 1999, 22). The press constantly emphasizes the successes of the funds but, in the words of a successful local industrialist, the 2626 Fund and Banque Tunisienne de Solidarité are a "catastrophe" because most beneficiaries use the loans for quick-return commercial activities (appendix A: I-42T).

[7] A businessperson close to Ben Abdallah claimed that the fine amounted to $27 million. In addition, after the arrest, the government allegedly seized the defendant's thread factory, Bacofil, and sold it to a group of Italian investors for $4 million. The original cost of the project approximated $67 million (appendix A: I-49T).

many years.[8] Although the details of Ben Abdallah's crime were unclear, the official reason for his condemnation was falsification of bills. Ben Abdallah allegedly inflated the capital equipment costs of his factories on paper in order to reduce his tax burden (appendix A: I-49T). A close associate of Ben Abdallah added that the businessman owed money to a state-owned bank but, nonetheless, transferred large sums of money overseas, violating the terms of his debt repayment agreement as well as regulations on currency transfers (appendix A: I-66T). The fact that these practices are both commonplace and widely acknowledged in the business community strongly indicates that the real reason for his imprisonment lay elsewhere.

Undoubtedly, the charges against Ben Abdallah were a pretext for other motives. Many businesspeople were convinced that Ben Abdallah's real crimes were political, namely that he criticized the regime and made contacts with opposition figures in Europe.[9] In addition, a textile manufacturer claimed, the workers in Ben Abdallah's factories openly demonstrated their hostility toward Ben Ali during an official presidential visit. "When Ben Ali passed through the village in the Sahel where the Bacofil factory was located," the informant attested, "the workers at the factory jeered at him and shouted anti-Ben Ali slogans" (appendix A: I-49T). Whether the details of these accounts are entirely accurate is irrelevant. The scandal and the harsh sentence indicate the extent to which the state will punish potential challengers and serve as a lesson for the business community.

The Ben Abdallah affair attests to the selective application of laws and regulations in Tunisia. A prominent businessman argued that the scandal had detrimental effects on the local private sector: "There are so many laws on the books that, were they to be fully implemented, it would be impossible to avoid breaking the law.... Laws effectively exist to provide tools to the administration to use whenever it needs an excuse to prosecute a particular individual" (appendix A: I-38T). The Ben Abdallah

---

[8] Ben Abdallah was extremely influential. At industry meetings, a manufacturer claimed, the former head of FENATEX had a larger escort of bodyguards than government ministers (appendix A: I-49T).

[9] Unpaid debts to private banks are common and therefore do not explain Ben Abdullah's imprisonment. Some claim that the scandal was "purely political." A businessperson admitted that "he would not be surprised if possible links to the political opposition prompted the affair because Ben Abdallah was a very powerful man who thought that he was immune to government prosecution and, therefore, it would be in character that he would take such risks" (appendix A: I-66T).

affair clearly exposes the climate of uncertainty in the Tunisian system, which potentially undermines business confidence and undoubtedly curtails private-sector mobilization against state policies.

The "Sliding Scale" Principle of Levying Customs Duties. The levying of customs duties, like the enforcement of tax policies and business regulations, is also unpredictable in the Tunisian system. An economist at a government-run think tank emphasized the distinction between "real" and "theoretical" customs duty levels. "Theoretical" rates denote official duties, or rates published in the annual budget, and "real" rates indicate rates that are, in fact, levied. The analyst clarified that he did not mean the difference between "nominal" and "real" rates. Rather, the distinction refers to official, published rates versus actual rates levied on a firm-by-firm basis, implying that certain individuals benefit from more favorable duties than others. The Customs Authority, the economist alleged, maintains records of these differential duties, but they are not accessible to the public. The dispersion of customs duties in the trade regime ensures that the system remains complex and opaque. With more than 22 tariff rates and 35 categories eligible for exemptions in place, significant room exists for discretionary application of customs duties (World Bank 1996, 30).

Indirect channels are also important tools in the government's arsenal for controlling international business transactions. International treaty commitments, notably the GATT and the EU accords, compel the government to resort to tactics such as quality-control checks, demands for certificates of origin, antidumping charges, and requirements for import licenses to maintain official control over foreign trade. Through these practices, the government attempts to cushion the local economy from exposure to global economic pressures while maintaining discretionary control over the business community and arbitrarily implementing customs-processing procedures and business regulations (appendix A: I-10T; I-18T; I-60T). A foreign diplomat noted:

Tunisia is a country filled with laws and appears to be complying with all demands of international lenders. It appears to be on the track to building a real market economy. The reality, however, differs a lot. Even though many laws exist, they are not necessarily enforced and certainly not applied equally to all. Even though customs duties are dropping inevitably because of engagements with the WTO and the EU, there are many other means at the administration's disposal to hamper free trade.... Application of procedures and imposing obstacles is arbitrary and very clearly depends on "who you are." (appendix A: I-33T)

Businesspeople claimed that the government imposes obstacles to trade in order to limit certain activities to a small number of operators with close connections to presidential circles. In some cases, customs officials allegedly call ministers from the ports to receive direct orders about what products can enter the country for a given importer (appendix A: I-10T; I-33T; I-42T).

Repression and discretionary application of business regulations help to ensure private-sector docility, demonstrating the importance of the state in explaining the lack of business responses to reform in the 1990s.

State Corporatism and the Co-optation of Organizational Resources: The Weakness of Business Representation

An important institutional effect of state repression in Tunisia is the poverty of organizations representing societal interests, such as businesspeople and even workers, who once boasted an influential and vibrant labor organization. The neocorporatist authoritarian system in Tunisia enables the state to create and penetrate the institutions channeling societal input in the policymaking process. Assuming that producers have real grievances – an assumption that I will examine more closely later in the chapter – state repression handicaps the ability of industrialists to respond to reform.

UTICA. The official representative of business interests in Tunisia, Union Tunisienne de l'Industrie, du Commerce et de l'Artisanat (UTICA) is the logical forum for disgruntled producers to express their policy interests. But the organization is thoroughly co-opted by the state.[10] It was created by the Neo-Destour during the struggle for independence as part of its strategy to mobilize diverse elements throughout Tunisia. The organization penetrates all regions and activities in Tunisia through an umbrella structure encompassing 15 sectoral subfederations that collectively represent 950 local sectoral chambers and 23 regional unions, which oversee about 200 subregional bodies with over 3,000 cells (*Réalités*, no. 270, October 26–November 1, 1990, 21). Rather than functioning as a real advocate for the business community, UTICA provides few, if any, benefits

---

[10] On the organization of societal interests in a "state corporatist" system, see especially Schmitter (1974) and Collier and Collier (1979). For a related yet distinct regime model, see the literature on bureaucratic authoritarianism, reviewed comprehensively in a volume edited by David Collier (1979).

in exchange for membership. Industrialists, including large-scale capitalists with multisectoral holdings and high-ranking positions in the UTICA administration, unanimously attested that they derived little value from the organization (appendix A: I-36T; I-54T; I-59T; I-64T). Often, respondents conveyed contempt and ridicule for the association. A prominent Tunisian industrialist who is also a member of the UTICA board declared, "All of these organizations are for show. They do not constitute a real force" (appendix A: I-54T).[11] Similarly, the manager of an apparel export firm contended that UTICA did nothing for its constituents: "What does it mean to be a 'member' of UTICA? There is a difference between registration and membership. All factories are required to register with UTICA but, in reality, our firm has nothing to do with UTICA and does not consider membership a serious obligation" (appendix A: I-43T). UTICA is not a real pressure group because it does not push the state to pursue policy demands.

Manufacturers enumerated their visions of a truly representative and effective business association, emphasizing that UTICA did not meet their expectations. The marketing director of one of Tunisia's most prominent textile firms lamented that neither UTICA nor any other business association provides reliable sectoral and macroeconomic data on Tunisian and global market developments. Crucial databases on investment, customs duty levels, and products have not been updated since 1992, he charged, preventing him from implementing a serious marketing plan. The manager's concerns became all the more critical as trade barriers began to fall. According to another manufacturer, UTICA also fails to coordinate production processes among disparate small-scale manufacturers, despite repeated requests for assistance in this area. For example, beginning in the mid-1990s, the organization discussed the possibility of assisting a group of apparel producers to found a jointly held company that would purchase a high-tech, expensive cloth-cutting machine, the *electrasystème*. Yet UTICA did not act on the proposal, nor did it respond to other producer demands, such as a proposal to open tax collection centers in more industrial zones (appendix A: I-56T).

Industrialists and local observers conceded that UTICA exercises some organizational influence in the official triennial wage negotiations held

---

[11] Local scholars concurred. A professor at the University of Tunis commented, "All institutions, such as the UGTT or UTICA, are simply empty, useless organizations now that do essentially nothing" (appendix A: I-72T). Bellin (2002) encountered similar portrayals of UTICA's ineffectiveness during field research conducted in the late 1980s.

with government and labor union officials (appendix A: I-54T; I-59T; I-64T; I-67T; I-84T). But manufacturers even expressed cynicism about the organization's role in the tripartite talks. An apparel subcontractor claimed that the directors of UTICA and the UGTT are state appointees who ensure that wage negotiations conform to state policy interests (appendix A: I-84T). Another garment exporter expressed similar cynicism about UTICA mediation in labor disputes: "Whenever I have a meeting to discuss a problem with a worker, representatives from UTICA, the UGTT, and the Labor Inspection Authority attend. As soon as the UGTT and UTICA representatives enter the room, they kiss each other, showing that they have a close personal relationship.... The organization does not represent the interests of industrialists as a whole" (appendix A: I-56T). Even UTICA's credentials as a representative of business interests vis-à-vis organized labor – an area that some respondents deemed praiseworthy – are questionable.

When Hédi Djelani, the current head of UTICA, assumed the presidency of the producers' union in 1988, the Tunisian press anticipated a new era in the organization's history. At first, expectations of a new UTICA under Djelani seemed warranted. In 1989, the organization undertook an extensive restructuring program designed to boost its effectiveness as a representative of producer interests vis-à-vis the state.[12] As part of this process, the organization beefed up its institutional infrastructure. With thousands of local and regional branches throughout Tunisia, the union developed a formidable organizational structure that, in theory, would enable it to maintain close contacts with its rank and file (*Réalités*, October 26–November 1, 1990, 21). By relying on its local branches, the UTICA leadership emphasized that the organization would increasingly focus on listening to the concerns of its constituents rather than act as an "echo chamber for governmental decisions, as in the past" (*Réalités*, October 19–25, 1990, 4; *Réalités*, March 19–25, 1993). A 1995 internal reform aimed to boost the organization's efficiency and increase accountability to its base. Innovations included the creation of a database to assist firm owners in business planning and an office to promote the

---

[12] After a key meeting of the National Council of UTICA, a prominent journalist wrote, "[UTICA] is listening to the largest and the smallest. It is in the midst of constructing a network of coordination, communication, defense and demand of the first order.... UTICA is looking to occupy the spaces left vacant until now to the profit of its other partners [i.e., the state and the UGTT]. As evidence, the business confederation is restructuring itself, organizing itself and basing its mode of operations on the model of political parties" (*Réalités*, no. 216, October 6–12, 1989, 10).

development of small and medium enterprises (*Réalités*, September 13–19, 1996, 22). The national press hailed the apparent restructuring of UTICA and the "new generation" of administrators running the organization. As evidence of Djelani's successes, supporters stressed that UTICA membership doubled during the new president's first term (*Réalités*, December 1–6, 1995, 23).

But Djelani did not revamp UTICA into an autonomous organization with the ability to challenge or oppose policies threatening its constituents. Instead, Djelani called for the "depoliticization" of associational life and took steps to ensure that the business community could not pose a significant challenge to state authority (*Réalités*, September 9–16, 1988, 27). The restructuring of UTICA merely enhanced its role as a vehicle for informing the business community about state policy rather than as a means of transmitting private interests to the state. A political weekly commented, "UTICA recently saw its role expand considerably, *with the blessing of the state*, in associating it more and more directly to business, and sought visibly to *sensitize* industrialists to the heavy responsibilities that fall upon them in the current economic strategy" (emphasis added) (*Réalités*, October 26–November 1, 1990, 21). Although official rhetoric praised UTICA's apparent transformation into a vehicle for the representation and communication of private-sector interests, in reality the state retained firm control over the organization.

By the mid-1990s, perceptions of UTICA within the business community had changed drastically. Even high-level UTICA members charged that the organization increasingly represented the personal interests of its leadership, and particularly of Djelani himself (appendix A: I-62T).[13] The president of a sectoral federation in UTICA declared, "The head of UTICA is simultaneously a parliamentarian, a party member, and part of the inner circle of the president." Another industrialist charged, "UTICA has a president who defends *his* interests." Respondents frequently cited Djelani's reliance on marriage ties and personal bonds to further his own interests. After Djelani assumed the UTICA presidency, his daughter married President Ben Ali's brother-in-law, convincing Tunisians from diverse social strata of Djelani's self-interested goals.[14] A Tunisian scholar argued that

[13] A Tunisian economist argued, "It's a closed club. It serves the interests of the people running it and, apart from that, has no real purpose. The head of UTICA has links to the party, the palace and all sorts of important personal networks" (appendix A: I-53T).
[14] The marriage was the subject of intense gossip. To highlight the alleged political goals behind the arrangement, respondents emphasized the renowned beauty of Djelani's daughter and the ill manners and poor appearance of her husband. Recently, another of Djelani's daughters married a close relative of President Ben Ali.

Djelani's ambition sacrificed UTICA's effectiveness as a representative of the broader private sector: "He is highly involved in marriage strategies. He married off his daughter into the president's family. This is perfectly logical since this activity is now the most economically profitable move possible – more profitable than engaging in traditional economic enterprises" (appendix A: I-72T). In a context where business–government relations were historically much less corrupt than in neighboring countries, the alleged political maneuverings of the inner circle of the president and the UTICA leadership outraged most respondents.

During Djelani's tenure, large capital holders became increasingly prominent in UTICA, reflecting a broader trend in the national political economy since Ben Ali took power. Small and medium-sized enterprises have traditionally dominated the association and constituted its backbone, in part because big capital did not emerge until more recently. Djelani's ascension to power in 1988 touched off a power struggle within UTICA. Owners of small and medium firms, as well as merchants and artisans, threatened to break off to form their own organization, while large capital holders complained that no organization adequately reflected their agenda (*Réalités*, August 12–18, 1988; *Réalités*, January 30–February 5, 1998, 17).[15] In 1988, a Tunisian businessman, Mondher Bel Hadj Ali, even collected over 400 signatures on a petition calling for the establishment of a new association to represent small-scale business interests (*Réalités*, August 19–25, 1988, 20; *Réalités*, October 26–November 1, 1990, 18). In the end, the UTICA leadership successfully defended the unity of the organization.

With the secession threats stamped out, UTICA became an organization of big business interests with ties to the state. Owners of small firms became increasingly cynical about UTICA. A knitwear exporter dismissed the utility of membership in the association for small firms:

---

[15] In the mid-1980s, a group of private businesspeople created the Institut Arabe des Chefs d'Entreprise (IACE) in an effort to create a truly independent business organization. The founders created the new organization as a forum to discuss common interests separately from UTICA and government institutions. At one time, the IACE was very active (Bellin 1991, 221–225). A Tunisian economist claimed, "There was a real dialogue and exchange within the organization and it posed an alternative forum to UTICA, which entirely lacked a vision to guide the private sector" (appendix A: I-88T). The government keeps tight control over private-sector organizations and, in 1994, the state effectively took over the IACE after its president and founder expressed his intentions to run for president. Chakib Nouira, who is the son of former prime minister Hédi Nouria and enjoys close linkages to high-level officials, took over the organization. Although the organization still exists, it is no longer as vibrant (appendix A: I-12T; I-88T).

"I am a member of UTICA, but since I joined the organization nobody from the Union has contacted me – not even to collect my membership dues of five dinars per year. In theory, UTICA speaks in the name of all industrialists, but in reality it is a club that represents the inner circle of the organization and its friends and associates" (appendix A: I-56T).[16] A foreign diplomat confirmed that small firms had little representation in the system. "UTICA works closely with the government and largely represents big business interests. But most Tunisian companies are small and medium-sized enterprises. Small and medium-sized enterprises constitute a huge proportion of the private sector, yet nobody or no organization really represents their interests" (appendix A: I-5T). Even large industrialists with high-ranking positions in UTICA admitted that big business had gained the upper hand in the organization (appendix A: I-36T).[17]

By the mid-1990s, the credibility of UTICA as a representative of broad business interests had been destroyed. In its public activities, the organization is most involved in organizing seminars to transmit information on state policies to the private sector (appendix A: I-36T). Even during the trade liberalization process, which the government itself admitted would jeopardize if not bankrupt almost two-thirds of all industrial firms, UTICA has not lobbied forcefully to block or temper reform. Association officials stressed that the organization does not pose demands upon the state. Djelani, elected just two years after Tunisia undertook an SAP, consistently emphasizes the importance of supporting state efforts to reform the economy. Indeed, at a 1997 meeting of the UTICA National Council, Djelani commented, "We are not really in a situation to pose demands" (*L'Economiste Maghrébin*, no. 187, July 30, 1997, 32–33; *Réalités*, no. 157, August 12–18, 1988, 19). Increasingly, UTICA rhetoric reflects the organization's status as a mere appendage of the state if not an outright advocate for Ben Ali's program. During the 2000 presidential election campaign, Djelani exhorted UTICA members to vote en masse for Ben Ali, in recognition of the "different economic reform policies implemented

---

[16] The director of an off-shore apparel firm echoed his concerns: "These associations are closed circles. I cannot benefit from referrals through these associations because I am not part of the inner circle. I am not known, I am not big" (appendix A: I-62T).

[17] A Tunisian economist commented, "Now UTICA is an elite club that is not at all representative of its purported constituency" (appendix A: I-88T). Djelani defended himself against such accusations. "Contrary to what certain people want to make believe, I am not a man of big companies. I belong to the family of big firms, of course, but I am tremendously involved with small and medium firms and small activities" (*Réalités*, no. 635, January 30–February 5, 1998, 17).

since the *Changement*"[18] and the "need to defend the futuristic program of the President Ben Ali, which represents the best track enabling [us] to face the challenges that changes in the global economy impose upon us" (*Réalités*, no. 719, September 30–October 6, 1999, 11; *Réalités*, no. 746, April 6–12, 2000, 20, 26). UTICA officials claim that the organization influences policymaking in important ways by sharing its views with the government on upcoming legislation and participating in the triennial collective negotiations over wages.[19]

By modernizing its operations and improving the training of its staff, UTICA appeared more effective than in the past, but this largely reflected official efforts to present a pro-business image to foreign investors and creditors. All civic organizations, including UTICA, remain entirely subject to state control and have no room for independent action (appendix A: I-76T). In Tunisia's neocorporatist authoritarian system, UTICA and its branches serve as an additional vehicle for mobilizing social actors behind the state and facilitating official monitoring of private-sector activity. In an ominous statement during a membership drive in 2000, Djelani commented, "There is no locality or neighborhood where economic, commercial, artisinal or industrial activities are practiced that was not visited by our representatives.... [T]his permitted us to have a list of all firms in the country. Those who did not agree to join us will be revisited in order to convince them to adhere.... This will permit us to know the reality of our base in a statistical manner, by sector and by region" (*Réalités*, September 27–October 11, 2000, 13).

FENATEX. UTICA rhetoric depicts the organization as active and dynamic, but many of its constituent bodies are all but dormant. Although it represents the most important national manufacturing industry, the Fédération Nationale du Textile (FENATEX), or National Textile Federation, is no exception. Indeed, even when apparel exports soared in

---

[18] The *Changement*, or the "change," refers to Ben Ali's ascension to the presidency, which supposedly heralded vast positive developments in Tunisia.

[19] One respondent, a high-ranking UTICA official and prominent businessman, claimed that UTICA focuses its attention on tax legislation, placing stricter requirements on private firms. Although the press did not report on its actions, the organization allegedly blocked several important tax laws before they were passed (appendix A: I-14T). Periodically, the UTICA leadership aired their concerns on relatively innocuous issues. For example, at the 1998 meeting of the UTICA National Council, Djelani responded to industrialist concerns by publicly denouncing a proposed law requiring the retention of accounting documents for 10 years rather than the previous 5-year period (*Réalités*, no. 643, April 3–9, 1998, 20–21).

the 1980s and 1990s, the association still did not develop codified voting procedures, and it lacked institutional channels that would enable its membership to take part in decision making. Respondents claimed that FENATEX meetings are held irregularly and members do not pay annual dues (appendix A: I-36T; I-49T). Yet the administrative director of FENATEX claimed that decisions are made "by consensus, which entails much discussing and arguing among participants" (appendix A: I-31T). Officially, the federation elects a new president, nominated by the Executive Council, every five years. A prominent member of FENATEX, however, admitted that the electoral procedure is just a formality (appendix A: I-60T). In reality, the appointment of the association's president is less democratic: the president of UTICA backs a particular individual and, invariably, the appointed successor wins the election (appendix A: I-81T).

Respondents unanimously attested that FENATEX is completely ineffectual, even as its leadership and main constituents face bankruptcy with trade liberalization. The organization neither holds regular meetings nor collects membership dues (appendix A: I-23T; I-36T; I-56T; I-70T). A French investor who has worked in the Tunisian apparel sector since the early 1970s commented, "[The FENATEX leaders] do nothing. They vegetate. The organization has no power. All members act independently" (appendix A: I-90T). Instead, local manufacturers stressed that the Centre Technique du Textile (CETTEX) and the Agence pour la Promotion de l'Industrie (API), both state-administered organizations, promote the textile and apparel sectors more effectively (appendix A: I-74T; I-90T). Although it was created in 1969 (the brainchild of a state-appointed commission to study the textile sector and make recommendations for a national growth strategy), many textile and apparel manufacturers, both local and foreign, were not aware of FENATEX's existence (appendix A: I-66T; I-67T; I-84T).

FENATEX's responses to trade reform demonstrate the extent of the organization's inactivity. Insiders attested that FENATEX does not play an active role in outlining strategies for dealing with global economic challenges to the local textile and apparel sectors. The organization repeatedly takes the credit for government proposals to assist the sector, but, in reality, has virtually no role in crafting or even militating for policies to aid local manufacturers. For example, neither UTICA nor FENATEX contributed materially to the "Livre Blanc," an official document published in 1999 that provided an overview of the Tunisian industrial sector and outlined a sectoral integration strategy for the textile and apparel sectors. Although the cover of the document lists UTICA as a contributor to the report, one of the document's authors claimed that neither the peak-level business association nor FENATEX participated in the study (appendix A: I-90T). A high-level CETTEX official corroborated these contentions, charging that FENATEX is not "well equipped" to face economic challenges:

Even the President of the Republic turns to us, not to FENATEX, when he wants to address an issue relating to the textile and clothing sectors. . . . FENATEX is not taking the responsibility for restructuring the sector. It is not very implicated in the restructuring process, nor is it very aggressive in its approach toward the current difficult economic situation facing the industry. CETTEX is the [organization] that is doing everything to save the sector, and CETTEX does everything on behalf of the association. CETTEX saves FENATEX! (appendix A: I-81T)

Even in the darkest hour for the Tunisian textile sector, the body that formally represents local manufacturers could not promote the interests of its constituents.

The stagnation of FENATEX in the face of profound economic change is surprising because textile manufacturers, who stand to lose the most from trade liberalization and access to cheaper thread and cloth on global markets, dominate the organization. Manufacturers from the textile and apparel sectors as well as government officials widely acknowledged that a clique of textile manufacturers controls the association (appendix A: I-81T; I-82T; I-85T). A CETTEX official claimed:

To see who really runs FENATEX, all you need to do is look at the Executive Bureau. There is a sixteen-member bureau, and all of its members are directors of Tunisian owned and resident companies. They mainly come from the textile sector – that is, thread and cloth producers – with a few heads of small-scale clothing companies. Just look at *who* is the president of the organization to determine where the real power lies. (appendix A: I-81T)

But, in reality, domination of FENATEX did not translate into control over the policy agenda during the reform period.

Among its principal official duties, FENATEX organizes seminars to promote awareness among industrialists of government policies and challenges facing the textile and apparel sectors. In reality, FENATEX is not instrumental in arranging these programs; the Ministry of Industry and CETTEX play a far more important role in designing and executing the events. For example, beginning in the mid-1990s, FENATEX officially cosponsored an annual workshop called the "Tunisian Textile Quality Tour." In 2000, FENATEX president Hachemi Kooli opened the event with a speech emphasizing the importance of cooperation among the state, business, and labor to face the "challenges of globalization," but he offered no substantive vision of how to meet this goal. Government officials, particularly from various departments of the Ministry of Industry, gave more concrete presentations outlining the supposed formidable efforts of the government to support industrialists in the adjustment process (appendix A: I-51T; I-65T).

Through a variety of channels, including the co-optation of business associations as well as the selective enforcement of taxation, business law, and customs-processing procedures, the state maintains control over private business activity. As many students of North African politics argue, then, the state has played a critical role in blocking societal dissent. A combination of outright repression and the distribution of incentives on an increasingly selective basis ensured the quiescence of the local business community during the reform period.

Carrots: Preemptive Support for Local Industrialists

Official rhetoric stresses that state responsiveness – in fact, *anticipatory* responsiveness – explains the apparent placidity of the private sector in the face of profound economic shifts. In essence, state assistance for adjustment and industrial upgrading obviated the need for business lobbying and pressure tactics. An alphabet soup of government programs designed to provide targeted support to firms experiencing financial and technical difficulties allegedly address the fundamental concerns of local manufacturers. The Programme pour la Mise à Niveau (PMN), the state-run support program for the industrial sector, is the jewel in the crown of local macroeconomic, sectoral, and firm-level upgrading programs. Parastatal agencies provide assistance to specific industrial sectors, such as the Centre Technique des Industries Méchanique et Electrique for the mechanical and electrical sectors and CETTEX for the textile and apparel industries. Individual firms can seek assistance from a variety of state-sponsored credit programs, which provide financial support for successful and ailing firms alike, and from an innumerable quantity of seminars and mini-courses to help managers acquire advanced technical and administrative skills. A Ministry of Industry official explained, "Textile producers initially tried to resist the reforms a bit. But the administration created the PMN to assist companies that experienced difficulties. The government also created CETTEX and other technical support institutions to help industrialists adjust and improve their production. These programs are working well." The local media supply near daily accounts of the successes of these programs, praising the president and his advisors for their visionary efforts to save the local industrial tissue in the "inevitable march" toward integration in the global economy.

In late 1995, after the signing of the EU free trade agreement, the Tunisian Ministry of Industry and the Economy launched the PMN to boost the competitiveness of firms operating in Tunisia. Allotted over two billion Tunisian dinars,[20] largely supplied through EU grants, officials initially planned to implement the program over a five-year period (*Réalités*, May 26–June 1, 1995, 15). A tripartite commission composed of industrialists, bankers, and government representatives formally oversees the program's administration and selection process (appendix A: I-11T; *Réalités*, June 16–22, 1995, 21). Officially, participation is voluntary and firms of all sizes and from all industrial sectors, regardless of trade orientation, receive equal consideration in the selection process. The government provides incentives for participation in the form of subsidies and loan guarantees for firms chosen to participate in the program. Once accepted, firms undergo a preliminary diagnostic exam to assess their strengths and weaknesses. Participants share the costs of the exam with the program. The PMN Commission then encourages beneficiaries to implement the recommendations of the diagnostic with the support of bank loans. To kick off the program, the Ministry of Industry launched a pilot program with approximately 100 participants drawn from Tunisia's most prominent and successful industrial firms (*Réalités*, June 16–22, 1995, 21).

The government portrays the PMN as the palliative for the challenges of global economic exposure, while high-level administrators insist that the program demonstrates state willingness to support the business community during the transition period (appendix A: I-11T; I-36T; *Réalités*, May 12–18, 1995, 20). Officially, ministry officials, business association representatives, and the PMN administrators claim that the business community demanded the creation of the restructuring assistance program. As evidence for alleged private voluntarism in the program, officials cite the fact that the PMN pilot committee incorporated representatives from the peak-level business association and also noted that a tax levied on private companies supplies a portion of the program's operating budget. In reality, the PMN was a state initiative with extensive EU assistance (appendix A: I-31T; I-68T).

The argument that government support ensured the quiescence of local manufacturers during the adjustment process hinges on the premise that

---

[20] In 2000, two billion Tunisian dinars equaled almost US$2 billion.

state aid is actually effective. At best, the success of the PMN is questionable. Observers and alleged beneficiaries of the PMN, as well as would-be participants in the program, criticized the program on several grounds. First, the program only accepts companies that already face good prospects for survival in a liberalized economy. Arguably, competitive firms would have survived without state aid. Some manufacturers even suggested that the PMN commission hand-picked participants for the pilot program to ensure an auspicious beginning for the effort (appendix A: I-23T; I-68T). As part of a marketing strategy, only firms that had already achieved a minimum level of success were selected to participate in the first round (appendix A: I-88T; Bédoui 1998, 16–17).

Many firm owners expressed cynicism about the PMN. For these manufacturers, the state feigns support for the local industrial tissue but in reality sets up a catch-22: only profit-making firms that can afford the fee and seem viable in the eyes of the selection committee can benefit from subsidized technical assistance (appendix A: I-17T; I-18T). The director of a small cloth-finishing firm noted, "The people who benefited from the upgrading program are those who are already strong. Banks only help those companies that are already strong." The respondent applied to the PMN, but the commission rejected her application on the grounds that she lacked sufficient collateral to obtain loans that would cover the costs of participation.

A second critique of the PMN also undercuts the contention that state assistance obviates the need for business pressure: many observers contended that the benefits of participation in the program were insignificant. To be fair, the participants themselves were often responsible for this shortcoming because many refused to heed the recommendations of the diagnostic exams. The director of a state-owned bank and a consultant for the PMN confirmed that the program progressed slowly and achieved little tangible success. "Very few companies have actually implemented the recommendations outlined in their diagnostic studies. I can say this with confidence because I work with the program, but there are no statistics to prove this at this time. Overall, the banks have the impression that few companies have actually carried out the upgrading plans." A major obstacle to the program's success was the reluctance of many factory owners to pay for consulting services to assist them in implementing upgrading strategies, even when heavily subsidized by the state (appendix A: I-17T).

The PMN undoubtedly generates some benefits, both for its participants and administrators, although these may be unintended. Some observers, including local consultants and economists as well as World

Bank and European Union analysts, suggest that the PMN became a subsidy program for local firms (appendix A: I-61T; I-67T; I-88T; Lynn et al. 1996, iv). State grants for participation in the program are calculated on the basis of a firm's total capital investment, which provides an automatic incentive to inflate this figure. Industrialists openly admitted that, once they obtained the automatic enrollment bonus, they applied the funds toward nonproductive investments, such as real estate, rather than the stated project.

From a macroeconomic perspective, the PMN does not provide a coherent vision for boosting national competitiveness in global markets. The program primarily works with firms in sectors that no longer reflect Tunisia's competitive advantage and does not aim to transform the national economic profile (appendix A: I-52T). A consultant who worked extensively with PMN participants and helped to design the program itself echoed these comments:

[The PMN's] excessive microeconomic focus is problematic because it underestimates the need for the economy to transform itself. It should have adopted a multisectoral approach, leading to the transformation of sectoral activities in the country as a whole.... The PMN gives the impression of a static transition to new economic realities. But industrial upgrading is a long-term process, a change in the overall culture of work. (appendix A: I-61T)

State support during the economic transition did not help to create a more competitive economic environment for local industrialists, but because the PMN conducts its own evaluations of its activities, program administrators overlook many of the criticisms just discussed.

In the 1990s, the state created several technical support centers to provide tailored support for specific industrial sectors deemed critical to the national economy. CETTEX, a parastatal organization founded in 1992, targets the textile and apparel sectors, working closely with the PMN to provide technical support for upgrading efforts for textile and garment factories. CETTEX has a 12-member executive board, which includes representatives from the Ministry of Industry, the Ministry of Finance, and a state-owned bank, as well as 9 private industrialists. The president of FENATEX, the official business association representing the textile and apparel sectors, presides over the board.

Official rhetoric as well as the legal statutes establishing CETTEX hold that the state created the center *in response to* industrialist demands. This account implies that Tunisian business proactively lobbied the state for assistance. But CETTEX was purely a state initiative. In the early 1990s, when the textile and apparel sectors were booming, the state decided to "organize" these activities by creating CETTEX (appendix A: I-81T). According to high-level CETTEX employees, officials from the Ministry of Industry conceived of the institution, relied on informal contacts with industrialists to obtain feedback on the idea, and launched the center. Industrialists themselves never pushed for its creation. The director of CETTEX himself emphasized that the government – not industrialists – was better equipped to mastermind the center. With access to extensive macroeconomic data, state officials had a more comprehensive view of the structure of the industrial sector, enabling them to identify and address the challenges of industrial development more accurately than the business community. The establishment of CETTEX and other technical support centers for the private sector bolsters the official line that state anticipation of industrialist needs precluded lobbying activity during the reform process.

Government officials and the state-sanctioned media also highlighted the battery of legislation enacted to assist companies as they adjust to new economic realities. The oft-cited law for "companies in difficulty" is a case in point. In 1995, in response to the reforms and the EUAA, the government passed legislation to assist companies that could no longer meet their financial obligations (*Réalités*, March 9–15, 2000, 24). The law established a set of legal procedures enabling companies to avoid bankruptcy and retain their employees while restructuring their managerial and production techniques and establishing a debt repayment schedule (*Le Renouveau*, May 7, 1996; *Conjoncture* [Tunisia], September–October 1996, 1–6; *La Presse*, August 20, 1999). By 1998, 400 firms, of which 70 percent were industrial enterprises, officially declared themselves "in difficulty" in order to take advantage of the law. Official estimates maintained that 40 percent of these applicants avoided bankruptcy by following the stipulations of the law, permitting the retention of 3,100 workers (*Le Temps*, January 2, 1998). In the absence of reliable data, assessing the real impact of the "companies in difficulty" law is impossible. But the legislation reinforced the appearance of the government's commitment to the local private sector during a challenging period.

Proactive state policies undoubtedly appeased some local industrialists during the difficult adjustment period. Indeed, Tunisia's regulatory and legal structures aggressively promote private investment in certain areas, particularly in the export sector. For example, both Tunisian and foreign investors praised the government for establishing the *guichet unique* system. Created in 1989 to facilitate entrepreneurship, *guichet unique* refers to a centralized office within the API, a parastatal organization that promotes national industrial development. The office includes representatives from all relevant government ministries and agencies required to authorize the firm-creation process. Essentially, the system created a "one-stop shopping" experience for potential investors, who overwhelmingly affirmed its utility (*Réalités*, April 12–18, 1991, 18–19).[21] In addition, manufacturers benefited tremendously in the early 1990s, when the government legalized short-term labor contracts in the off-shore sector. Businesspeople had called for the amendment to the Labor Code since at least the early 1980s (*Réalités*, November 2–8, 1990, 17).

In sum, government policies provide an array of fiscal and regulatory incentives for the private sector, even though capital did not historically play a predominant role in the state's social base. Nonetheless, in the mid-1990s, manufacturers had many outstanding concerns, which constituted potential issues around which business groups *could* – but chose not to – mobilize.

THE SOCIAL FOUNDATIONS OF BUSINESS BEHAVIOR

Given the formidable array of tactics available to the Tunisian state for maintaining social control, it is tempting to conclude that state repression and co-optation of civic associations ensured business passivity in the face of profound economic change. But this explanation presumes a latent – albeit frustrated – desire among local business factions to mobilize around the issue of trade liberalization. State promotion of the off-shore, export zone since the early 1970s ensured that a substantial portion of the local private sector was relatively unscathed by the initial round of trade liberalization in the 1980s and 1990s and, consequently, entirely disengaged from struggles over the domestic trade regime playing out in the domestic economy. Exporters therefore had little incentive to organize in response to the reforms and economic opening in the 1990s did not become politicized. Studies of Tunisian politics tend to emphasize the role of the authoritarian state in quashing expressions of societal discontent. The sociology of Tunisian capital – a product of struggles within the anticolonial movement that shaped postindependence state-building and

---

[21] At the same time, some Tunisian businesspeople complained that it unfairly favored foreign investors. While foreigners could create industrial or commercial businesses in Tunisia within a 48-hour period, they argued, locals were obliged to undergo a comparatively complex bureaucratic process that took much longer (*Réalités*, March 7–13, 1997, 19).

economic policymaking – is a neglected but equally important explanation for the muted responses of local industrialists to economic opening in the 1990s.[22]

Economic "Democracy" and the Common Origins of the Tunisian Industrial Class

Overall similarities in the social origins of most capital holders, as well as the relative equality of access to capital, helped to depoliticize the economic adjustment process in Tunisia. As chapter 3 describes, access to capital was relatively democratic after independence in 1956. Because of the social composition of the anticolonial movement and its effects on postindependence state-building, an economic or political elite did not monopolize business opportunities, and individuals from modest social backgrounds were able to advance economically. Within the Tunisian private sector, businesspeople developed varied relationships with international capital. While some Tunisian "captains of industry" worked extensively with international companies, others did not cultivate linkages with foreign capital.[23] Thus, Tunisian manufacturers had diverse holdings and positions in the local economy.

Large-scale protectionist manufacturers never enjoyed overriding influence in the domestic political economy. The vast majority of Tunisian companies were small enterprises: in 2000, the industrial sector contained about 4,500 companies, of which half employed 10 or fewer employees (appendix A: I-42T; I-63T). The bulk of private businesspeople with stakes in the postindependence economy did not come from especially privileged families, and access to economic opportunities was historically far more equitable than in most developing countries (appendix A: I-52T; I-87T). Tunisia's comparatively egalitarian social policy ensured that many successful industrialists came from modest social backgrounds, particularly in activities with low barriers to entry such as apparel exports.

---

[22] In arguing that the predominance of small and medium firms prevents the rise of an effective private-sector challenge to state control, Bellin (1991, 57–59) is a partial exception. But firm size alone does not explain the ability or inability of business to organize collectively, as successful mobilization among small firms in Morocco attests and critics of Olson's theory of collective action contend (Oliver 1993).

[23] For example, Mohamed Ali Darghouth, a prominent textile manufacturer whose factories target the local market, faced different challenges from economic opening than other big business owners, such as Chakib Nouira and Hédi Djelani, who have extensive linkages with international firms.

Export-promotion policies embodied in the 1972 Law and various fiscal incentives were a major catalyst for entrepreneurs in light manufacturing industries. The state-sponsored Fond pour la Promotion du Developpement Industriel (FOPRODI) played a key role in promoting entrepreneurship, in some cases supplemented by loans from relatives and friends (appendix A: I-56T; I-62T; I-70T). Access to credit ensured that entrepreneurs from diverse social origins invested in the industrial sector. The celebrated middle class was a cornerstone of the Tunisian model of economic development touted by government officials and representatives of international financial institutions alike (Bras 1996). The comparable social backgrounds of Tunisian producers in the on-shore and off-shore zones deterred conflicts among producers in the two segments of the economy. Because producers could not frame their disputes in terms of sharp socioeconomic differences or privileged ties to the state, struggles over trade liberalization among manufacturers in the domestic and export markets did not ignite.

The average dispersion of capital holdings also shaped business responses to reform. Investors tended to confine their holdings to a limited range of activities, if not a single industry.[24] Indeed, Tunisian law explicitly limited the size of business empires by forbidding the establishment of holding companies. On several occasions, the Tunisian parliament considered a series of laws that would legalize the juridical structure of a *groupe*, or holding company, but none were adopted (appendix A: I-63T). In 1988, the parliament passed a law creating the Société d'Investissement du Capital Fixe (SICAF), which essentially permitted an equivalent form by enabling shareholding in diverse companies. Ostensibly adopted to invigorate the local financial market by providing alternate funding sources for companies, the SICAF law facilitated the rise of larger-scale holdings. Nonetheless, the government continued to ensure that assets remained circumscribed. The head of a local consulting firm commented, "The minute that a relatively large *groupe* arises, the government sends auditors to the company because it thinks there is something fishy going on in the

---

[24] The Poulina group was an exception. Few families had holdings in multiple sectors. Another exception was the Hachicha family, which owned Randa, a food-processing plant; LG, a consumer electronics dealership; and Unoplast, a plastics manufacturing business (appendix A: I-42T). The director of a textile firm noted, "Private businessmen in Tunisia did not have millions, as in Morocco. Furthermore, business holdings were divided by branch. That is, businessmen generally did not control holdings throughout the economy, but rather confined their holdings to a specific branch" (appendix A: I-27T).

company, such as embezzlement."[25] The legal framework also supported
this de facto government policy by providing vast incentives to create
companies but few inducements for firm restructuring or mergers. As a
result, the few large capital holders in Tunisia managed their interests separately and their businesses were not formally linked (appendix A: I-40T;
I-61T).

Nascent private-sector "dynasties" and large fortunes have emerged
only recently, particularly in the 1990s, and many enjoy close linkages to
the president and his inner circle. In part, liberalization may have convinced Tunisian policymakers to encourage capital consolidation because
big business conglomerates are, theoretically, more competitive in a globalized economy. In an interview with a weekly news magazine, the head
of UTICA declared, "The country needs big industrial groups. The government is aware of this imperative. There is no doubt that incentives
were put in place for the constitution of these groups. What remains is
that juridically we must deepen and create real legislation for these holding companies because the legal void limits the spirit of industrialists"
(*Réalités*, January 30–February 5, 1998, 16). A French embassy official
also argued that economic reform and liberalization encouraged some
diversification of assets among large holders. For example, "There are
some businessmen or groups who have got involved in various, diverse
activities across different sectors. Poulina, for example, is diversifying. The
major groups are presently in the process of getting rid of their unprof-
itable holdings" (appendix A: I-47T). A local textile manufacturer commented, "Multisectoral holdings in private hands did not really arise until
after 1987 [when Ben Ali came to power]." The last decade has witnessed
a trend toward enlargement of private holdings. "All of the new large-
scale holdings, however, are in the hands of new industrialists, such as the
Poulina group, the Chaibi group, which has invested heavily in malls and
shopping centers, and the Mabrouk family, which has invested in cookies
and other food products. These families are all part of a new generation
of industrialists in Tunisia" (appendix A: I-40T). These groups, including
the Ben Ayed, Chaibi, Mzabi, and Cherif groups, trace their origins to
the 1970s, when they benefited from state industrial promotion policies,

---

[25] Rumors and some evidence abound that this is changing, as close associates and family members of the president and his wife have allegedly enjoyed privileged access to
economic opportunities since the mid-1990s (Donze 2002; Hibou 1999). See also the
Web site of the opposition group Audace, which aims to document the holdings of the
close associates of the president and his wife: www.audace.free.fr (accessed February 7,
2006).

but they have developed and prospered extensively since the late 1980s (appendix A: I-54T).

Resentment toward increasing capital concentration, particularly in the hands of close associates of the president, emerged in the late 1990s. Small apparel exporters consistently articulated dissatisfaction, in particular by citing the system for referring foreign investors to local subcontractors. The client referral process through the API was a major source of resentment. Owners and managers of small firms claimed that they did not benefit from API efforts to match up local producers with foreign clients. The owner of a small knitwear factory claimed, "API opportunities are all distributed to friends and associates of the agency's administration." Another small-scale garment exporter concurred: "Ultimately, it is best to find clients through direct channels. The 'big cheeses' in the sector gobble up all opportunities listed through organizations such as API [Industrial Promotion Agency]." Managers of multinational garment firms sourcing in Tunisia, as well as the directors of large firms, corroborated these contentions (appendix A: I-66T; I-67T; I-70T). The manager of a major lingerie factory in Sfax stated that her firm obtains many client referrals through API and Centre pour la Promotion des Exportations (CEPEX). Still, there is some economic logic to the API referral process: because multinational firms prefer to work with larger local subcontractors, institutions such as the API direct them to Tunisian factories with 200 or more employees.[26]

Still, the recent trend toward greater capital concentration concerns only a handful of local investors and generally involves sectors that require high minimum capital holdings. Because smallholders still generate substantial wealth in off-shore processing zones, most do not feel that this trend threatens their businesses directly – even if they dislike cronyism. Continued state support for capital dispersion through access to credit for new and small investors undercuts producer interests in collective

---

[26] Multinational firms often perceived that small subcontractors were unreliable because they could not always complete orders on time and sometimes sub-subcontracted part of their orders to even smaller firms, adding further uncertainty to the production process. Instead, foreign companies such as the Sara Lee group, which sourced for the Playtex label in Tunisia, sought contracts with large Tunisian companies. When it first began producing in Tunisia, Sara Lee obtained lists of potential subcontractors from the API and the local chamber of commerce, which provided information on the structure and size of potential suppliers. Sara Lee representatives then visited prospective suppliers to conduct on-site inspections. Through these channels, the Sara Lee group initially established contacts with the Ben Abdallah group, which began as a subcontractor and later supplied workers to Playtex through its temporary personnel service.

mobilization. How increasing capital concentration affects ongoing responses to reform, however, remains to be seen.

The Semiopen Economy: Separate Spheres of Production

The construction of parallel on-shore and off-shore markets also helps to explain the virtual absence of Tunisian business mobilization in the 1990s. The creation of the export sector soon after independence not only enabled Tunisian investors to profit financially but also shaped their political responses to reform decades later. The rise of off-shore processing effectively split local capital into two segments – one targeting the local market and the other oriented toward international markets – and prevented the rise of an entrenched protectionist elite. The importance of foreign capital in the off-shore economy, another by-product of the relatively early development of the export sector, dampened opposition to reform, while the small size of the domestic market preempted battles between exporters and domestic producers. With such a small consumer base, the relatively early turn to export promotion was logical, and many local manufacturers who emerged in response to this policy had little interest in targeting the local market (appendix A: I-90T).[27]

Exports have been an important mainstay of the Tunisian economy for decades, in large part because officials perceived that the small domestic market precluded import-substitution policies. Just as small domestic markets in Western European countries such as Austria, Switzerland, and Belgium compelled policymakers to adopt outward-oriented industrial policies (Katzenstein 1985), Tunisian officials quickly perceived the need to develop the export sector. In the early 1970s, a time when most developing countries were firmly entrenched in policies of import-substitution industrialization, Tunisia constructed a profitable off-shore zone, which gradually attracted substantial local and foreign capital. Both large and small capital holders have important stakes in the off-shore processing zone. The share of off-shore production in total exports attests to the importance of this sector in the national economy: in 1997, exports from off-shore companies accounted for 63 percent of total exports (République Tunisienne, *Annuaire Statistique*, 1998).[28]

---

[27] A large textile manufacturer surmised that liberalization did not become politicized in Tunisia because the local market was small: "In Morocco, there is actually something at stake for local clothing producers."

[28] In 1988, the head of UTICA observed, "Exports constitute an essential and fundamental route for the development of our economy given the limited size of the internal market and [domestic] population control campaigns" (*Réalités*, August 12–18, 1988, 18).

Since the passage of the 1972 Law, which created the off-shore zone, the government has actively promoted off-shore production and ensured that the system worked efficiently.[29] Liberalization only reinforced incentives for off-shore manufacturing (appendix A: I-70T).[30] Businesspeople repeatedly attested that the off-shore regime operates smoothly, with few bureaucratic glitches and minimal corruption on the part of customs officials. Government officials rarely obstruct the in-bond, reexport trade regime, which constitutes the regulatory foundation of the off-shore sector (appendix A: I-85T; I-90T). From the state's perspective, the export economy has both economic and political advantages. The off-shore sector generates some local value-added and creates jobs, an important asset for a regime obsessed by the potential political dangers of high unemployment rates among young people.[31]

The continuing significance of foreign capital in Tunisian manufacturing – another notable feature of local capital structure – also explains the lack of private-sector mobilization. The relative importance of foreign capital in the Tunisian economy meant that a significant portion of private investors were not only divorced from local politics but also could easily exercise an "exit" option by divesting. Many foreign garment producers and buyers operating in Tunisia's off-shore zone had little or no contact with Tunisian-owned firms and minimal linkages to the domestic economy. For example, Levi's, which sources 75 percent of its supply for European markets in Tunisia, works with nine subcontractors in Tunisia, of which only one is fully Tunisian owned. European companies, with factories operating in the Tunisian off-shore economy, own the eight remaining firms (appendix A: I-84T). The editor of a Tunisian economic weekly commented, "The fact that there is a high degree of foreign investment in the industrial sector has also affected industrialist responses to opening.

---

[29] The director of a garment-sourcing office for a major international clothing retailer noted that Tunisian law provides many fiscal incentives for exports. Export companies do not pay a value-added tax on many items, including items as mundane as office supplies, and the same holds true for factories that subcontract for exporters (appendix A: I-37T).

[30] In the 1999 budgetary law, the government introduced further tax deductions to benefit exporters, including a measure permitting tax deductions for international marketing of Tunisian products.

[31] Abuses of the off-shore trade regime limited its value for the Treasury. Investment regulations allow off-shore companies to operate tax-free for their first 10 years of operation and provide other attractive terms to export firms, whether local or foreign. In practice, however, foreign companies often nominally shut down their factories while changing the official name of their local company after 10 years of operating in Tunisia in order to profit from an additional 10-year package of fiscal incentives. The government was well aware of this illegal practice but overlooked it to retain foreign direct investment, which provided about half of all manufacturing jobs in Tunisia (appendix A: I-66T).

In the textile and apparel industries, over 50 percent of investment comes from multinationals. These companies can leave their production operations in Tunisia easily if the business climate deteriorates" (appendix A: I-85T). Because the off-shore economy contains a significant portion of foreign investment, many manufacturers are not committed to maintaining operations in Tunisia and therefore have little incentive to mobilize politically on local business policies (appendix A: I-90T).[32]

Foreign investors expressed little commitment to Tunisia, which is attractive to multinational firms as long as it provides a compelling investment climate. For industrial manufacturing, Tunisia's greatest asset is its semiskilled and unskilled labor, although geographic proximity to major end markets is an additional attraction. Foreign investors, particularly multinational corporations with interests in diverse labor-rich countries, are prepared to shift their investments and business relationships to lower-cost production sites in Eastern Europe and Asia. Furthermore, Tunisian law provides little incentive for foreign firms to establish joint ventures with local partners, which would arguably increase their commitment to the local market and engage them more directly in business politics. Because investment laws greatly facilitate the process of *creating* companies on Tunisian soil, most foreign investors opt to set up their own companies in the off-shore sector. According to a French exporter in the apparel sector, the only tangible reason for a foreign company to seek a Tunisian partner is to save time in establishing local operations. Working with local intermediaries or business brokers obviates the need to seek local partners.

The government maintains a sharp division in the local economy between parallel on-shore and off-shore sectors. Legally, domestic and export production are entirely separate. In this way, the state shelters local producers from outside competition while encouraging local investors to seek their fortunes in global markets and attracting foreign capital. The 1972 Law officially permits off-shore firms to sell 20 percent of their production on the domestic market but, in reality, the state blocks local sales to protect Tunisian industry (appendix A: I-5T; I-61T).[33] The strict

---

[32] Of course, the relationships of different multinational corporations to the Tunisian market vary. Some international firms have direct ownership stakes in local factories, while others, such as Gap International or Levi's, subcontract their work to local firms but maintain local sourcing offices (appendix A: I-35T; I-37T).

[33] Foreign investors operating in Tunisia's off-shore zone reportedly wanted to exercise this right, but bureaucratic obstacles and "quality control checks" repeatedly inhibited local sales. For example, foreign diplomats attested that the American multinational firm Nabisco wanted to sell some of its production in Tunisia but has been blocked repeatedly (appendix A: I-5T).

separation between on-shore and off-shore production leads to paradoxical sourcing patterns for local retail sales. For example, the American jeans manufacturer Levi's has plants in Tunisia but does not sell on the domestic market. Instead, retail stores marketing the company's brands are obliged to adopt the same procedures as all importers to obtain merchandise. Tunisian subcontractors for Levi's send finished products to a warehouse in Brussels, where the parent company's retail sales department sorts products and ships to retailers worldwide, including to Tunisia (appendix A: I-84T). The government maintains the distinction between the on-shore and off-shore economies in all sectors of the economy. In the financial sector, for example, the government consistently refuses to issue licenses for foreign banks to operate in the domestic market (Cammett 1999).

The split between export and local production, well established before the reform period, muted the impact of liberalization by ensuring that the substantial export segment of the private sector was not immediately harmed by the process. Economic reform had different effects on different components of business. While export manufacturers and subcontractors benefited immensely from the off-shore trade regime and would gain even more from liberalization, locally oriented producers faced declining profits.

The division between on-shore and off-shore activities has built-in limits because of negligible backward linkages to the local economy for export activities. Politically, however, the dual market model has great advantages: by dividing the private sector and ensuring that many local investors could profit on global markets, the system promoted complacency and, hence, stability in the face of economic change.

Export manufacturers were largely satisfied with the duty-free trade regime and, if anything, believed that trade reform would strengthen the regulatory framework guiding their activities. In many cases, exporters seemed blissfully unaware of the detrimental impact of global economic exposure for the local textile industry. The director of a major textile firm commented, "The EU Agreement did not pose a big problem for the majority of producers because a big percentage were already export-oriented." The attitudes of the manager of a large lingerie factory in Sfax were representative of the views of most exporters. The respondent expressed no concern about the long-term effects of trade liberalization and indicated only a partial knowledge of regulations governing the on-shore economy. In discussing impending changes in trade policies, she supported the reform process, particularly the prospect of greater access to textile inputs and streamlined customs-processing procedures, but reacted as if these were inevitable trends in the Tunisian institutional environment. In her view, the deepening of the trade liberalization process with the EU Agreement only reinforced a key pillar of the Tunisian economy. Similarly, the director of production of a major lingerie subcontractor in Sfax commented, "I have no contact with firms working for the local market so I cannot talk about the impact of the EU Agreement for domestic firms." Exporters adopted a short-term view on trade liberalization while downplaying the longer-term threats of Asian competition on global markets.

Exporters were much more focused on boosting the international competitiveness of their individual products than in participating in collective action strategies to change national trade regulations, which might boost long-term prospects in world markets. The primary concerns of management in off-shore factories were improving quality and upgrading production and management techniques within the factory. The manager of an apparel export factory listed the firm's priorities, including "financial restructuring, modernizing of equipment, developing new marketing strategies, improving management methods, computerizing firm records, implementing the ISO9000 Quality Assurance system, and rationalizing human resources." For a significant portion of the local business community, therefore, economic change elicited internally focused efforts to restructure the firm rather than struggles to obtain overt state protection from global pressures. Even the politically charged issue of labor costs, a primary component of apparel assembly costs, did not compel exporters to mobilize collectively against rising wages.[34]

The detachment of Tunisian exporters and representatives of multinational firms from the on-shore economy also helps to explain the stagnation of producer organizations such as UTICA and FENATEX. Unlike in Morocco, which had a lower rate of foreign investment, manufacturers in Tunisia had fewer vested interests in the domestic market and therefore in national politics. With so many producers divorced from local struggles, few tensions erupted between textile and apparel manufacturers. Managers of international apparel firms expressed little, if any, need to join or participate in producer associations (appendix A: I-66T; I-67T; I-84T). The marketing director of a Belgian garment export firm claimed, "Since

---

[34] Triennial state-led wage negotiations set official wage levels in a variety of sectors, but businesspeople felt they had little control over the process. At the same time, the state instituted more "flexible" labor regulations in the late 1990s, which greatly appeased off-shore manufacturers and obviated the need for lobbying around this issue. For background on Tunisian labor politics, see Alexander (1996).

the company is linked to a European company, we turn to our Belgian parent company if we need something."

The dismissive attitudes of Tunisian exporters toward local business associations reflected their relative satisfaction with the status quo as well as their perception that such organizations could not further their goals, notably to boost their international competitiveness. A longtime investor in the Tunisian apparel sector noted, "Apparel producers have direct contacts with global markets. They do their own business prospecting and, thus, have little need to participate in FENATEX. They just do assembly work." Owners of off-shore garment firms were more closely linked to foreign associations, such as the European or American chambers of commerce in Tunisia, or state agencies, such as the API, than to local manufacturers' associations. A Tunisian apparel exporter exclaimed, "I am heavily involved in the Tunisian-British Chamber of Commerce, and other foreign business associations. I have no time for organizations such as FENATEX." With a battery of state export incentives promoting their activities, apparel exporters felt no need to organize in professional associations.

Off-shore apparel manufacturers were completely divorced from political struggles within FENATEX. Although apparel exporters far surpassed domestic textile manufacturers on a variety of criteria, including total number of firms, exports, investment, and production, they did not adhere to the organization that officially represented their interests. In the mid-1990s, trade reform elicited fierce battles within FENATEX between thread and cloth manufacturers over reductions in duties on thread imports, yet exporters were entirely divorced from these conflicts (Cammett 1999). Apparel manufacturers continued to export at a rapid clip and steadily expanded their clientele, while conflicts consumed their counterparts in the thread and cloth industries. Confined to the on-shore economy, the battles raging in the textile sector had no impact on off-shore apparel subcontractors.

Tunisian manufacturers expressed a variety of competing concerns and fears about trade reform that were typical of manufacturers in many developing countries and paralleled those of their Moroccan counterparts. What prevented domestic textile producers and apparel exporters from vilifying each other as occurred in Morocco? I argue that the dispersion of capital as well as the state's relatively equal treatment of factions of the industrial class with different trade orientations undercut the impulse to organize collectively in response to trade reform. A pattern of state-sponsored industrialization, which grew out of the postindependence state-building project, ensured that industrialists did not develop the organizational skills or desire to represent their own interests.

Interviews confirmed that on-shore and off-shore producers harbored no resentment against each other. A few respondents in the textile and apparel industries even sympathized with their would-be opponents. A textile manufacturer described the mounting pressures facing apparel exporters: "The least affected subsector is the ready-to-wear garment industry, especially off-shore factories. But the situation is getting worse for them as well. Even some small ready-to-wear factories have closed" (appendix A: I-26T). Further, cloth and thread manufacturers did not belittle the apparel production process, which requires less capital and technical expertise than their own activities. Instead, many recognized the difficulties of establishing relationships with foreign clients in an increasingly competitive global marketplace. A textile factory owner declared:

Sure, it is easy to open an off-shore facility. The state is really pushing this and has set up an extensive legal and institutional support system to encourage off-shore enterprises. The main problem is getting clients. It's meaningless that it's so simple to open off-shore facilities if a firm does not have clients because then it won't do any business! And it is very hard to get clients. (appendix A: I-26T)

Although Tunisian cloth manufacturers wanted local garment subcontractors to purchase cloth from their factories, they neither begrudged apparel exporters for their input sourcing choices nor invoked a moral obligation to buy locally.

Domestic and export manufacturers did not hold each other responsible for their economic woes. Instead, their resentment focused on nebulous and distant enemies such as "globalization" or Asian countries with cheap labor and "aggressive" export policies. The director of a textile firm emphasized that liberalized textile imports posed the greatest challenge to local producers. She commented, "Now foreign textiles enter Tunisia almost freely and there is a lot of clandestine importing, which evade taxation and thus can be sold at much cheaper prices." The director of FENATEX, an organization dominated by cloth weavers, blamed the global economy and cloth weavers themselves for the decline of the textile sector:

In general, the weaving subsector is not able to survive in a competitive environment. Many have already closed due to falling prices for their finished products and the fact that their quality-level is quite poor.... The cloth sector slept for the last 25 years, despite the fact that weaving firms should have approached consumers and apparel producers a long time ago to learn about their needs. If they had done so, they could have averted the influx of imported cloth.

As in Morocco and many other developing countries, Tunisian textile manufacturers favored greater integration with the local apparel sector to save their factories. The de facto rejection of this strategy by apparel exporters, however, did not vex proponents in the thread and cloth industries. Domestic and export-oriented manufacturers believed that they shared the same intangible enemy – globalization. Industrialists largely perceived that globalization and even national trade reform were out of their control. For local manufacturers, the real "perpetrators" of global economic competition – international financial institutions and low-wage Asian countries – were remote and seemingly undefeatable. Hence, mobilization against economic change seemed futile. Furthermore, state creation and continued active support for industrial development meant that producers in both the export and domestic economies relied on proactive state policies rather than their own initiative to adjust to economic change.

From the perspective of standard trade and interest group theories, Tunisian business apathy vis-à-vis new opportunities and challenges from global markets is counterintuitive. Why would local manufacturers facing bankruptcy and dwindling material wealth do little to resist detrimental domestic economic reforms? Conversely, why would exporters who faced mounting challenges from Asian competitors not take more initiative to promote popular long-term development strategies based on sectoral integration and clustering, as government officials and development consultants advocated? The absence of channels for societal expression is an obvious and somewhat justified answer. In the first instance, state repression deterred the politicization of the industrial class. As the chapter has argued, however, state repression does not address characteristics of the local industrial class and its historic ties to the state that made collective mobilization improbable. Postindependence state-sponsored industrialization and, relatedly, the structure of the industrial class obviated potential conflict among producer factions over economic policymaking.

6

Fat Cats and Self-Made Men

Class Conflict and Business Collective Action in Morocco

> *Le patronat est devenu plus revendicateur que les syndicats!*
> (Business has become more demanding than the labor unions!)
> Abdelmajid Bouzoubaa, official, Confédération
> Démocratique du Travail, February 10, 2000
>
> *Signe des temps, ce sont les patrons qui revendiquent et non les employés.*
> (As a sign of the times, it is business that makes demands and not workers.)
> *Maroc-Hebdo*, May 12–18, 2000, 18

The political economy of Morocco is often depicted as unshaken in the face of challenges from abroad and at home. The literature focuses overwhelmingly on the primary place of the monarchy and palace politics in determining economic and social outcomes. A tenet of the literature on postindependence Moroccan politics is that the private sector most effectively lobbies decision makers and influences policy through opaque personal channels, and that patronage is essential for any transaction. (Hammoudi 1997; Hibou 1996; Layachi 1999; Leveau 1985; Leveau 1987; Waterbury 1970).

But the preponderant focus on the palace in the scholarly literature on Morocco has masked pockets of change initiated by emergent social actors.[1] A tendency to treat social groups as aggregate wholes in studies of Morocco skews analyses of the postreform Moroccan political economy

---

[1] Catusse (1999b, 367) makes a similar argument: "The question arises of how a new 'political actor' appears in a relatively closed [political] configuration or system: the thesis of 'manipulation' or of a [deliberate] state strategy is seductive and remains important. But, many indicators support the hypothesis of a penetration of the political system by a category of entrepreneurs, which itself is demanding access to the political sphere."

148

and overlooks the role of "self-made men," a new class of industrialists who modified existing patterns of business–government relations that had been entrenched for decades.

THE CONSTRUCTION OF AN INTEREST GROUP

Events in the 1990s, notably an economic bust and the signing of a bilateral trade agreement with the European Union, highlighted mutual interests among exporters and compelled them to organize within the existing producers association for the textile and apparel sectors. A shared perception that a bloc of large-scale protectionist businesspeople stymied broader access to economic opportunities, however, provided the real spark for an aggressive mobilization campaign by emerging export manufacturers.

Economic Crisis, Business Cleavages, and the Politicization of AMITH

The 1990s were tough for Moroccan producers. East Asian textile man-ufacturers gained increasing global market share and progressively pen-etrated the local market. Regional shocks, largely a result of the First Gulf War in 1990–1991, also had devastating effects on the local econ-omy. Trade liberalization only furthered the vulnerability of Moroccan textile manufacturers to world price fluctuations. Hence, they opposed trade reforms implemented as part of the 1983 SAP. The umbrella pro-ducers organization, Conféderation Générale des Enterprises du Maroc (CGEM), often conveyed the viewpoints of domestic manufacturers. Its leaders cited the inability of Morocco's fragile industrial tissue to survive the "dumping" of goods by international exporters. Macroeconomic dif-ficulties, the confederation leadership contended, necessitated an immedi-ate pause in the SAP, notably a halt to import-liberalization policies (*LVE*, March 23, 1990, 12; *LVE*, May 31, 1991, 10; *LVE*, December 20, 1991, 4; *LVE*, February 14, 1992, 2; *LVE*, April 12, 1992, 31; *LVE*, April 16, 1993, 3–8). Similarly, the textile producers association, the Association Marocaine de l'Industrie du Textile (AMIT), issued a statement calling for "liberalization with prudence," drawing critical attention to the commer-cial practices of Morocco's competitors in global textile and clothing mar-kets. Official AMIT rhetoric maintained that liberalization would benefit local firms by compelling them to improve their production techniques. But the association's president, Mohamed Lahlou, a high-level manager in the Kettani group and the director of a Kettani-owned textile firm, argued that an "overly brutal" opening might wipe out the "dynamism" within this key sector of the Moroccan economy (*LVE*, December 14, 1990, 33).[2] Recognizing the futility of resisting the reforms, the CGEM leadership abandoned its open appeals to block tariff cuts by the mid-to-late 1990s. Local industrialists also outwardly resigned themselves to the "inevitability" of the liberalization process. A major textile producer in Ain Sebaa noted that it was no longer possible to fight liberalization because "it is too powerful and it is a worldwide trend. There is too much external pressure" (appendix A: I-41M).[3]

As local textile manufacturers complained about trade liberalization in the early 1990s, emergent apparel exporters also faced mounting constraints in world markets. By this time, the explosive growth in the Moroccan apparel industry had come to a screeching halt. The negative repercussions of the Gulf War and the downturn in global consumer demand highlighted shared interests within the nascent class of apparel exporters. In 1991, apparel exporters embarked upon a number of missions – individually as well as in organized groups – to seek new clients and convince existing clients and suppliers that business was running smoothly in Morocco. After returning from a European promotional tour in February 1991, Lahlou, along with several prominent industrialists in the apparel sector (such as Abdelali Berrada, who would play a decisive role in the association over the course of the next decade), publicly stressed the urgency of the situation. An AMIT committee established in 1990 and charged with boosting local apparel exports decided to institutionalize these efforts by launching an official trade show to promote the Moroccan clothing export sector. Thus, the biannual Salon du Vêtement Marocain (VETMA) was created. The first VETMA was held in May 1991, followed by a second show in November 1991, with a group of 120 apparel and knitwear companies selected to participate (*LVE*, December 14, 1990, 33; *LVE*, March 1, 1991, 9–10; *LVE*, March 29, 1991).[4]

---

[2] Other professional association demands included an appeal for state efforts to curtail black market activities, the establishment of a fund to assist firm-level upgrading efforts, tax reform, reduced interest rates on bank credit, the institution of a more flexible labor code, and restructuring of the social security system (*LVE*, January 25, 1991, 4).

[3] Industrialists felt powerless to stop the process, expressing dissatisfaction with the administration's decision to adopt the policies without consulting the private sector writ large (*LVE*, April 16, 1993, 4). Another director based in Ain Sebaa voiced similar resignation in the face of liberalization. He claimed that the Moroccan government was compelled to sign international trade agreements in order to "sell its tomatoes and phosphates to Europe" (appendix A: I-72M). In his view, this was not fair to local manufacturers.

[4] AMITH's official description of VETMA noted, "Since [the event's] creation in 1991, industrialists wanted to make VETMA a veritable tool for promotion and public relations.

The decision to launch VETMA constituted a radical break from prior association activities. Overwhelmed with orders following the shows, Moroccan producers credited VETMA with "saving the situation" for apparel producers after the Gulf War (*LVE*, June 28, 1991, 4). In 1993, Berrada became the full-time director of the exposition and the executive director of AMIT. Within a year, Berrada and his staff began planning international VETMA events. Toward this end, AMIT established several overseas offices with full-time staff members who relied on mailings, advertising, and press releases to foster direct contacts between European clients and local producers. Furthermore, the VETMA organizing committee often traveled to Europe to promote Moroccan exports. The state did not provide any funding for the overseas version of the trade show until two years after its inception (appendix A: I-34M).[5]

At the same time, professionals from all constituencies within AMIT called for a more proactive role for the association, and previously marginalized apparel exporters again took the initiative. In an autumn 1991 meeting, clothing producers decided that restructuring AMIT was a priority. The producers had three main goals: opening opportunities within the profession to young entrepreneurs, recruiting qualified administrative personnel for AMIT, and acquiring a new headquarters for the organization (*LVE*, October 11, 1991, 14). This effort gave rise to a number of important changes that strengthened the association's ability to actively represent all of its constituents. In 1991, AMIT moved from its small, informal office in the old Derb Omar quarter of Casablanca to its new headquarters in the posh Anfa neighborhood (appendix A: I-108M). Significantly, in 1993 – the same year that Berrada was appointed executive director – AMIT officially added the word *habillement* (apparel) to

Thus, they were the initiators, conceptualizers, executors, and promoters of this trade show. The first VETMA show, organized in 1991, was the expression of the will of Moroccan industrialists and of the Association to take the promotion of the sector into their own hands. This first edition took place right after the Gulf War, which was the challenge that the professionals wanted to face along with international competition that was becoming stronger" (http://www.amith.org.ma/Amith/VETMA.asp). At this time, the association also created a standing commission of French and Moroccan textile manufacturers to discuss their business relations and, specifically, EU policies on export quotas for North African apparel.

5 In a public statement during a VETMA show in 1994, Berrada emphasized that the private sector fully funded the event and called upon the state to devote more resources to it. He commented that, "This is a unique instance where the private sector pays for expenses that normally should fall upon the state" (*Maroc Economie*, November 14–20, 1994, 3–4), suggesting that the government had shirked its responsibility in this area. Accordingly, Berrada supported a proposal for the 1995 budgetary law to create a state export promotion fund that was subsequently adopted.

its name, changing its acronym to AMITH (appendix A: I-108M). Henceforth, the association headquarters had 13 permanent staff members, of which 4 were management-level employees. Four subcommittees represented the major branches of the sectors, including weaving and finishing, thread spinning, knitting, and apparel assembly, headed by an industrialist from the respective activity. Ad hoc committees were also established to address issues of concern to AMITH constituents, notably energy costs and labor code reform.

By the mid-1990s, AMITH had almost 700 members, who collectively accounted for about 79 percent of all workers, 84 percent of production, and 97 percent of total exports in the textile and clothing sectors.[6] Members paid 3,000 Moroccan Dirhams (DH) (in 2007, about US$349) in annual membership dues, which constituted the bulk of the association's funding source and subsidized participation in overseas trade shows (appendix A: I-71M).[7]

In 1995, the AMITH membership adopted an amendment limiting the tenure of the association's presidency to three years, with a maximum of two terms. Previously, the official presidential term was two years, but Lahlou had presided over the organization for more than 20 years. Until the early 1990s, association members attested, AMITH was an ineffective representative of its constituent sectors and its leadership largely used the organization to serve their personal interests; that is, to represent the interests of certain big textile producers. In effect, AMITH was a mouthpiece for large firms. "Previously, it was a club of the most powerful *groupes* in the industry," said one manager of a textile firm. The marketing director of a large thread firm in Berrechid corroborated these assessments, contending that AMITH has never been representative of its constituent sectors. "The problem is that it is always the same people who engaged in discussions with the administration, so basically everyone else knew or at least thought that only the personal interests [of the AMITH leadership] were represented" (appendix A: I-69M).

Apparel exporters in particular stressed the importance of membership in the organization. A founding member of the Fès AMITH office and a local CGEM official claimed, "There are many advantages to being a member of these associations, but you need to have an 'associative spirit'

---

[6] AMITH was unable to supply cross-time data on its membership.

[7] In 1999, 10 Moroccan dirhams equaled approximately 1 U.S. dollar. In 1996, the government began contributing to the AMITH operating budget by providing partial funding for export promotion measures and activities through the 0.25 percent *taxe parafiscale* levied on exports.

first. The main advantages are that members are au courant on important events and can participate in the big decisions taken by the administration. Small-scale firms – particularly those headed by relative newcomers – could not have this kind of influence" (appendix A: I-67M). With a growth in membership since the early 1990s, particularly due to the influx of apparel manufacturers and small textile industrialists, the interests represented in the organization diversified. The owner of a medium-scale cloth factory joined the association only recently, although he had been in the industry for decades. In his words, "There was an incredible upgrading of the association." A knitwear exporter in Settat, who had believed in the past that the association merely served the goals of a narrow group of industrialists, had altered his view in recent years: "AMITH is not an exclusive club representing insider interests." Even large, fully integrated firms, which faced few of the challenges and constraints confronting most manufacturers, began to participate in AMITH events and support its lobbying activities (appendix A: I-60M; I-63M). Regardless of firm size or sectoral orientation, members unanimously attested that AMITH remade itself into an active and influential organization during the 1990s.

The growing politicization and mobilization of textile and apparel producers through AMITH was palpable. A former member of the organization's executive board noted that business associations – and AMITH in particular – were unquestionably more powerful than in the past. He asserted, "Moroccans do not like to volunteer their time to participate in associations," but during the bust of the late 1980s, they began to understand the importance of professional associations. He had been closely involved with AMITH since 1985 and, during much of his experience there, the same three or four individuals would attend most meetings. Since the late 1980s, every time a major crisis with the Customs Authority arose, the room would be filled. When the crisis situation acquired a quasi-permanent status, AMITH became increasingly powerful (appendix A: I-41M). Another long-term member in the textile sector also attested that AMITH became one of the strongest business associations in Morocco: "Now that industrialists feel threatened in the current economic climate, they are much more active [in professional organizations] than before, when they were protected. There was no need then" (appendix A: I-61M). The director of a multinational joint venture firm based in Settat concurred: "The big groups still try to defend their own interests and privileges through associations, but the situation has definitely changed" (appendix A: I-63M). Working through the association, AMITH officials agitated on a variety of issues affecting their expanded constituency. By lobbying on issues of broad concern for the private sector, AMITH promoted business interests both within and beyond the textile and clothing sectors.

Defending the Ranks: AMITH and the Government Antifraud Campaign

Until the mid-1990s, exporters and domestically oriented producers maintained a delicate balance within AMITH. A crackdown on black market activity, in part a response to EU pressure to curb corruption, exposed the radically different concerns of export and domestic producers and fueled the formation and articulation of distinct producer interests among these groups.[8] In January 1996, the government initiated the *Campagne d'Assainissement*, or "purification campaign," which ostensibly aimed to improve Morocco's international image in light of the recently signed EU trade agreement. A high-level commission headed by the powerful former interior minister Driss Basri[9] led the campaign, and many suspected him of abusing his position to target specific businesspeople to "settle scores" (appendix A: I-54M).[10] Terrorizing small and large industrialists alike, the operation entailed repeated raids throughout the country and the confiscation of large quantities of illegal imports such as textiles, clothing, consumer electronics, household appliances, gasoline, cigarettes, and pharmaceutical products. Scores of private businesspeople were arrested, including some from prominent families (appendix A: I-55M). The campaign elicited fierce condemnation from the private sector. It was clear that such extensive black market operations could not have developed in the first place without complicity from customs officials and, many

---

[8] The crackdown also had the important effect of galvanizing the private sector through the CGEM to become an organized political actor on the national stage. See Catusse (1999a; 1999b) for a comprehensive exposition of CGEM politicization.

[9] King Mohamed VI, who took power after the death of his father, Hassan II, in July 1999, removed Basri in November of that year. Basri had presided over the ministry for over 20 years and wielded tremendous power through his tight control over internal security and the system of provincial governors.

[10] One textile manufacturer in Casablanca termed the event "absolutely insane" and an "enormous scandal" on the part of the government. The local business community welcomed King Mohamed VI's abrupt dismissal of Basri in November 1999. Many industrialists and bankers never forgave Basri for the "famous and violent 'purification campaign' that he led against them and which had for its sole consequence 'to traumatize business owners and crush their will to invest." Not surprisingly, the news of Basri's dismissal had a positive impact on portfolio investment in Morocco (*Le Journal*, November 13–19, 1999, 5).

speculated, without Basri's consent if not his outright participation.[11] Economic activity took a sharp downturn during the first half of 1996.

A primary target of the campaign was abuse of the AT system, which allowed producers to obtain duty-free inputs if they exported the goods made from these inputs within six months. However, many producers amassed large fortunes by illegally selling part or all of their production on the local market. Most local apparel producers imported a small amount of cloth, paying full customs duties on the material in order to sell "legally" on the local market, but then sold the bulk of their production through the local black market (appendix A: I-40M).[12] Buyers came directly to the factory to bid on the apparel. As a result of these practices, only a handful of clothing manufacturers supplied the local market through legal channels.

The crackdown on the AT system resulted in long delays in customs-processing procedures and delivery times, as well as bottlenecks at ports in Casablanca and Tangiers, which prevented local manufacturers from fulfilling their sales contracts. In addition, problems in the system for measuring inputs imported and subsequently reexported resulted in a substantial number of false accusations against apparel exporters. When customs authorities measured textile inputs entering Morocco through the AT system, they measured their quantities in meters, yet they assessed the reexported finished product in pounds. European suppliers adopted the meter as their unit of measurement, but the formula used by the authorities to convert the amount into pounds provided only a ballpark figure. Discrepancies sometimes arose simply due to measurement issues rather than intentional violations of the system. Furthermore, local firms often accepted the declared amount of imported inputs at face value without

---

[11] Indeed, Ali Amor, then director of the Customs Authority, was convinced of participation by customs and local officials because dealers had never been harassed in the past, despite the fact that the police knew the locations of warehouses storing illegal imports (*LVE*, January 12, 1996).

[12] Black market sales affected textile products as well as apparel. A cloth manufacturer based in Casablanca was enraged about illicit sales of thread on the black market, arguing that a number of thread producers, including some members of the AMITH executive board, sold substantial quantities of thread on the black market to local, unregistered cloth factories. Although the alleged perpetrators were well known, AMITH turned a blind eye to their activities, presumably because the owners were influential and well connected. The incensed cloth producer threatened to expose the situation by writing open letters to the press or by informing the director of the Tax Administration. He ultimately disavowed these threats by pledging to resolve the issue through AMITH channels before resorting to such extreme measures.

verifying it in the presence of customs officials.[13] Because the administration did not previously enforce the stipulations of the AT system, the AMITH president argued, industrialists did not feel obliged to observe the letter of the law strictly. For these reasons, Lahlou insisted, both the administration and local industrialists were at fault, and AMITH called for the settlement of alleged AT violations on a case-by-case basis (*Conjoncture* [Morocco], no. 774, October 1997, 16–18).[14]

The business community sharply denounced the strong-arm tactics employed to seek out and prosecute tax evaders, compelling the government to initiate talks with the private sector to resolve the crisis. Producer associations called for more efficient management of the campaign and condemned the near absence of specialists in the commission overseeing the operation to evaluate the AT system (*LVE*, February 16, 1996, 5–6; *LVE*, June 28, 1996, 27).[15] Under the leadership of Abderrahman Lahjouji, CGEM spearheaded these negotiations (*LVE*, January 12, 1996, 3; *LVE*, January 19, 1996, 3; *LVE*, February 23, 1996, 5). The CGEM and AMITH took leading roles in negotiating the release from prison of many businessmen arrested for fraud during the campaign, became active partners in efforts to reformulate the customs code with administration officials, and represented producer interests in the process of settling outstanding AT accounts (*LVE*, February 14, 1997, 16). Because so many

---

[13] The debate over how to measure imported inputs was especially sticky. Customs officials insisted on maintaining the weight declared by foreign suppliers as the basis for their calculations, while industrialists argued that imported goods should be weighed upon entry. Officials claimed that limited warehouse space precluded this solution. AMITH representatives then asked the administration to assign a customs official to each factory, as the Tunisian system stipulates. But customs officials preferred to keep operations centralized, instead opting to construct a new headquarters with more space. Exacerbating the crisis, officials treated samples as imported merchandise. At times, representatives of European firms were detained at the airport for bringing in samples, which were then confiscated. One frustrated subcontractor cried out to customs authorities in desperation, "[Apparel exports are] the oil of Morocco!" (*Conjoncture* [Morocco], no. 774, October 1997, 29).

[14] Lahlou claimed that companies that consciously abused the AT system were not members of AMITH and therefore the government was not justified in cracking down on the entire sector to detect the illegal practices of a few firms. Although some businesspeople were prosecuted unfairly, his comments attempted to mask the extent of AT fraud in Morocco. Years earlier, Lahlou had charged that "technical contraband" was a widespread practice among apparel producers and declared that it must be stopped (*LVE*, February 19, 1988, xi). "Technical contraband" refers to the practice of importing merchandise under the AT system and selling it on the local market while reexporting empty containers or containers with other merchandise (*LVE*, February 26, 1988, 14).

[15] For further discussion of the campaign, see Hibou (1996) and Catusse (1999b).

of those facing imprisonment or already imprisoned on fraud charges came from the apparel sector, AMITH was critical in the talks with the government and won the release of many of its constituents (appendix A: I-54M; I-67M). On June 21, 1996, after about 40 hours of negotiations, the CGEM executive bureau and a ministerial delegation headed by Basri reached an accord to resolve the crisis. The agreement addressed many producer concerns regarding fiscal and customs-processing issues. The major components of the accord included the establishment of a mixed public–private commission to study revisions of the customs code, the institution of a six-month grace period for settling outstanding AT accounts, the creation of new agencies to promote more efficient commercial regulations, and the reform of legal codes and administrative practices regulating business activities (*LVE*, June 28, 1996, 27).[16]

The state campaign to prosecute black market activities coincided with a national debate over trade liberalization. The 1996 EUAA initiated a far-reaching liberalization process that aimed to fulfill and even surpass the goals of the SAP.[17] As the Moroccan government pursued trade liberalization with increased vigor, the fragile equilibrium between on-shore and off-shore markets was threatened. The reform effort exposed issues around which factions of textile and apparel manufacturers could organize.

Increasingly, local manufacturers began to feel the effects of Morocco's international treaty commitments to liberalize the national trade regime. By the early 1990s, Moroccan producers had already lost a significant measure of competitiveness on global clothing markets on a pure price basis as lower-cost producers from Thailand, China, and other Asian countries entered the market (*LVE*, October 2, 1992, 27). The 1997 Asian financial crisis exacerbated the situation as Asian producers flooded global markets with low-cost goods. Because Asian producers lowered their

---

[16] With CGEM and AMITH intervention, the grace period for settling AT accounts was delayed a number of times (*LVE*, November 21, 1997, 23; *LVE*, December 26, 1997, 22). Furthermore, black market activities subsequently returned with a vengeance. Within two years of the dreaded *Campagne d'Assainissement*, the Casablanca neighborhood Derb Ghallaf, famed for its enormous open-air market with hundreds of stalls selling illegal merchandise, was fully stocked and open for business. Nonetheless, falling customs duties on many products meant that the range of goods available was more limited and in some cases products were less expensive in retail stores (*Conjoncture* [Morocco], no. 789, January 1999, 16–17).

[17] Morocco adhered to the GATT accords in June 1987 and signed a bilateral free trade accord with the European Union in 1996. See chapter 2 on the substance of these agreements.

prices and devalued their currencies after the crisis, they could afford to use faster transportation methods such as airfreight for delivery to European clients, enabling them to penetrate certain niche markets in which Morocco formerly had an advantage. Accordingly, European buyers began to complain about Moroccan prices, forcing local exporters to drop their prices by 10–20 percent. One apparel subcontractor bemoaned that Moroccan apparel exporters were forced to coordinate the production process perfectly to remain competitive, compelling them to seek easier access to textile inputs with shorter time delays. In effect, the manager of a Berrechid textile firm argued, "Asian producers exported their crisis to other countries" (appendix A: I-69M).

By the late 1990s, many factories in all branches of the textile and apparel sectors had closed. The thread and cloth industries, which largely targeted the local market, were affected most adversely. Several major thread companies shut down, including ICOSE, a state-owned enterprise, as well as privately owned companies such as PBK, FILCOF, and SATFIL-LAGE. Other prominent firms were on the verge of bankruptcy, notably COTEF and SETAFIL. Many apparel factories closed as well, in part because they were managed poorly and founded on flawed business plans but also due to mounting global competition. Several large-scale textile firms that launched adjacent apparel export factories were forced to shut down their clothing assembly units and focus exclusively on their primary activities (appendix A: I-42M; I-68M).[18]

As exporters gained increasing clout in AMITH beginning in the mid-1990s, apparel manufacturers emphasized that AMITH was their undisputed representative and main channel to policymakers. Badr Berrada, the head of AMITH's apparel subcommittee, was the most vocal and powerful spokesman for their interests and, increasingly, he became the mouthpiece of the most vehemently pro-liberalization, export interests. Expressing dissatisfaction with the executive board's reluctance to push for rapid trade liberalization and elimination of the AT system, Berrada threatened to split off from the organization on several occasions. A textile factory owner and AMITH executive bureau member claimed that he and others locked horns repeatedly with Badr Berrada in association meetings (appendix A: I-54M). The balance of power began to change dramatically within the organization and, one producer based in Fès claimed, an extreme, pro-liberalization faction of apparel exporters nearly expelled textile manufacturers from AMITH in 1998 (appendix A: I-98M). This

---

[18] The government Statistics Bureau estimated that 44,642 jobs were lost in the textile and clothing sectors between late 1999 and late 2000 (*L'Economiste*, March 13, 2001).

contention was striking because textile producers originally founded the association and had dominated it since its inception.

By organizing within a preexisting yet virtually inactive producer association, they launched their offensive from a ready-made organizational structure. The timing was particularly auspicious because the World Bank began to take an interest in producer associations at this time, offering funding and technical support to strengthen formal representation of business interests in the domestic political arena. Working through an extant organizational structure saved significant start-up costs, and AMITH was already the official representative of the apparel sector.[19] Furthermore, organizing within the peak-level association would dilute their lobbying power by mingling policy concerns specific to the apparel sector with those of many other industries.

The Hyper-politicization of Trade-Based Cleavages

Tensions erupted in full force within AMITH in the mid-1990s. The most visible disputes occurred between domestic textile manufacturers and an extreme pro-liberalization faction of apparel exporters. As seen in figure 6.1, policy preferences between textile and apparel manufacturers were sharply divided.

Badr Berrada, along with other pro-liberalization producers, launched an offensive to accelerate the tariff dismantling process in 1997. Although the EUAA stipulated total liberalization phased in over a 12-year period, Badr Berrada was skeptical that the agreement would be fully implemented without pressure from local exporters. Concerned that protectionist interests would devise alternative obstacles to free trade, he contended that the EU Agreement and the GATT agreement were not faits accomplis (appendix A: I-74M).[20] With the support of Abdelali Berrada, these exporters sought the abolition of reference prices, claiming that they

---

[19] For most apparel exporters, the CGEM was not a logical forum for political mobilization. The CGEM had a subfederation for small- and medium-sized firms as well as a textile and clothing division, which was also headed by Lahlou, but new economic interests widely regarded the confederation as a club for elite business executives. Discussions with small-scale operators in other sectors confirmed the perception that the CGEM only represented the interests of a few well-connected investors. All the leading figures in the CGEM, including Lahjouji, Chami, and Benkirane, came from big families and were "insiders." While the CGEM presented itself as the indisputable representative of private-sector interests, small-scale apparel exporters turned to the sectoral association to press their claims.

[20] He cited quality-control measures and health restrictions, such as French limitations on British beef imports, as possible protectionist tactics.

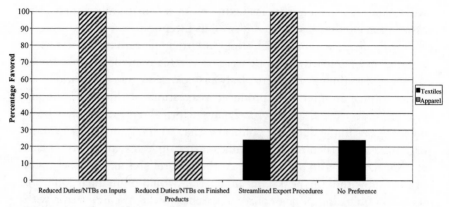

FIGURE 6.1. Trade Policy Preferences of Textile and Apparel Manufacturers in Morocco.

increased production costs unnecessarily and discouraged investment in the sector (appendix A: I-34M; I-54M; *Conjoncture*, [Morocco], no. 774, October 1997, 26).[21] Ultimately, they sought to eliminate duties and protective barriers on all upstream products in the textile sector, notably cloth and thread. Protective trade policies, they reasoned, gave rise to vigorous black market activities and fueled a vast market in used clothing, threatening the sector overall. The most extreme proponents of liberalization in AMITH favored the total liberalization of inputs originating from any country, not just those from the EU, as stipulated in the bilateral agreement signed with Europe in 1996.[22]

A group of apparel exporters prioritized the abolition of the controversial AT program. Dismantling the in-bond trade regime would enable producers to gain considerable time in the production and delivery process

---

[21] "Reference" or "floor" prices establish a minimum price against which duties are calculated for a given import. Textile products represented 82 percent of the goods protected by reference prices in Morocco (*LVE*, April 6–12, 2001; *LVE*, June 22–28, 2001). As a compromise, apparel manufacturers proposed to pay a nominal 1 percent tax on all imported inputs in order to create a fund to assist cloth weavers and thread spinners in upgrading their factories.

[22] Apparel exporters maintained that liberalization of textile inputs would improve their competitiveness in global markets, and most had little interest in producing for the local market. Dominated by the informal sector, distribution was undeveloped in Morocco. Purchasing power was depressed, and local consumers preferred to purchase foreign brands – or at least less expensive copies from the black market. One of the most prominent local clothing companies, Icomail, created a retail chain – Les Boutiques 303 – which met with little success. The rampant black market undercut the viability of retail sales in the formal sector (*Conjoncture* [Morocco], no. 774, October 1997, 32–33).

while eliminating economic "distortions" and problems with the customs authorities (appendix A: I-65M).[23] Claiming that firms are now "under the control of the customs administration," an apparel subcontractor in Marrakesh hoped that trade barriers would drop so he could "escape from the control of the authorities" (appendix A: I-65M). Every year, he complained, he loses money as customs officials find minor problems in his accounting records, forcing him to keep a full-time staff to handle customs-processing issues. To press his point, in 1997 he published an editorial in the Moroccan economic weekly *L'Economiste* arguing against the AT system (appendix A: I-65M).[24]

Not surprisingly, textile manufacturers vehemently opposed the demands of apparel exporters to dismantle protective trade barriers. Justified by the infant industry argument, customs duties calculated against reference prices rather than the billing price were an important source of protection for the local textile sector (*Conjoncture* [Morocco], no. 774, October 1997, 24). The lack of integration across the local textile and apparel sectors was a key issue for textile interests, many of whom had invested large sums in their factories. In 1996, the local apparel export industry imported nine times more textile inputs than it bought locally (*Conjoncture* [Morocco], no. 774, October 1997, 26). Majid Boutaleb, the head of the textile subcommittee, repeatedly emphasized the negative effects of the lack of sectoral integration. Although a local apparel

---

[23] Another problem with the AT system was that the government compels local producers to pay customs duties on imported inputs even when a foreign client declares bankruptcy and cannot pay for the order. With no import barriers, all of these problems would be eliminated.

[24] The informant contrasted the Moroccan and Tunisian regulatory environments. In Tunisia, he noted, customs officers were placed in the factories "so the delivery truck arrives directly at the factory and the customs officer processes incoming merchandise on location." The merchandise was then stocked at a warehouse. Hence, "the Tunisian entrepreneur is not at all bothered with customs processing. Because of this, the Tunisians were able to benefit immensely and outpace Moroccan clothing producers." Arguing that the Moroccan in-bond export regime is "illogical" from a "rational, economic perspective," he contended that it introduces many possibilities for manipulation: "Capitalists are wolves. If cloth entering duty free under the AT program is worth 100DH per meter, the producer can export clothing made from cloth acquired on the local market for 20DH per meter. Or the producer can simply economize on the material, and make more items than the foreign client requested while selling the leftovers illegally on the local market. Factory owners can either alter the accompanying documents or bribe customs officials. . . . None of this can happen in Tunisia, where the customs officials are on site and thus control all activities closely." Ultimately, he concluded, the AT will only benefit exporters until the day when the customs authorities decide to conduct a "purification" campaign.

industry developed in the mid-1990s and customs duties remained in place to protect local cloth production, thread and cloth manufacturing did not experience much growth during this period. The fact that the cloth industry did not benefit from the AT system and depended on local market sales for 90 percent of its production were major handicaps (*Magazine Maghrébin du Textile*, no. 14, 1995). Resisting rapid cuts in customs duties, Boutaleb and his colleagues argued for an adjustment period of at least 10 years (appendix A: I-64M).

Reducing factor costs, particularly energy prices, was another concern for textile producers. Textile manufacturing consumes a great deal of energy. High energy prices in Morocco hurt local producers and deterred foreign firms from relocating to Morocco or investing in Moroccan cloth and thread factories. In the mid-1990s, many French textile firms went bankrupt.[25] According to the French Chamber of Commerce, the high price and scarcity of industrial land, expensive electricity and energy costs, and Morocco's overvalued currency deterred French capital investment in Morocco (*Conjoncture* [Morocco], no. 774, October 1997, 25).

In 1997, a bitter war erupted within AMITH between pro-liberalization apparel subcontractors and thread producers, nearly resulting in a split within the organization. The efforts of Badr Berrada and his supporters to accelerate reductions on thread and cloth imports beyond the stipulations of the EU Agreement sparked the crisis (appendix A: I-71M; I-92M). The various industry-specific subcommittees of the association held separate meetings, largely focusing on the debate over reference prices (appendix A: I-54M).[26] Tensions reached an all-time high in mid-1997, when textile producers and apparel manufacturers lobbied the government separately – particularly the Ministry of Finance, which oversees the Customs Authority, and the Ministry of Industry – to ensure that

---

[25] In 1997 alone, 17 French textile firms declared bankruptcy (*Conjoncture* [Morocco], no. 774, October 1997, 25).

[26] Big textile interests profited from reference prices, and sometimes illegally. Mohamed Lahlou, appointed to head the Office Chérfienne des Phosphates (OCP), the state-run phosphate company, also owns a major thread-spinning factory in Berrechid and comes from a prominent family that initially built its wealth in the textile industry. Critics charge that he used his political influence to benefit personally from industrial policies. With the help of government loans, which he allegedly acquired through personal connections, he expanded his business to include the production of "pol," the primary material in polyester thread and fabric. He then gained control of 70 percent of Moroccan pol production and used his influence to institute reference prices on imports of the material. Deterred from buying on world markets, local spinners of polyester cloth were obliged to purchase from Lahlou's firm at "inflated" prices.

their trade policy interests would be included in the 1998–1999 Finance Law, which establishes the annual government budget. The apparel producers actively targeted these ministries in order to lobby for access to cloth imported from Asian suppliers, who offered much lower prices than local suppliers (appendix A: I-64M; I-66M). In response, textile producers called for adherence to the schedule delineated in the EU Agreement at a bare minimum, if not a delay in the tariff dismantling process (appendix A: I-64M). Active members of the AMITH executive committee from the apparel sector rejected the appeal, claiming that textile producers had squandered the ample time allotted to them for adjustment to Morocco's commitments to liberalize its trade regime (appendix A: I-71M; I-92M). At the same time, Badr Berrada's faction threatened to secede from the organization (appendix A: I-54M; I-68M; I-92M). By refusing to resolve the conflict within the association, the warring parties repeatedly ignored the stipulations of the AMITH charter.

Despite vigorous lobbying by apparel subcontractors, the administration did not adopt immediate reductions in customs duties and reference prices on textile products in the 1998 Finance Law. The textile lobby temporarily staved off the demands of clothing exporters, ensuring that the tariff dismantling schedule established in the EU Agreement remained in force (appendix A: I-61M).[27] The minister of finance at the time, Driss Jettou, had previously supported exporter demands for reduced tariff barriers, pledging to enact accelerated cuts in customs duties and a 15 percent drop in reference prices.[28] Apparel subcontractors were therefore taken by surprise when certain thread and cloth manufacturers successfully

---

[27] Government officials claimed that the cuts would aggravate the budget deficit and noted that the EU agreement was not yet ratified (*LVE*, February 20, 1998 23). The proposal would have lowered import duties on three categories of products: tariffs on capital equipment would drop from 2.5 percent to 0 percent, products subjected to a 10 percent rate would also face duties ranging from 2.5 to 0 percent, and the maximum tariff level would fall from 35 percent to 25 percent (*LVE*, May 29, 1998, 7). To make matters worse for Badr Berrada and his supporters, Morocco received an additional two-year delay from the WTO for reducing reference prices in July 1998. In July 2000, the government received a further delay (*LVE*, April 6–12, 2001).

[28] Jettou told the pro-liberalization faction that the government would implement the cuts before the parliamentary vote on the Finance Law. During a VETMA fair in late 1997, Jettou discussed the possibility of resolving the AT dispute once and for all by lowering tariffs to 2.5 percent across the board. Furthermore, in mid-1998, during parliamentary deliberations over the 1999–2000 Finance Law, apparel manufacturers did not even succeed in getting the reductions on the agenda (appendix A: I-27M). Exporters feared that the incoming socialist government, which was appointed in November 1997 and had close links to the labor movement, would be less amenable to eliminating protective barriers (*LVE*, January 16, 1998, 26).

stalled the process. In an interview with the economic weekly *La Vie Economique*, Badr Berrada expressed his sense of betrayal. "We do not understand why what was already expected will not figure in the budget.... It is a bit bizarre that for some there will be no changes while for other industrialists, instead of receiving the expected cuts [in tariffs], they will be obliged to pay 15 percent more. This is not logical." Berrada then speculated that the administration continued to protect some business interests over others. These conjectures reflected the widespread perception that the textile lobby had exerted its allegedly vast influence on key government officials, if not directly on the palace. The strength of this perception among exporters fueled a shared sense of opposition to big, protectionist capital in the textile sector, facilitating collective action. Disputes between factions of textile and apparel producers continued in this vein for at least a year.

The Construction of Interests: The Creation of a Cross-sectoral AMITH Lobby

The way these conflicts ultimately unfolded and were resolved reveals a complicated story that goes beyond predictable struggles between businesspeople with competing economic interests. The political behavior of manufacturers did not correspond neatly to market orientation or trade preferences. Instead, interests – that is, concrete strategies used to pursue policy goals – developed gradually through a negotiated process and resulted in alliances between producers who initially held opposing trade policy preferences. Producers hammered out a set of shared concerns over the course of several years, and their interests shifted. This bargaining process demonstrates that interest groups based on *expected* cleavages do not arise automatically and, once in place, do not necessarily remain fixed.

The mobilization of export-oriented manufacturers within AMITH did not lead to the organization's irreparable fracture along sectoral lines, as analyses based on simple trade-based cleavages might predict. By mid-1998, tensions cooled to some degree and, at the annual AMITH General Assembly meeting in July 1998, a growing number of industrialists appealed for a more conciliatory approach. These voices of restraint within the association argued that the only future for both textile and apparel manufacturing in Morocco lay in cross-sectoral integration as an important step toward creating a local, innovative industrial cluster (Porter 1990; 2000). Much of the meeting avoided potentially divisive issues, such as the fate of the AT system, and instead turned to areas of common ground, including customs code revisions, mounting labor unrest and the "inflexibility" of the labor code, financial guarantees for temporary imports, support for small and medium-sized firms, and reduced customs-processing time (appendix A: I-54M; I-71M; I-92M; *LVE*, July 24, 1998, 23).[29] Accordingly, AMITH focused its attention on lobbying for improved business conditions in order to attract French capital investment in the textile sector as well as customs and labor code reforms (appendix A: I-54M). The turn toward moderation within the organization culminated in a compromise embodied in a document called the *contrat-programme*. From mid-1998 through mid-1999, a special committee within AMITH worked on the formulation of an integrated growth strategy for the textile and apparel sectors.

In August 1999, an AMITH delegation formally presented the strategy outlined in the *contrat-programme* to a group of government ministers and high-ranking officials (*L'Economiste*, July 19, 1999; *LVE*, March 10, 2000, 18). The document called upon the government to implement a number of measures to save the sector in the shortest possible time frame. The proposed strategy would reduce indirect production costs such as social security payments and company taxes, create a fund to help companies restructure, institute a special devalued "export dirham," cut energy costs, reduce transportation costs, establish industrial zones providing land at affordable prices, revise the tax code to reduce local taxes and allow for reimbursement of the value-added tax for exporters, set up a centralized investment administration, and promote a more flexible labor code. In return, producers pledged to create 125,000 new jobs over a five-year period, double their export capacity, increase value-added by 50 percent, and boost production by 3 billion DH (*L'Economiste*, August 16, 1999, 4).

The varied attitudes of apparel exporters toward the *contrat-programme* attested to the potentially diverse array of interests or policy goals among manufacturers, even those within the same industry. Although they almost unanimously expressed pro-liberalization views, apparel manufacturers did not always act as a unified front. Some thoroughly opposed AMITH's strategy of sectoral integration, claiming that the *contrat-programme* stressed the concerns of textile producers by emphasizing the need to reduce energy costs (appendix A: I-91M;

---

[29] There is some evidence that labor unrest also prompted the articulation of shared interests, particularly in the labor-intensive apparel sector. Moroccan industrialists did not necessarily face more labor unrest than Tunisian firm owners.

I-93M).[30] Many of the most vociferous critics of protectionist textile interests, however, found real utility in the proposed strategy. Both textile and apparel producers, they reasoned, would benefit greatly from reduced social security charges and bank loan interest rates (appendix A: I-77M). Even a notoriously pro-liberalization exporter who had repeatedly called for the elimination of the AT program supported the *contrat-programme*. From his perspective, the textile and clothing interests *must* stay together in order to "fight the state." He asserted, "Together, the two groups have significant weight.... The state fears us because we are united" (appendix A: I-65M). Ultimately, Badr Berrada also accepted the *contrat-programme*. Negotiations within AMITH compelled him to temper his opposition to the proposal. As a result, he conceded that local access to high-quality textile inputs would enable apparel exporters to improve their production time and thus boost their international competitiveness. Difficulties with the AT program also made access to local high-quality thread and cloth more appealing (appendix A: I-74M). Thus, even though anti-protectionist producers periodically threatened to split off from AMITH, most key players rejected this approach. Instead, many clothing producers opted to encourage local textile manufacturers to modernize their factories through a sectoral integration strategy (appendix A: I-65M).[31]

To garner support for the *contrat-programme*, moderates within AMITH resorted to several arguments. In part, the appeal of the proposal lay in an economic logic founded on policy measures designed to create a more attractive overall regulatory environment for manufacturers from diverse sectors. For textile producers, making the local business environment more compelling to foreign investors would enable them to establish partnerships with European textile manufacturers seeking overseas production sites (appendix A: I-71M; I-72M). Conversely, an increasingly vocal wing of moderate exporters recognized that rising Moroccan labor costs would one day destroy subcontracting opportunities, inducing them to support efforts to upgrade local textile inputs. With European textile firms poised to undertake a "third wave" of relocation to lower-cost

---

[30] An exporter in Tangiers claimed that the proposal was tantamount to "forced integration" of the textile and clothing sectors. Comparing the strategy to the "arranged marriages of young Moroccan girls at the age of sixteen," he associated it with the interests of textile producers (appendix A: I-91M).

[31] A Ministry of Industry official in Rabat denied that the *contrat-programme* focused solely on the concerns of protectionist textile manufacturers. In his view, the document embodied "something for all branches within AMITH" (appendix A: I-107M).

production sites in the late 1990s, the formulators of the AMITH document aimed to attract foreign investors (appendix A: I-42M).[32] Favorable changes in the business and investment climate, they argued, would also promote the rise of a dynamic industrial growth pole. AMITH lobbyists emphasized that their proposals dovetailed with the strategic goals of the government in promoting Moroccan competitiveness in global markets. *Maroc Compétitif*, a report commissioned by the Ministry of Industry with support from the World Bank and the European Union, identified four primary clusters for development, including tourism, maritime products, electronics and Internet technology, and textiles and apparel (DRI/McGraw-Hill et al., 1996). With over 200 state officials and businesspeople participating in the research, the report emphasized that public–private cooperation was essential to promote the industrial clusters targeted for promotion. In response to AMITH pressure, the prime minister's office created an interministerial commission to examine the propositions of the document in detail as well as a joint public–private commission to discuss issues facing the textile-clothing sector.[33]

The presentation of the *contrat-programme* was a major milestone in the politicization of AMITH. The formulation of the proposal remolded cleavages among industrialists and effectively constructed a cross-sectoral interest group that was organizationally prepared to act collectively. After the various factions reached a compromise embodied in the document, the organization became increasingly vocal, issuing a series of demands that spanned the interests of its diverse constituents and, at a minimum, did not directly oppose the interests of key association members. AMITH's major policy goals became the settlement of alleged AT violation cases prosecuted during the *Campagne d'Assainissement*, reform of the AT system, devaluation of the dirham to promote exports, reduced energy costs, and the creation of industrial zones (*L'Economiste*, June 17, 1999). The question remains, if exporter mobilization was a primary impetus for AMITH's politicization, then what enabled apparel producers to act as a group?

---

[32] Chapter 2 discusses the "waves" of European overseas firm relocations.

[33] The commission met for the first time on August 11, 1999, under the direction of Alami Tazi, then minister of industry, and created three subcommissions charged with examining taxation and customs duties, investment and exports, and factor costs. The subcommissions met several times in the weeks after AMITH's presentation of the document to consider concrete ways of fulfilling its proposals. As the following discussion demonstrates, the government did not meet many of the demands within the stipulated time frame.

THE CATALYST FOR MOBILIZATION: FROM CLASS IDENTITY
TO CLASS FORMATION

Structural economic conditions, which were similar in Morocco and
Tunisia (as well as in many other textile- and apparel-producing countries), cannot explain why business groups mobilize differently in different countries. Trade liberalization provided the backdrop for producer
conflict – and subsequent compromise – but the construction of a collective identity based on distinct "cultures of production" was an essential
ingredient for political mobilization among a key faction of exporters.
Although producers in the same industries would be expected to favor the
same strategies for pursuing common goals, this study revealed a diversity
of perspectives among Moroccan manufacturers. To mobilize effectively,
manufacturers needed both a catalyst for action and a sense of cohesion.
Dense networks of relations through personal and business connections
gave textile manufacturers from prominent families an intangible political advantage. But apparel exporters, who emerged recently, did not have
the benefit of preestablished cohesion and therefore needed to construct
a lobbying bloc. Paradoxically, the postindependence legacy of a concentrated protectionist elite that monopolized economic opportunities and
cultivated close links to the state propelled a sense of unity among export
entrepreneurs. Perceived marginalization in the local political economy
promoted unity among new business elements.

Fat Cats versus Self-Made Men: The Self-Image of the New Exporter

The perception that established big capital, including textile producers, dominated policymaking circles promoted cohesion among smaller,
marginalized producers. A twofold rhetoric of the textile "fat cat" juxtaposed with the "self-made man" articulated in interviews with apparel
subcontractors reflected an emerging class identity. Apparel manufacturers depicted thread and cloth producers as *rentier* industrialists who benefited from state protection for decades without investing in their businesses. Instead, textile producers allegedly kept their excessive profits for
personal consumption without concern for the competitiveness of their
own firms and, by extension, Moroccan industry writ large (appendix A:
I-34M).

This image of the *rentier* industrialist permeated descriptions of the
origins of the Moroccan textile industry as told by new exporters. In
describing the trade regime that gave birth to the local textile industry, a

clothing exporter in Tangiers stated, "In the past, reference prices reached as much as 200 percent, which led to a system of hyper-protection and encouraged an effective monopoly by local textile interests" (appendix A: I-92M). Similarly, an apparel manufacturer in Salé recounted:

When the textile and clothing businesses first developed in Morocco, the cloth weavers and thread spinners got all the laws passed in their favor. Initially, they represented 90 percent of the field. They became complacent and dependent on the favorable policy regime. After independence, businessmen took over companies left by the French, became fat cats, obtained easy money, and didn't hesitate to screw other people over. . . . Thread and cloth producers benefited from years of protection but in recent years have complained about declining profits, which are due to the fact that they now pay taxes and social security charges, whereas in the past they did not do so. (appendix A: I-40M)

Exporters charged that a small elite of "big families" dominated the textile industries and enjoyed special connections to policymakers. When asked about the development of textiles and apparel production in Morocco, an apparel manufacturer who launched his business in 1996 was visibly agitated:

It was ten families that we have protected in this branch. These companies do not export. I would prefer that they would disappear. They should all go to Switzerland. We will contribute to their chateaux there. If it's a question of money, then fine. They can all go live a nice life and never work again. We [apparel manufacturers] and the French and the Americans can donate some money, too. (appendix A: I-91M)

In his view, privileged elites had monopolized economic opportunities for too long. The local director of a European textile firm based in Morocco also emphasized that a small number of families benefited for years from the "captive national market," selling at inflated prices and reaping enormous profits. Because these interests ensured that protectionist policies remained in place for a long time, he argued, the private sector reacted slowly to economic opening and continued to earn large margins without investing. "Everyone knew for a long time that liberalization was inevitable, but they waited until the last moment to react and consider upgrading." The investor claimed that families such as the Lamranis and Berradas, whose members held high-ranking positions in the government – including prime minister, minister of finance, and director of the national phosphate company – used their positions to protect their personal business holdings (appendix A: I-103M).

The apparent enduring strength of the textile lobby played into the "fat cat" rhetoric, reinforcing group solidarity among exporters. Apparel

exporters alleged that an amorphous lobby of protectionist textile interests perpetuated outdated trade policies, prevented the passage of liber-
alizing reforms, and continued to dominate AMITH. A former AMITH
professional staff member claimed that each time clothing manufacturers
tried to lobby the administration to lower input costs by eliminating reference prices, cloth weavers and thread spinners used their "connections
with people in high places" to block their efforts (appendix A: I-34M).
Referring to the debate over the pace of tariff dismantling, an apparel
exporter based in Salé charged, "Last year, when the debate was raging
before the passage of the Finance Law, textile producers had the ear of the
president of AMITH" (appendix A: I-65M). Others echoed the perception
that large-scale textile interests enjoyed significant influence in the association. Implying that a pro-Kettani faction prevented real trade reform,
another apparel exporter emphasized that a key group of textile interests
in AMITH monopolized high-level management positions in the CGEM
and other national associations to prevent real change (appendix A: I-
77M). Articles in the local economic press supported these contentions.
Journalists covering the textile and clothing sectors expressed bewilder-
ment about the government's continued protection of the thread and cloth
industries at the expense of production, which constituted 90 percent of
the combined sectors in terms of revenue, employment, and production
(appendix A: I-27M). An article in *La Vie Economique* made vague references to powerful lobbying efforts by the "Route de Mediouna," a district in Casablanca where many weaving and thread-spinning firms were
located.

Textile producers undoubtedly benefited from their decades of experience to develop effective lobbying strategies and behaved collusively at
times to pursue their policy interests. Because they had been in business for
decades and had cultivated personal ties to policymakers or had close relatives in high offices, locally oriented thread and cloth manufacturers were
able to construct a formidable lobbying group (*LVE*, February 20, 1998,
23).[34] Yet representations of a cohesive, impenetrable textile lobby were

---

[34] Even the monthly magazine of the French Chamber of Commerce in Morocco, *Conjoncture*, corroborated these assertions. The magazine contended that having developed in
a *cocon douanier* – or "protectionist cocoon" – textile producers constituted a strong
lobby in Morocco (*Conjoncture* [Morocco], no. 774, October 1997). A knitwear producer based in Ain Sebaa who adopted a moderate stance on the dispute over reference
prices also supported these claims. He noted, "Although there are fewer textile manufacturers, they have traditionally been more organized and powerful because they were
forced to make higher capital investments for their production" (appendix A: I-71M).

exaggerated. Splits within the thread and cloth industries have emerged, as evidenced by mutual accusations of black market sales, and most textile firms did not forge durable alliances across business groups to pursue their interests in the era of liberalization. Instead, most textile manufacturers favored internal restructuring and integration strategies in the face of trade reforms, or even planned to divest from their textile holdings (appendix A: I-54M; I-60M; I-73M; I-83M).

The counterpart to the idiom of the textile fat cat was the image of the "self-made man." Exporters contended that they earned their profits in "legitimate, respectable" ways. Hard work and self-initiative rather than state beneficence or privileged family background, they claimed, enabled them to amass fortunes, which were invariably depicted as far inferior to those of textile manufacturers (appendix A: I-34M; I-77M). Unlike the textile sector, which was dominated by wealthy families, exporters claimed that the apparel assembly sector provided many examples of middle-class nonelites who started successful companies, enabling them to improve their social status. The manager and joint owner of an apparel factory in Salé described himself as the consummate self-made man. Indeed, 2M, a popular national television station, interviewed him for a documentary on Morocco's new entrepreneurs. The factory owner's father was a teacher, and his mother did not work outside the home. In his words, they "sacrificed themselves" to send him to Paris to earn a PhD in marketing. Two years into his studies, he refused to accept additional financial support from his parents and instead earned money through odd jobs supplemented by loans from banks and wealthy friends he had met in Paris. After completing his studies, he performed his civil service duties by serving in the Centre Marocain pour la Promotion des Exportations (CMPE), a state agency designed to promote exports, as a marketing analyst. Several years later, he began working at an apparel factory owned by a wealthy Moroccan he had met during his studies in France. He then left the company to start his own assembly firm with support from friends and bank loans. Thanks to his experience at the CMPE, he developed a small initial client base from contacts in Europe. When he founded the company in 1990, he had only 30 employees. By 2000, he had acquired four factories employing a total of 720 workers (appendix A: I-76M).

In reality, many new exporters did not fit the profile of a self-made entrepreneur. The image functioned more as a unifying device among emerging exporters than as a true reflection of social origins. According to the director of a British international apparel-sourcing firm that works with multiple Moroccan subcontractors, "money and contacts" were essential to setting up a clothing export business. All of her suppliers were well-connected, affluent individuals, and some even had close family members in high-level government positions. While most did not come from the wealthiest families in Morocco, few, if any, boasted a true rags-to-riches social trajectory (appendix A: I-74M).[35] Because wealth concentration and income disparities were and remain extreme in Morocco, almost anyone with sufficient capital to launch an export-oriented business undoubtedly enjoyed a modicum of social privilege. Nonetheless, the vast majority of apparel exporters and subcontractors did not hail from the upper echelons of the Moroccan elite, which has controlled key sectors of the national economy since independence.

Exporters repeatedly stressed that state incentives played no role in their decision to found their businesses and that they received little if any government support for their firms. The owner of an apparel factory in Salé that supplies the British market noted bitterly that the state did nothing to help him launch his business. On the contrary, he faced massive bureaucratic red tape in state agencies and often paid bribes to administration officials and judges in order to facilitate his business transactions (appendix A: I-40M). Another manufacturer based in Marrakesh noted, "The only tangible [state] incentives were total fiscal amnesty for the first five years of production in export firms followed by 50 percent remission during the subsequent five years" as well as exemption from paying the import tax during the first seven years of operation. In his view, these were not substantial incentives (appendix A: I-65M).[36] Another producer also argued that state policies did not influence his decision to open the factory. Although a new investment code was enacted in 1983 to promote exports, it provided few real incentives. In his view, the only meaningful state inducements were the bonuses promised to local firms for

---

[35] A possible exception to this statement was the director of the Petit Poussin, a highly successful apparel export firm that supplies the Gap and Old Navy clothing chain stores. The owner allegedly worked his way out of poverty to head this vastly lucrative apparel subcontracting business. Legend has it that he was an employee in a factory managed by a French woman, who took a liking to him and nicknamed him "mon *petit poussin*," or "my little chick." Eventually she helped him to launch his own factory, and through hard work his business grew exponentially. Even in this exceptional case, however, the subject benefited tremendously from his former employer's assistance (appendix A: I-74M). Although multiple informants repeated this story, it was difficult to confirm the details.

[36] The informant claimed, "This is no real help."

hiring workers as part of an employment promotion program. In effect, he argued, even these bonuses were immaterial because the state rarely disbursed them.[37] While certain industrial upgrading programs existed, usually in the form of educational seminars sponsored by producer associations and local banks to sensitize the business community to the need to modernize, little financial assistance was available. Even the CMPE provided limited support. Describing the organization as "totally useless," informants claimed that they were unable to forge links with potential clients through CMPE events (appendix A: I-66M; I-67M).

The rhetoric of the "self-made man" versus the "fat cat" postulated a modern, export-oriented culture of production that contrasted sharply with the alleged ethos of manufacturers who developed in the context of a protected national market. Apparel exporters claimed to possess greater business acumen than their counterparts in the textile industries. According to the marketing director of a large knitwear firm that subcontracts for large international chains such as Gap and Stefanel, "Almost all producers are export-oriented, which means they are obliged to follow global fashion trends, quality requirements, world prices, and thus need to adopt a 'reactive logic'" in their business dealings. He then contrasted this approach with the attitudes of cloth weavers, who "follow the mentality of the local market and thus lack creativity and quick reaction, and are accustomed to selling at high prices" (appendix A: I-70M). Describing the mentality of most textile producers, a member of the apparel subcommittee in AMITH declared, "They have a permanent orientation toward protectionism," and "competitiveness and productivity are not their concerns" (appendix A: I-74M). Speaking of clothing producers as a coherent group conscious of their interests, an apparel manufacturer in Salé claimed, "Now there is a younger generation that is educated and very technologically savvy.... Now things are starting to change. Now the apparel subcontractors are starting to really lobby, especially to get reference prices lowered" (appendix A: I-40M).

Apparel exporters even blamed local textile producers for their own woes following the bust in international clothing markets. After the Gulf War, when the apparel industry experienced a severe downturn, some clothing manufacturers tried to adopt a new business plan by creating their own collections. Because this strategy required access to local textile

---

37 Another exporter based in Fès claimed that the state owed him five million DH in bonuses for job creation in his factory (appendix A: I-67M).

inputs, they encouraged thread and cloth manufacturers to boost the quality of their production. An apparel exporter based in Salé observed:

We pushed textile owners to invest but they were not interested because they were reluctant to spend money on investment. Tariff barriers protected them and thus they did not feel the need to take initiative. Their production tends to be oriented toward the local market, including the black market. For example, in 1996 Marks & Spencer came to Morocco and took a tour to see the [local] textile [production] facilities. M&S offered to buy textile products guaranteed for three years in return for certain upgrading changes, but the textile producers refused. (appendix A: I-77M)

One vehemently pro-liberalization apparel exporter in Tangiers argued that signing the EU Agreement was essential because it would force local textile manufacturers to upgrade and enable him to purchase inputs on world markets. He contended:

In Morocco, we have protected a lot of people – not sectors, but people. . . . The country suffered from this because these companies did not reinvest their earnings and did not seek to improve their production. We fight. We have no protection. . . . The textile manufacturers profited from forty years of privileged access to and control over the local market. They have not helped the apparel subcontractors to export and they have not evolved. They continue to use old equipment and poor, outdated production techniques. But apparel producers are obliged to improve their production and those that have remained in operation have invested. The [textile producers] are late and we cannot wait any longer for them to catch up. (appendix A: I-92M)

Many exporters were incredulous that the internationally uncompetitive textile sector remained protected despite nearly two decades of government efforts to liberalize the economy. In their view, struggles between textile and apparel manufacturers over national trade policies were therefore illogical. A foreign investor who established an apparel export firm in Morocco reasoned, "There are 285,000 workers in the apparel industry, while the textile industry only employs 50,000, and of this only 20,000 are in the woven cloth branch.[38] Thus, [continuing protectionist trade policies] that block the entry of European goods means we're protecting maybe 10,000 jobs" (appendix A: I-85M). The "fat cat" idiom resonated well among the emerging class of small-scale exporters who had long felt cut off from business opportunities in the local economy by the notorious Moroccan private elite.

---

[38] Moroccan production of woven cloth was no longer internationally competitive on a pure price basis, while knitted cloth remained a successful export industry.

The "Greedy Upstart": *Textilien* Responses to Exporter Identity

By the late 1990s, textile manufacturers were expressing increasing alienation from the organization that had once represented their interests almost exclusively. These producers claimed that apparel exporters had more power in AMITH and that Abdelali Berrada and his supporters merely pretended to work in the interest of all constituent groups (appendix A: I-54M; I-97M; I-103M). A former manager in the Kettani group observed, "Clothing producers clearly have the upper hand now [in the association]. They are stronger, more dynamic, more numerous, and have a different mentality," which purportedly gave exporters an organizational advantage in the current climate. Firm closures and bankruptcies diminished the absolute number of thread and cloth producers, who tended to come from an older generation that was less disposed to participate in formal associations and less apt to adjust to new conditions.

Some textile producers were enraged by the virtual takeover of AMITH by apparel subcontractors. According to one textile manufacturer whose family expanded its holdings to include apparel manufacturing for export, "AMITH deviated from its mission. It is entirely under the influence of the apparel assembly lobby. It has done nothing for the upstream component. VETMA should have been the business of the CMPE, not the major task of AMITH." Because of the shifting balance of power within the association, he argued, Morocco's developed textile infrastructure was deteriorating. "Textile producers have not even tried to block what is happening inside of AMITH because the organization effectively tells them that they are nothing compared to the apparel subcontractors.... AMITH thinks in terms of jobs, not investment" (appendix A: I-102M).[39]

In reaction to the increasing cohesion among apparel exporters, textile manufacturers developed their own rhetoric. In their view, producers were newcomers who lacked an appreciation for the sacrifices that textile producers incurred in building the local industrial base. Displaying little commitment to their *métier*, new apparel exporters viewed it as a means to acquire wealth rapidly rather than as a profession. A textile producer sarcastically referred to apparel exporters as "*coutourriers*"

---

[39] Other textile producers belittled the association. An owner of a cloth-finishing firm in Casablanca claimed that the association was no longer effective, labeling it a "speck or a fly on the world stage with no power." He gauged the strength of the association on its power to resist economic reform imposed by international financial institutions. He added that the Moroccan government cannot afford to lose customs duties, which are a key source of government revenue.

because most subcontracted for foreign clients, merely supplying the labor power to assemble precut apparel rather than designing clothing themselves. In his view, they were "slaves" of their clients (appendix A: I-73M). Another textile manufacturer in Meknes said, "The main problem with local producers is that their *savoir faire* is very low. What textile producers invest every two months in their companies is sufficient to create an entire apparel assembly plant. It is extremely difficult to acquire the necessary know-how in textile production; it is highly technical and specialized" (appendix A: I-97M). Many textile manufacturers spoke with pride about their profession, implying that they rendered a great service to the national economy that merits special consideration in the economic adjustment process.[40]

Textile manufacturers perceived exporters as greedy. The marketing director of a large cloth factory in Mohammedia observed that his firm lost a number of local clients, who switched to overseas suppliers. Pointing to the avarice of these manufacturers, he claimed that price differences were negligible – only one or two dirhams per unit – but many apparel manufacturers nonetheless abandoned local suppliers. In his view, exporters were unjustifiably concerned about their own business relationships without regard for broader economic interests (appendix A: I-76M). Although they undoubtedly underplayed the price and quality differences between locally produced and imported textiles and expressed unwarranted expectations about the magnanimity of profit-seeking entrepreneurs, these judgments reflected a commonly held view among textile manufacturers. Citing a Moroccan proverb – *Sahib al-hagati a'ma* ("He who wants something is blind") – the director of a large thread factory claimed that apparel producers had overly narrow perspectives, neglecting the shared interests of

---

[40] The director of a large thread factory in Casablanca claimed, "Not just anyone can operate in the sector" (appendix A: I-59M). Thread and, above all, cloth production are particularly difficult to launch because the requisite capital goods are extremely expensive and complex and production requires extensive know-how. Factories require complicated ventilation and air-conditioning systems as well as a large piece of land. Hence, only very wealthy families with long histories in the textile business were involved. Conversely, a director at a state-owned textile firm in Fès noted that subcontracting attracted "anyone" – not people from the profession – and, as a result, it was "difficult for textile and apparel producers to sit at the same table" (appendix A: I-98M). The marketing director of a Berrechid thread firm noted, "Yes, apparel production contributes a lot of value added, but there are other industries in Morocco that have existed since the 1960s" (appendix A: I-69M). For this reason, many textile interests claimed that textile and apparel producers must pursue a joint, integrated strategy at the present juncture.

the textile and clothing sectors (appendix A: I-83M).[41] For many textile producers, the "greediness" of exporters poisoned AMITH. According to the director of a large, state-owned textile firm in Fès, the apparel subcontractors are "opportunists" and mere "traders" who are "manipulating AMITH for personal gain" (appendix A: I-98M).

Elite manufacturers maintained an implicit separation between the domestic and export markets in their articulation of fair business practices within the national economy. The real reason that exporters agitated for the abolition of customs duties and reference prices on textile imports, they argued, was not because of the bureaucratic complications of administering the AT system – as many exporters contended – but rather because of an insidious desire to penetrate the local market. In their beliefs about what constitutes legitimate activity within the national market, textile producers suggested that the desire to target the local market reflected "greed" on the part of new export interests (appendix A: I-54M).[42]

Shared material interest alone did not bring about collective action. Instead, consciousness of a group or class identity was a prerequisite for mobilization (Katznelson 1986; McAdam et al. 1996; Stryker 2000). Unlike established textile families, emergent apparel exporters had few social or professional ties to each other before organizing through AMITH. A group identity as "self-made men," promoted by apparel exporters in the AMITH leadership and disseminated through discussions in AMITH meetings and elsewhere, was critical for transforming a group of disparate exporters into a lobbying bloc and overcoming potential

---

[41] The marketing director of a large thread factory further declared that "clothing exporters must not be fickle like a weathervane but must be more loyal" to save both the textile and apparel sectors. His company, and textile manufacturers in general, invested a lot to meet the needs and demands of clothing producers who then did not buy from them. "Their advantage is that they are more flexible than we are. Weaving and spinning are heavier industries that cannot respond to changes as quickly. The weaving production process can last up to six months, in addition to the standard three-month credit draft that producers often demand. That makes a total of nine months of investment and financing. The more the production cycle shortens, the more it costs. The apparel producers do not understand this. They have a short turnaround time. But they should help us, even if it costs more by a dirham or two. We have asked them to do this but they don't get it. Here in Morocco they search for quick return profits" (appendix A: I-76M).

[42] Hence, some informants claimed that the divisions within AMITH were founded on "false problems" because the AT program effectively eliminated trade barriers for subcontractors, obviating the need for comprehensive trade liberalization (appendix A: I-97M). Others echoed this contention, arguing that exporters agitated for reduced duties on textile imports to avoid penalties for breaking the rules of the AT system (appendix A: I-61M; I-98M). A few apparel exporters admitted an interest in targeting the local market, claiming that it has untapped potential (appendix A: I-65M; I-92M).

obstacles to collective action among large groups of smallholders (Olson 1965). Exporter mobilization catalyzed changes in Moroccan business–government relations.

PRODUCER MOBILIZATION AND NEW MODES
OF BUSINESS POLITICS

Producer politicization through AMITH marked a shift in the political behavior of the Moroccan private sector and its relationship with the state. In the late 1990s, interactions between the administration and manufacturers became increasingly formalized. The rise of new exporters, notably in the apparel sector, and their virtual takeover of a preexisting professional association, brought a new style of interest transmission as well as new kinds of demands. For decades, a small, relatively cohesive elite had dominated the Moroccan economy, largely relying on informal personal channels to convey its preferences and gain access to economic opportunities. The rise of new, smaller-scale export subcontractors did not supplant the traditional elite, nor did informal modes of interest transmission and patronage politics disappear. But the growing importance of new private-sector elements in the national political economy brought a distinct style of placing demands on the state.

Changes in business–government relations were manifested in multiple ways, including the rising salience of producer associations as lobbying vehicles, increased access to public officials for a broader cross section of the private sector, growing reliance on public modes of interest transmission, and the adoption of more confrontational pressure tactics (see figure 6.2). Together, these developments indicate the nature of shifts in business–government relations in the postreform period and suggest a trend toward more formalized interactions between public officials and private economic actors.

The data demonstrate that Moroccan industrialists adopted a proactive approach in pushing for their interests. Exporters were even more vigilant than their counterparts in the textile sector. In almost every tactic category, apparel subcontractors exceeded textile manufacturers in their lobbying tenacity. Importantly, the only approach that apparel exporters relied on to a lesser degree than textile manufacturers was personal contacts. This outcome almost certainly reflects the fact that apparel exporters emerged much more recently than thread and cloth producers, who benefited from established connections to high-level palace and ministry officials. The data reveal other important findings as well. First, neither *textiliens* nor

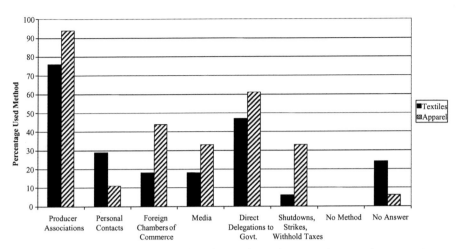

FIGURE 6.2. Lobbying Methods of Textile and Apparel Manufacturers in Morocco.

apparel manufacturers claimed that they resorted to "no method" of lobbying. In other words, both groups freely admitted that they employed pressure tactics to pursue their interests. Second, although few informants in either camp refused to address questions on lobbying strategies, textile manufacturers were comparatively less forthcoming in their answers, suggesting a reluctance to openly acknowledge the practice of lobbying consistent with a tendency to resort to more opaque channels of influence.

The increasing importance of business associations was the most obvious indicator of the altered business–government relationship in Morocco. In a setting where for decades producer organizations were at best utterly ineffectual and at worst fronts for the interests of a few families, broad political mobilization through formal organizational structures was striking. The politicization of new exporters and their construction of a lobbying bloc within an established organization demonstrated the newfound importance of these structures. For an older generation of elites, who profited from personal – and often family-based – ties to palace officials, formal organizations were not the primary vehicles for interest transmission and demand making. Their strong reaction to AMITH's takeover by apparel exporters reflected fears about the growing influence of manufacturers with opposing interests rather than concerns about losing control over the association per se. New business interests, on the other hand, had been excluded from many economic opportunities and lacked high-level sponsorship in a system founded on patronage. Organized and structured modes of political action were essential to construct a critical mass of producers capable of exerting pressure on the administration and to increase the visibility of their lobbying efforts. Hence, owners and managers of small and medium apparel factories repeatedly emphasized that AMITH and, to a limited degree, the CGEM were their main vehicles for transmitting policy interests to relevant ministries and government officials (appendix A: I-41M; I-54M).[43]

A second measure of the new style of business–government relations was increased access to administration officials and information on state policies for private actors and, importantly, for a broader range of business interests than in the past. Interactions with government officials, particularly from the ministries of Industry and Finance as well as the Customs Authority, became regular events. Since the *Campagne d'Assainissement*, reforming the trade regime and the AT system was increasingly urgent for private business owners, particularly for exporters and subcontractors for multinational firms. Negotiations with the Customs Authority became a major preoccupation of AMITH beginning in the mid-1990s, and a standing committee within the association held regular meetings with government officials.[44] The monthly AMITH newsletter, first published in 1995, informed the association membership of scheduled meetings with the administration and provided extensive information on policy developments and prospects relevant to manufacturers in its constituent industries.

The institutionalization of contacts between AMITH representatives and government officials had important consequences for the regulatory environment, especially with respect to the customs regime. Interlocutors from the textile and apparel sectors, as well as journalists and bankers, agreed that AMITH played a critical role in accelerating the reform of the national customs-processing system, which improved dramatically during the late 1990s. The efforts of exporters agitating through AMITH

---

[43] See Shadlen (2002) on the importance of formal organization for political mobilization among small firms.

[44] A 1997 study jointly executed by the National Commission for Simplifying Procedures, a working group within the Moroccan Ministry of Industry, and the World Bank determined that the average amount of time needed for customs processing in Morocco was two weeks. In certain Asian countries, the process took only fifteen minutes. Part of the reason for the lengthy processing time in Morocco was the extensive number of agencies and parties involved, notably the Customs Authority, transporters, shippers, and banks, which were not well adapted to the requirements of international commerce. The consensus among businesspeople at the time was that the Customs Authority was the most inflexible of these parties (*Conjoncture* [Morocco], no. 774, October 1997, 28).

further altered the national context for business–government interactions by consistently pushing for continued integration in global production circuits.

Anecdotal evidence also indicates that emerging export interests tried to exert lobbying pressure on a broader range of government bodies than did domestic industrialists, who traditionally relied upon high-level connections in the palace, ministries, and regional governorships. Studies of postindependence Moroccan politics have demonstrated that elected representatives wielded little power in a system largely controlled by the monarchy. But because manufacturers who emerged in the late 1980s and early 1990s generally lacked privileged access to influential officials, they were forced to exert pressure through alternative channels, including elected representatives and legislative bodies. The marketing director of a large thread firm in Berrechid claimed that exporters increasingly tried to push their demands through parliamentarians as a way of transmitting their preferences and particularly as a means of targeting the prime minister's office and key ministries. He complained that the growing number of apparel manufacturers and their allies in parliament, particularly in the second legislative chamber, gave this business faction greater political influence in the legislative branch than their counterparts in the textile industry (appendix A: I-69M).[45] In the Moroccan political system, ultimate decision-making authority unquestionably resides in the monarchy, but the parliament ostensibly passes important laws, including the annual law establishing the budget for the upcoming fiscal year. Emerging exporters exerted pressure wherever possible. The decision to lobby elected bodies did not signify a trend toward political liberalization or democratization. New entrepreneurs were not the champions of liberalism, nor did they favor fundamental changes in the political system. Rather, like most industrialists everywhere, they simply aimed to further their interests.

A third consequence of new styles of private-sector mobilization for business–government relations was the increasingly public mode of conveying interests, particularly through the media. In the late 1990s, AMITH officials and prominent industrialists frequently relied on press releases and television appearances to express demands and air grievances. Furthermore, producer associations regularly contacted journalists at various

---

[45] Other anecdotal evidence corroborated the assertion that exporters gained influence in the parliament. For example, the former speaker of the parliament has a son who owns an apparel export firm.

local newspapers to publicize their concerns and suggest topics for articles. AMITH pressure on the government to fulfill the demands of the *contrat-programme* demonstrated the association's increasing reliance on the media. Soon after the presentation of the document, it became clear that the administration's response was not forthcoming. By 2000, the apparel export sector was in crisis, with factory closures and reduced working hours, due in part to the overvaluation of the Moroccan dirham. Industrialists – and particularly export subcontractors – became increasingly impatient and began to expand their repertoire of lobbying techniques.[46] AMITH officials expressed mounting frustration about the delay through the national press. To underscore the urgency of the situation, Abdelali Berrada stressed to a major economic weekly, "The more time passes, the more opportunities we lose." Without rapid implementation of the proposals, AMITH officials lamented that foreign investment would go to competitors such as Tunisia (*LVE*, March 17–23, 2000). Condemning the administration's capitulation to union demands for a 10 percent wage increase in the face of producer calls for labor market "flexibility," Berrada openly declared that the government's treatment of industrialist demands in the *contrat-programme* was unacceptable (*LVE*, April 28–May 4, 2000; *Maroc-Hebdo*, May 12–18, 2000, 18). In an interview with *La Vie Economique*, Badr Berrada emphasized the importance of immediate joint action by public officials and private operators to save the sector. In particular, he decried the negative repercussions of currency overvaluation for local exports (*LVE*, March 24, 2000, 18).

AMITH press releases emphasizing the urgency of the situation continued throughout 2000 and 2001 (*L'Economiste*, February 1, 2001; *LVE*, December 22–28, 2000). In an article in *L'Economiste* in early 2001, an increasingly exasperated and resigned Abdelali Berrada declared, "The ball is in the government's camp" (*L'Economiste*, January 3, 2001). At key moments in the ongoing negotiations with the administration over policies to boost the textile and apparel sectors, AMITH ensured that the local economic press printed a constant stream of articles stressing the government's inaction and, by implication, irresponsibility. For example, an editorial in the widely circulated and controversial weekly *Le Journal* severely criticized the administration for its failure to respond, noting

---

[46] Industrialists even blamed the CGEM and AMITH for failing to defend their interests adequately. Their frustration was noteworthy because it demonstrated the growing importance of producer associations. By the late 1990s, industrialists viewed these associations as their rightful representatives and evidently expected them to defend their interests (*Maroc-Hebdo*, May 12–18, 2000, 20).

that "the injection of a dose of decision-making capacity in the executive branch seems necessary" (*Le Journal*, March 18–24, 2000). During the same week, articles and editorials appeared in other local publications highlighting the challenges facing the sector and calling for proactive government policies to address the situation. Officials were visibly annoyed by the openly confrontational tone of AMITH demands. AMITH officials initially decided not to publicize the *contrat-programme* but subsequently opted to publicly pressure the administration through the national media to implement the document's proposals. Ministry of Industry officials argued that the association's change in tactics unnecessarily damaged Morocco's international "brand image" (appendix A: I-113M).[47]

The most striking indicator of a shift in Moroccan business–government relations was the expansion of the producer lobbying repertoire to include more confrontational tactics, notably threats of management "strikes" and acts of civil and fiscal disobedience. Increasingly outspoken in their demands, AMITH members searched for more radical strategies to convey their interests and press their demands. At a June 2000 General Assembly meeting of the association attended by about 100 members, industrialists condemned the AMITH bureau for failing to act aggressively in the face of the administration's inaction and proposed to take matters into their own hands. A faction of producers suggested that the association stage a producers strike and wage a campaign of civil disobedience. In explicit terms, they proposed to stop production for two hours twice per week and withhold social security payments and taxes. The proposals evoked a thunderous round of applause at the meeting (*LVE*, June 30–July 6, 2000).

Following a meeting on July 7, 2000, with Khalid Alioua, then minister of labor, Lahlou addressed AMITH members in a well-attended

---

[47] According to a top Ministry of Industry official, the substantial budgetary expenditures needed to implement the *contrat-programme* constituted the main obstacle to adoption of the proposal. The government was reluctant to devalue the dirham because of budgetary constraints, notably persistent debt problems and the import bill (*LVE*, May 12–18, 2000). An administration official in Rabat argued, "I don't want capitalism to kill the working class!" (appendix A: I-113M). Furthermore, the document called for exclusive incentives for the textile and apparel sector and, he emphasized, "I have never heard of a country where people in one sector pay [fewer taxes] than those in another sector" (appendix A: I-107M). Government officials also claimed that some of the document's proposals, such as the creation of a firm restructuring fund and subsidized industrial zones, were already available to Moroccan industrialists. Furthermore, the concessions that AMITH offered, notably literacy training for workers at the firm level, could be considered investments in firm productivity rather than expenditures and therefore were not real sacrifices (appendix A: I-113M).

extraordinary session of the General Assembly. The association president openly called upon industrialists to compensate *themselves* for a recent hike in the minimum wage by decreasing their social security payments by 9 percent (*LVE*, July 7–14, 2000). Lahlou declared, "We are proposing to wait until the first of August. Until then, if we do not receive a single response, we will compensate ourselves by deducting nine points from management's contributions to the CNSS. This should cover the 10 percent increase of the minimum wage" (*Maroc-Hebdo*, July 28–September 7, 2000).[48] Lahlou's proposal of "self-compensation" initiated a debate at an AMITH General Assembly about the wisdom of adopting this illegal measure. In the end, the assembly voted to adopt the proposal by a significant majority.

Outwardly, Lahlou declared that all AMITH members respected the minimum wage increase enacted in June 2000. Officials from the Social Security Administration, however, declared that it was nearly impossible to verify whether this was true because social security payments were remitted monthly, while wages were paid on an hourly basis. Furthermore, firm owners often underreported labor hours by filing only 10 to 15 working days per month per employee (*LVE*, April 6–12, 2001). Privately, AMITH officials implied that industrialists intended to resist the latest hike in the minimum wage by ignoring it. The association president asked suggestively, "We are not against the 10 percent minimum wage increase, but do they have the means to implement the raise?" (*LVE*, May 12–18, 2000). In an interview with the Moroccan weekly *Maroc-Hebdo*, which is linked to a major national labor union, the Union Marocaine du Travail (UMT), Lahlou stated, "I am perfectly aware that the minimum wage in Morocco is insufficient. I admit this. But foreign companies do not understand this" (*Maroc-Hebdo*, May 12–18, 2000, 18).[49]

In addition to the threat of a management strike, the AMITH assembly adopted several other innovative strategies to press its claims. Emulating tactics often employed by national labor unions in Morocco, the association planned to stage a sit-in in front of AMITH headquarters and organize a march to relevant ministries. Equally important but less confrontational lobbying measures included the decisions to draft an open

---

[48] In a July 7, 2000, meeting between AMITH and the Ministry of Labor, the administration proposed to compensate owners for the minimum wage increase up to 1,826 DH. AMITH rebuffed this offer and instead proposed the sum of 2,500 DH, which officials subsequently rejected (*Maroc-Hebdo*, July 28–September 7, 2000).

[49] Because some sectors do not rely heavily on labor, Lahlou echoed a CGEM call for the institution of sector-specific minimum wages (*Maroc-Hebdo*, May 12–18, 2000, 18).

letter to Prime Minister Youssoufi and to seek royal arbitration. AMITH also pledged to continue its widespread media campaign to publicize its demands. Lahlou maintained that these actions would not "politicize" the situation but would merely "sensitize" the public to producer concerns, claiming, "We are industrialists and we simply want to defend our interests" (*LVE*, July 7–14, 2000). His remarks were both disingenuous and ignored the reality of the situation. Producer mobilization was indeed political, and it altered the tacit rules of interest transmission and lobbying in postindependence Morocco.

The most immediate and concrete result of AMITH mobilization was on customs-processing procedures and regulations. The lobbying efforts of export subcontractors through the association compelled the administration to streamline customs-processing measures. By the end of 1998, shortly after manufacturers organized in earnest to press their demands, a Moroccan weekly deemed 1998 "the year of the easing of customs procedures" (*La Nouvelle Tribune*, January 21–27, 1999). At the same time, the AMITH leadership made frequent statements praising the efforts of Abderrazaq El Mossadeq, the new director of the Customs Authority, in facilitating the improvements and stressed the openly cooperative dynamic between customs officials and local manufacturers. Recounting the accomplishments of AMITH under his stewardship, Abdelali Berrada pointed to the vast simplification of customs procedures and the institution of an ongoing dialogue between business associations and administration officials. Previously, he argued, the customs authorities focused on "collecting taxes," but since the beginning of 1998, their efforts have shifted to a more "economic" role, which both respects the concerns of the private sector and streamlines international business transactions. A tangible outcome was the drastic reduction of the maximum customs-processing time for imported inputs from several weeks to only six hours. Equally important, extensive and ongoing negotiations between business and government representatives ensured that the AT system ran smoothly (appendix A: I-21M). These changes, Abdelali Berrada noted, allowed industrialists to "free themselves from some persistent problems [that undercut their competitiveness] and devote more time to client relations" (*La Nouvelle Tribune*, September 1999).

Lobbying pressure from exporters brought about other improvements in customs-processing procedures as well, notably the establishment of a new system of providing collateral for temporary imports under the AT system and the computerization of customs inspection measures. For years, small-scale industrialists who subcontracted for international firms complained about their inability to provide the requisite guarantees for imported inputs. Firms needed a financial guarantee equal to the value of the imported goods, but local banks would not extend credit beyond $100,000. Furthermore, the authorities took over three weeks to return the guaranteed funds, which meant that the money was not available in the interim for investment or to purchase additional inputs. By preventing producers from obtaining inputs, bank policies deterred production and shut out many small-scale capital holders. As a direct response to producer lobbying, the Customs Authority introduced new types of *cautions*, or collateral guarantees for exports, such as the *caution mixte*, which reduced the required collateral on imported goods to only 20 percent of their value, and the *caution mutuelle*, which enabled groups of firms to act as joint guarantors for imported merchandise. In addition, the reforms permitted international sourcing firms to provide collateral for inputs imported under the AT system by registering with the Moroccan customs authorities (appendix A: I-40M; I-48M; I-67M).

The computerization of the system streamlined customs-processing procedures significantly. Local authorities no longer checked every imported good but instead worked selectively, based on a random sample of goods entering through the in-bond regime. By 2000, over 75 percent of all inputs entered Morocco without inspection, and the Customs Authority instituted a policy of continuous upgrading of the system (appendix A: I-48M). Because delivery dates were crucial in the fast-turnaround global apparel supply chain, these changes were vital for local producers and their international clients.

Relations between private investors and government officials have improved since the *Campagne d'Assainissement*. Tensions that arose during the 1996 antifraud campaign thawed in large part due to the willingness of the Customs Authority to heed producer concerns (*La Nouvelle Tribune*, February 3–9, 2000; *LVE*, November 12–28, 1999). By the late 1990s, private businesspeople as well as professional association representatives uniformly expressed the conviction that the customs authorities listened carefully and responded to the demands of industrialists. Business association leaders worked in conjunction with customs officials to formulate new customs procedures and rules. During August and September 1998, CGEM and AMITH representatives worked with officials on each article of the new legal code regulating customs procedures that was up for parliamentary ratification in 1999. The new director of the Customs Authority, a former high-level official in the Ministry of Industry, was intimately familiar with the problems plaguing industrialists. Emphasizing that he and his staff worked closely with private-sector representatives to modernize customs operations, El Mossadaq observed, "Everybody knows that today people listen at the Customs Authority and that everyone can benefit from an attentive ear." El Mossadeq also credited the vast improvement in customs operations in the late 1990s to joint private- and public-sector efforts. He noted:

Since the constitution of a joint [customs] simplification committee . . . all the members of the Commission noted delays. But nobody took responsibility for these delays. . . . In 1997, we declared that the Customs Authority was responsible for a delay of five and a half days, an exorbitant period of time, and we worked on the following issues: We eliminated superfluous inspections, we reduced other inspections, we began to computerize the handling of certain accounts in real time. The result: In 1998, customs delays dropped to less than one day. Today, we count in hours, in single digits, less than six hours, and more precisely to 4 hours and 37 minutes in Casablanca, on average, recognizing that 89 percent of these operations take less than two hours. (*LVE*, November 12–28, 1999)

El Mossadeq's comments reflected the cooperative dynamic as well as the increasingly formalized interactions between the government and private businesspeople that resulted in substantial changes in both the nature of business–government relations and key institutions regulating the national economy.

AMITH's lobbying efforts brought about other concrete changes in the regulatory environment as well. For example, in mid-2000, the government announced a 9 percent cut in energy costs to be implemented in increments of 3 percent over a three-year period. The decision was a direct response to demands articulated in the *contrat-programme* and was particularly beneficial for the textile sector. The reduction supplemented a prior cut of 11 percent in energy prices (*LVE*, September 22–28, 2000; *Maroc-Hebdo*, May 12–18, 2000, 20). In response to the demands of exporters and subcontractors for multinational firms, the administration announced a currency devaluation of 5 percent in April 2001 (*LVE*, April 27–May 3, 2001).[50]

---

[50] Because the vast majority of Moroccan exporters worked with European clients, the devaluation would be implemented by increasing the weight of the euro in the basket of currencies against which the dirham was pegged. Although it had hesitated in the past, the Ministry of Finance decided that a devaluation was tenable because the national debt was largely denominated in dollars (*LVE*, April 27–May 3, 2001). The administration did not implement the measure sooner because of persistent differences between the Ministry of Finance and the Central Bank, which held that a lack of productivity and competitiveness rather than currency overvaluation was the prime handicap for Moroccan exporters (*LVE*, April 27–May 3, 2001).

The government also attempted to address producer concerns about social security charges despite vociferous opposition from labor unions. At an AMITH General Assembly meeting in November 2000, Khalid Alioua, then minister of employment and official government representative, announced a major concession to textile and clothing producers. To compensate manufacturers for a recent increase in the minimum wage, the government granted a 50 percent reduction in social security charges to firm owners. The concession was a direct response to AMITH threats to wage a campaign of "fiscal disobedience," which Alioua nonetheless termed "excessive on the part of the textile community" (*Temps du Maroc*, August 11–17, 2000). Alioua's replacement as minister of labor, Abbas El Fassi, subsequently abrogated Alioua's promise, declaring that his predecessor did not have the right to make the announcement (*L'Economiste*, April 16, 2001). Nonetheless, the fact that the administration conceded – even temporarily – on such a highly controversial issue that would have engendered massive opposition from Morocco's active labor movement revealed the mounting strength and organizational capacity of producers in AMITH.[51]

The politicization of new exporters in Morocco created a vocal constituency for further integration in the global economy and brought about palpable changes in the rules of the game governing certain business activities by enabling greater access to economic opportunities in the highly concentrated Moroccan political economy. Under the leadership of a few key individuals, exporters organized collectively to ensure access to economic opportunities because they viewed themselves as marginalized in a political economy historically dominated by an entrenched, protectionist elite.

---

[51] Negotiations over the *contrat-programme* continued until 2002, when a plan was finally signed that incorporated some AMITH demands. The 2002 plan was widely viewed as a failure, and ongoing negotiations between the Ministry of Commerce and Industry and AMITH representatives focused on improving the business climate for domestic textile and apparel manufacturers. On October 18, 2005, the *plan emergence textile-habillement* outlined a series of policy measures designed to boost Moroccan competitiveness on global markets. The plan allocated funds to assist firms with debt restructuring and provided support loans to new and young investors, issued credit to support firm-level upgrading of equipment and management training, earmarked 1.8 billion Moroccan dirhams to worker vocational and literacy training, subsidized the construction of production facilities, and prioritized the construction of export platforms. Importantly, the plan stressed the importance of integrating the local apparel supply chain and targeted subsidies to upgrade firms in the upstream textile industries (*L'Economiste*, October 18, 2005 and October 19, 2005, www.l'economiste.com, accessed December 12, 2005; MoroccoTimes.com, October 19, 2005, accessed December 12, 2005).

To be sure, the Moroccan economic system remains highly oligarchic, particularly in key sectors such as finance and telecommunications (Alaoui 2000, 43; appendix A: I-1M; I-52M; Sobh et al. 2000, 36–42). But new investors who emerged in the export sectors in the 1980s brought a new style of interest transmission and demand formulation that carved out a margin of space for mobility in a system notorious for its rigid social structure. In a system where opaque informal networks of privilege were the dominant channels for lobbying and interest transmission, interactions across the public and private spheres became more formalized, visible, and institutionalized in producer associations and official business–government commissions. By effecting changes in the rules of doing business in Morocco, they secured their own share of the economic spoils and constituted a new domestic lobby for industrial development based on sectoral integration and clustering.

7

Globalization, Business Politics, and Industrial Policy in Developing Countries

How do industrialists in developing countries respond to globalization and trade liberalization? It is almost a truism that businesspeople are motivated by profits. Thus, it seems logical that exporters would support trade liberalization, which increases access to opportunities and inputs on global markets, and domestically oriented producers would resist efforts to dismantle protectionism, to which many manufacturers in the developing world owe their very existence. What, then, explains different patterns of business collective action in different countries?

This book has developed a model of business responses to global economic integration and tested it through a comparative analysis of business politics in Tunisia and Morocco, where investors in the same industrial sectors reacted very differently to economic opening. Tunisia and Morocco had parallel episodes of economic liberalization, are both highly dependent on trade with the EU, and have comparable linkages to the global economy and production profiles. In response to trade liberalization and global economic changes in the 1990s, Tunisian industrialists avoided collective lobbying efforts, focusing instead on firm-based upgrading or exit strategies, while a handful of larger industrialists conveyed policy preferences to state officials through informal channels. Moroccan producers, however, organized vigorous collective lobbying campaigns through producer associations and increasingly relied on public channels such as the media to convey policy interests.

On the surface, distinct Tunisian and Moroccan business responses defy a materialist logic. In fact, the material interests of manufacturers in the two countries were nearly identical, but the historical development of business–government relations mediated the processes of forming interest groups and mobilizing collectively. Patterns of business–government relations are constituted through protracted processes of building states and national markets, such as nationalist struggles to establish who controls the state or iterated conflicts between the state and business elites over economic policies.

Business–government relations can be broken down into two constitutive dimensions that affect the capacity and incentives for business collective action in response to economic opening. The first dimension is power relations between business and the state; that is, the extent to which private capital holders intervene in policymaking through personal ties to officials or holding government office, and conversely, the degree of state control over the private sector through outright repression or incentives. The second dimension is capital concentration, or control over vast holdings throughout the national economy by a few private capital holders.

These two dimensions combine to establish distinct configurations of business–government relations. I focus on two possible configurations: "close" and "distant" business–government relations. "Close" business–government relations arise when capital is concentrated and a faction of private capital holders penetrates state decision-making channels, while state control over business is restricted. When capital is concentrated and, relatedly, state control over business is low, the small elite is more likely to penetrate the state and influence policymaking. "Distant" business–government relations arise when capital is dispersed and state control over the private sector is high, reducing the likelihood that private capital holders can penetrate decision-making channels and facilitating state capacity to control business.

Different configurations of business–government relations set distinct contexts for business responses to economic liberalization. In political economies with distant business–government relations – that is, where capital is dispersed and the state exerts control over private capital through repression or economic incentives – deepened trade liberalization creates or expands an export class. But, because the state has not cultivated privileged ties with any faction of the private sector, export and domestic producers do not feel more or less advantaged than others in the domestic political realm. Furthermore, state control over the private sector undercuts the institutional foundations of private-sector interest articulation because states preempt industrialist interests, thereby obviating the need for firms to organize collectively. In this vein, the state may try to manage the economic liberalization process itself by encouraging firms to rely on state support in adapting to economic change. The combination of balanced state relationships with different factions of the private sector and state anticipation of private-sector interests reduces the likelihood that business will mobilize collectively in response to economic liberalization.

A close pattern of business–government relations is typical of countries that pursued classic ISI development strategies, in which the discretionary distribution of production and import licenses tended to create privileged domestic bourgeoisies with close ties to state officials, and hindered the rise of an export sector (Waterbury 1994; Waterbury 1999). Trade liberalization and exposure to production opportunities for global markets can foster the rise of new small and medium-sized export firms. New exporters perceive themselves as marginalized in a system where ISI elites historically monopolized local economic opportunities through close ties with top political officials. This shared sense of exclusion forms the basis of a collective identity in opposition to ISI elites, facilitating collective action in favor of greater access to economic opportunities.

The Tunisian case illustrates how distant business–government relations deter business collective action. At independence, the leaders of Tunisia's nationalist movement marginalized existing economic and political elites in state-building processes. State policies reinforced and perpetuated a dispersed capital structure of small firms by forbidding the formation of holding companies and granting balanced incentives to the export and ISI economies from the 1970s onward. These factors facilitated state control over the private sector. Co-optation in the form of fiscal incentives and credit as well as participation in policymaking councils were key mechanisms of state control, although on rare occasions the state resorted to repressive measures such as smear campaigns and imprisonment of top businessmen. Preemptive state sponsorship (Bellin 2002) of the export and domestic economies meant that producers were state-dependent and less organized than would be expected had they forged and pursued their own interests. Deepened trade liberalization in the 1990s did not incite business mobilization, in part because the state signaled its support for firm-level upgrading efforts and in part because both export and domestic producers did not fear exclusion given the relatively egalitarian ties between the state and these different private-sector components.

In Morocco, the regime's tolerance for societal dissent was less circumscribed than in Tunisia. But political opportunity alone does not guarantee collective action. Instead, close ties between the palace and ISI elites, established over decades before and after independence in 1956, mediated business responses to globalization. In the 1980s and 1990s, trade liberalization and shifts in global manufacturing processes greatly expanded the local export-oriented manufacturing industries. New export subcontractors with small and medium-sized firms believed that protectionist elites blocked their access to state decision-making channels. A shared sense of marginalization among a cohort of Moroccan apparel manufacturers coalesced in a self-image as "self-made men" opposing protectionist "fat cats," galvanizing them to organize collectively through an existing producer association. Lacking personal connections, these new exporters relied on public and formal channels such as the economic press and business associations to lobby for their interests. Their efforts were rewarded with certain policy changes and greater access to officials in relevant government agencies.

The Tunisian and Moroccan cases highlight linkages between class formation and collective action and show the merits of a political-sociological approach, which stresses that state–society interactions mediate the organized expression of collective material interests. Sectoral models of business aggregation based on trade orientation accurately depict producer preferences (Frieden and Rogowski 1996), but Tunisian producer quiescence and cross-national variation in business responses to trade liberalization present anomalies to these models. Political mobilization among small Moroccan export firms and the inability of a core group of protectionist elites to defend their program contradict sectoral models based on Olsonian notions of business collective action (Offe and Wiesenthal 1980; Olson 1965; Shafer 1994).

Institutionalist models of national responses to global economic change (Hall 1986; Hall and Soskice 2001; Vogel 1996; Zysman 1983) usefully emphasize that context-specific institutions lead to cross-national variation in both the preferences and political behavior of business groups. Based on evidence from advanced, industrialized countries, however, such approaches minimize the impact of globalization on class formation and business–government relations (Bellin 2002; Schneider 2005).

Statist models usefully show that state-imposed constraints and incentives structure business politics, although they do not sufficiently problematize the internal dynamics of business collective action. How different factions *within* the business community perceive each other and appear to threaten each other's ability to influence decision makers affects whether and how capital holders pursue collective action. These patterns of business politics are the product of historical state–business *interactions*. This political-sociological argument, then, fits within the new wave of research on developmental states, which emphasizes that distinct development paths in countries such as India and South Korea emerged as much because of business responses to policy initiatives as to conflict within the state elite (Chibber 2005; Underhill and Zhang 2005; Waldner 2003).[1]

DISMANTLING PROTECTIONISM AND BUSINESS POLITICS BEYOND NORTH AFRICA

Does the historical development of business–government relations shape the responses of industrialists to economic change beyond North Africa? Is business collective action less likely where the state did not establish tight relations with privileged segments of the industrial class and, instead, states sponsored the rise of a dispersed capital structure? Conversely, does the existence of a dominant elite with close ties to the state spur group mobilization among other producers? This section aims to extend these arguments in time and space. Morocco and Tunisia have many traits in common with other historical and contemporary developing country cases, including the adoption of trade regimes based on varieties of ISI (Chaudhry 1994; Richards and Waterbury 1996; Waterbury 1993) and similar positions in global manufacturing chains (Gereffi 1994; Gereffi 1999). Testing the arguments in additional comparable cases from diverse regions, notably Taiwan, India, and Turkey, will enable a preliminary assessment of the broader applicability of the framework.

The selected cases vary according to the "distance" or "closeness" of business–government relations. A brief analysis of business politics in pre-democratic Taiwan supports the claim that distant business–government relations, characterized by state sponsorship of a dispersed industrial capital structure, limit the possibility for business collective action. Next, I test the argument that close business–government relations induce reactive cycles of mobilization among different segments of the industrial class in response to global economic opening. Evidence from India and Turkey, where concentrated elites cultivated ties with state officials and economic

---

[1] Chibber (2005) argues that statist arguments for the emergence of the developmental state focus excessively on conflicts within the political elite. A more accurate explanation would incorporate the attitudes and actions of local industrialists: "While the orientations of state managers and their political leaders are indeed important, the preceding arguments suggest that their ability to successfully install developmental states may be mediated by the reactions of local firms to the project" (Chibber 2005, 28). The same can be said for responses to trade liberalization, which, if implemented to any degree, amounts to a reconstitution of the relationship between the state and industrial capital.

policies consolidated and expanded elite holdings through ISI policies, corroborate this claim.

Three caveats about the scope of the argument are in order. First, the argument is most relevant to developing economies that have adopted and implemented a minimum degree of trade liberalization such that a locally based export sector emerged or was reinforced.[2] Second, for cases with distant business–government relations, I focus on "state-sponsored" (Bellin 2002) business classes, in which the state provided credit and generous fiscal incentives to create and consolidate both domestic and export economies.[3] In some countries with dispersed capital structures, however, exporters may be relatively independent of the state thanks to capital amassed in other sectors, such as agriculture. Third, in countries with close business–government relations, the argument is most applicable where most exporters who emerged after trade liberalization are sociologically distinct from existing ISI elites.

Business–Government Relations and Business Politics in Taiwan: From Distant to Close?

Historical evidence from Taiwan supports the argument that state sponsorship of a dispersed class of industrialists ensures the political quiescence of business. In Taiwan, the virtual absence of indigenous capital after World War II enabled state-builders to forge a dispersed local industrial class and set the stage for distant relations between business and the state. Democratization after 1987 and consequent shifts in business–government relations permit an additional test of the broader argument that historically constituted patterns of business–government relations shape business responses to economic change. In the 1990s, a business

---

[2] This condition implies that the argument is less relevant to much of the Middle East and sub-Saharan Africa, where trade liberalization and structural adjustment have not advanced as much as in other developing and postsocialist regions (Abed 2003; Henry and Springborg 2001, 66–74; van de Walle 2001; World Bank 2003). Of course, many countries in these regions have implemented major reforms, particularly if assessed relative to prior levels of protectionism within a given country. (I thank Steve Heydemann for the latter point.)

[3] Although I expect that the argument is relevant to Latin American countries, I did not extend the analysis to this region because, in many cases, states interacted with already established business classes and therefore did not directly sponsor their creation. In addition, labor and leftist groups were generally more organized in Latin America than in other developing regions, adding another dimension to business collective action (Collier and Collier 1991; Schneider 2005, 203).

class structure became more concentrated and political and economic elites developed close, even collusive, ties. At the same time, evidence indicates that collective business mobilization increased throughout the decade.

When Chang-Kai Shek retreated to Taiwan from mainland China in 1949, the leaders of the Kuomintang (KMT) pursued an ISI strategy that included the standard battery of overvalued exchange rates, restrictions on foreign investment, and protective tariffs, particularly against Japanese products (Vogel 1991, 13–15). The emerging class of local industrialists therefore emerged in the context of protectionist trade policies. Yet when the government enacted transformative economic policies in the 1950s and 1960s, undercutting domestic economic protection, the nascent business class put up little resistance.

By the late 1950s, Taiwanese government officials increasingly advocated a shift to export-led industrialization[4] and greater competition in local markets, in part due to the saturation of the small local market with goods produced under the ISI trade regime but also due to a push for military preparedness, which required a strong economic base (Stallings 1990; Wade 1990).[5] The partial liberalization of the domestic economy was disruptive to indigenous elites because the reforms abolished direct foreign exchange budgeting and reduced nontariff barriers (NTBs), and, unlike many other countries that subsequently promoted export-led industrialization, the government encouraged competition in the domestic market (Wade 1990, 126).

The historical construction of business–government relations explains the relative political quiescence of the Taiwanese private sector in response to disruptive economic change. The KMT political leadership that fled from mainland China in 1949 encountered little indigenous industrial capital, giving the new leaders wide scope to shape industrial policy (Gold 1986). A handful of locals had developed industrial ventures under Japanese colonialism, but all significant enterprises were Japanese -owned, and, in 1945, the remaining firms were taken over by the Chinese

---

[4] In 1965, Taiwan established the world's first EPZ at Kaohshing, followed by others shortly thereafter (Cumings 1987, 70; Haggard and Cheng 1987, 116; Vogel 1991, 31; Wade 1990, 113, 116–117). Firms in the EPZs were required to export all production in return for duty- and tax-free access to imported inputs, well-developed infrastructure, and simplified administrative procedures for trade and remittances.

[5] In addition, U.S. aid linked to geopolitical objectives was critical in facilitating East Asian export-led industrialization, while the Japanese model of export promotion was clearly in the minds of bureaucrats (e.g., Vogel 1991, 23, 28; Wade 1990).

government (Vogel 1991, 13, 29).[6] Land reform, facilitated by the fact that the KMT had few linkages to local landlords and therefore was not vulnerable to political resistance from rural elites, further diluted potential opposition to the KMT economic agenda (Haggard 1990; Vogel 1991, 19). Other government measures, such as a regulation blocking the establishment of conglomerates, also prevented or undercut indigenous capital concentration (Chaponnière and Lautier 1998, 228; Cheng and Chang 2003, 5; Fields 1995, 6–7, 27; Noble 1998, 44).[7] The relative importance of state-owned enterprises in the economy further inhibited large-scale private capital accumulation. By 1946, the Chinese government that ruled Taiwan had reorganized and consolidated all industrial enterprises into 22 public-sector firms and retained government ownership in key sectors such as steel, shipbuilding, and electric and nuclear power (Kim 1997, 78; Vogel 1991, 29). Establishing and preserving autonomy from business influence was paramount for KMT officials (Cheng and Chang 2003, 4–5; Noble 1998, 15).

Given the wide scope for state action vis-à-vis the private sector, industrial policy beginning in the 1940s created and sustained a diffuse industrial capital structure, in turn perpetuating state control over private capital. A "diffuse industrialization" pattern developed (Chaponnière and Lautier 1998, 229), in which a large number of small and medium-sized firms were primarily export-oriented, while the largest companies, mainly public enterprises, focused on the domestic market (Cheng and Chang 2003, 11; Noble 1998, 44). The importance of the public sector in the economy helped to promote small-scale local capital accumulation by supplying basic inputs at subsidized prices in order to promote exports.[8] Sometimes, state officials even selected particular entrepreneurs to run factories and supported them with tax incentives and loans (Vogel 1991, 30–31). Taiwan's capital structure prior to the 1990s, then, was

---

[6] Some argue that the Japanese colonial legacy created the foundation for the emergence of a "developmental" state in Taiwan. The Japanese constructed a well-organized and penetrating colonial bureaucracy that remained intact after independence (Cumings 1987, 54). Kohli (2004) makes a similar argument with respect to South Korea.

[7] The anti-inflation division of the Economics Ministry also monitored private collusion. While the South Korean government granted credit at concessionary terms to general trading companies that were affiliates of large conglomerates, the Taiwanese government would only promote trading companies that were independent of large industrial firms (Noble 1998).

[8] In 1949, the private sector accounted for only 28 percent of production value; in 1985, 85 percent of production came from private investment (Vogel 1991, 29).

characterized by the predominance of small and medium-sized enterprises and the relative absence of large-scale, private conglomerates.

State sponsorship of the private sector does not necessarily imply cozy business–government relations: as in Tunisia, Taiwanese business–government relations were distant (Noble 1998, 14). Indeed, the separation between business and government was institutionalized in regulations forbidding officials from investing in their own private enterprises (Vogel 1991, 18). This distance between private investors and government officials was also in part a function of ethnic divisions between the mainland-dominated KMT and indigenous Taiwanese, who had little leverage on the state for much of the period after World War II, while perceived threats from mainland China helped to maintain a high degree of unity among the political elite. These factors may help to explain why the state was not "captured" by patronage networks (Brautigam 1994, 136; Fields 1995, 235; Noble 1998, 27, 32–35; Vogel 1991, 17).

The state had a high capacity to formulate and implement policies, in part due to the existence of an effective bureaucracy but also because of authoritarian, single-party rule under the KMT.[9] Taiwan's brand of authoritarian rule facilitated tight control over the population but required little use of brute force, particularly after the late 1970s (Noble 1998; Vogel 1991, 17). Instead, the state institutionalized its control over societal groups through a combination of preemptive economic measures and co-optation of social organizations. Business associations and industry, which were largely dominated by native Taiwanese, had little influence on the state and served a consultative rather than a lobbying role (Brautigam 1994, 136; Fields 1995, 21). Business representation conformed to a state corporatist model (Collier and Collier 1979; Schmitter 1974), in which state control over the associations took place through a combination of repression, compulsory membership, and monopolization of leadership positions by party allies and members (Cheng and Chang 2003, 10; Noble 1998, 45). As a result, industry associations were largely ineffectual and were little more than mouthpieces for government policy.[10]

---

[9] As in Tunisia and other comparable regimes, single-party rule in Taiwan effectively mandated party membership to hold high-level positions in the state, business associations, trade unions, schools, and other prominent institutions, as well as tight control over the media (Noble 1998, 32).

[10] State-controlled business associations are not necessarily ineffective. Foster (2001) argues that businesspeople in China perceive them as effective ways to seek favors and information from local officials.

The literature on the Taiwanese political economy provides little detailed information on business responses to the creation of the export sector and the introduction of greater competition in the domestic economy. But available evidence points to the quiescence of local capital holders in the face of these changes and links this outcome to the historical development of distant business–government relations, manifested in statist control over industrial development, a dispersed capital structure, and the absence of privileged ties to economic elites.

Studies of post-democratic Taiwan corroborate this general claim by pointing to shifts in business–government relations and linking them to new patterns of business organization and collective action. Beginning in the late 1980s, Taiwanese politics underwent a radical transformation with the gradual dismantling of single-party, authoritarian rule. In 1986, a formal opposition party, the Democratic Progressive Party (DPP), emerged, which explicitly attacked the KMT for manipulating state-owned enterprises and orchestrating monopolies in strategic sectors, and in 1987 Taiwan eliminated martial law (Noble 1998, 149).[11] The period of democratization roughly coincided with a new wave of economic liberalization. In the mid-1980s, Taiwan further liberalized finance, trade, and foreign investment (Cheng and Chang 2003, 20–21; Chu 1996; Noble 1998, 39, 153).

Democratization facilitated changes in local capital structure and gave rise to new kinds of ties between business and the state, which in turn led to new patterns of business organization and interest articulation.[12] First, democratization blurred the boundaries between business and politics by breaking down the separation between mainland Chinese and indigenous Taiwanese, who played a growing role in domestic politics. Second, the introduction of competitive electoral politics also enabled greater access to decision-making channels for the business community and the emergence of many new industry associations, while existing organizations developed more democratic internal governance (Kondoh 2001, 16–19; Noble 1998, 17, 151). Third, political liberalization was directly responsible for altering the domestic capital structure by reducing restrictions on capital concentration. Some local investors who founded large, diversified business groups in the domestic real estate and construction markets lobbied

---

[11] By December 1992, the legislature had been completely reelected, and in 1996 the president was freely elected (McBeath 1998; Noble 1998, 32). In 2000, the KMT lost the legislative elections, consolidating Taiwan's status as a multiparty democracy.

[12] Kang (2002) makes a similar argument with respect to South Korea.

successfully for the reform of investment laws and increasingly established close ties with state officials. Thus, post-democratization Taiwan exhibited a trend toward closer business–government relations, particularly between KMT officials and emergent big capital. Some evidence indicates that these new patterns of "cozy capitalism" sparked reactive mobilization by small firms, while the opposition capitalized on accusations of "black and gold politics," or collusive, corrupt relations between the KMT and big business (Chu 1996, 76–77; Kuo 2001; Underhill and Zhang 2005, 14, 18).[13]

Business associations became more important sites of business interest aggregation and articulation after democratization was initiated. Although big firms with close ties had less need for formal business associations, some producer groups, such as the National Federation of Industry and Commerce, were seen as representing the interests of prominent families (Kondoh 2001). But small and medium-sized exporters also began to work through the many associations that emerged in the 1990s.[14] Even exporters, who were based mainly in small and medium enterprises and tended to stay out of electoral politics, organized collectively, largely to push for greater economic exchange with mainland China (Cheng and Chang 2003, 12–14). To be sure, democratization did not totally transform business politics in Taiwan. Institutional legacies of statist economic development made firm owners question the value of producer organizations (Cheng and Chang 2003, 32; Kondoh 2001). But businesspeople increasingly used producer associations and even targeted the legislature directly to convey collective interests (Cheng and Chang 2003, 31–33; Chu 1996, 77).

Available evidence tentatively corroborates the claim that the historical development of business–government relations explains Taiwanese business quiescence during initial moments of trade liberalization in the 1950s and 1960s. Changing business–government linkages in the post-democratization era also support the argument by showing that increased business collective action through formal channels accompanied

---

[13] These accusations helped to undercut the KMT's hold on power and partly explain why the party lost the 2000 legislative elections (Cheng and Chang 2003, 25–27). Pressure from other social groups, such as environmental organizations and other antibusiness social movements, compelled the state to construct more transparent linkages with its allies in the private sector. Nonetheless, some claim that the extent of corruption depicted in the media was exaggerated (Cheng and Chang 2003, 28, 31; Tsai 2001, 372–373).

[14] About 1,800 industrial and commercial associations existed in 1998 (McBeath 1998, 4).

a shift away from distant business–government relations. The apparent construction of closer ties between the KMT and big domestic capital incited resentment and lobbying by small and medium-sized export firms as well as other interest groups. The next section tests this pattern of reactive mobilization in more detail in countries where established ISI elites had long-standing close ties with key decision makers.

ISI, Concentrated Capital Structure, and Business Politics in India and Turkey

Integration in global production chains and trade liberalization engender distinct business responses in political economies with established ISI elites, who enjoy close ties to policymakers. In these contexts, competing factions of the industrial class can engage in reactive cycles of mobilization in response to trade liberalization and deepened integration in global production chains. India and Turkey are appropriate cases for evaluating the argument because both pursued ISI development strategies until the 1980s, and, as a result, entrenched ISI elites dominated their respective economies and enjoyed tight links to the state. Both countries then pursued trade liberalization programs in the 1980s and 1990s, and new entrepreneurs took advantage of the reforms to participate in global production chains in industries such as textiles, apparel, and footwear. Importantly, many new, export-oriented investors who emerged with trade liberalization were sociologically distinct from established economic elites in both countries.

Indian collective business responses to economic liberalization in the 1980s and 1990s resembled patterns of business politics observed in Morocco in roughly the same period. New regional and export-oriented entrepreneurs pushed for greater liberalization of a system dominated by ISI elites with ties to the ruling Congress Party. Their efforts spurred cycles of reactive mobilization, producing a more vibrant business associational life. While new, well-structured producer associations emerged, existing associations revamped their internal structure and activities to be more effective and vocal representatives of their constituents.

What were the mechanisms of business group mobilization in India? Studies of Indian business politics affirm that preexisting business–government ties shaped producer responses to economic change. Economic reforms and trade liberalization enacted from the 1980s onward gave rise to a new class of export-oriented and regionally based entrepreneurs.

These new capital holders believed that their access to economic opportunities was impeded in a system dominated by established ISI elites, galvanizing collective mobilization.

The politics of India's protectionist postindependence trade regime are well documented (Chibber 2005; Frankel 2005; Jenkins 1999; Kochanek 1987; Kohli 2004). By the time India gained independence in 1947, it had developed an industrial base and a corresponding industrial class, which was increasingly vocal in its opposition to British laissez-faire trade policy (Chibber 2005, 107–108; Kohli 2004, 254). The nationalist movement, led by Mohandas K. Gandhi, championed the demands of indigenous industrialists, even if they were only one part of a diverse and fragmented coalition supporting the Indian National Congress (INC). Although the industrial elite was not unified on many issues, in part because of persistent divisions along family, caste, regional, and ideological lines (Frankel 2005, 1; Kochanek 1987, 1279–1281; Kohli 2004, 245), big business elites cultivated close relations with elements of the Congress Party and increasingly constituted a key source of campaign and party financing.[15] This relationship was, at times, precarious: business–government relations varied under different administrations and were fraught with tension during the period of Jawaharlal Nehru's rule (1947–1964) and, especially, during much of Indira Gandhi's tenure as prime minister (1966–1977). Nonetheless, an alliance between business groups and elements of the INC, the Congress Party, emerged out of the struggle for independence and remained a defining feature of India's political economy (Chibber 2005, 29–30, 45, 142–150; Kochanek 1987, 1283; Kohli 2004, 252–255).

State control over investment regulated access to economic opportunities, giving officials discretionary power and establishing a group of privileged industrialists.[16] The "license-permit raj," a system of exchanges in which private business obtained state authorization for investment, virtually guaranteed profitability in exchange for campaign contributions,

---

[15] Chibber explains the high degree of unity among industrialists in opposing the construction of a disciplinary developmental state by pointing to the effects of an ISI-based development strategy, which presents little incentive for industrialists to seek efficiency gains and upgrade production while demanding fewer sacrifices and less risk-taking (Chibber 2005, 45, 85). This argument is compelling but incomplete because it begs the question of why the Indian state adopted ISI instead of a more disciplinary, developmental approach to industrial development in the first place. For a more extensive critique, see Schrank (2007).

[16] State control over investment was never as complete as some officials had hoped (Kohli 2004, 261; Waterbury 1993, 54), even in the industrial sector (Chibber 2005, 127–129, 136).

donations, and jobs for relatives of government officials (Kochanek 1987; Kohli 2004, 264; Waterbury 1993, 57). This system, which first emerged in the early 1950s but expanded over subsequent decades, became the key nexus of the business–government relationship in India, ensuring that some had greater access to the economic spoils than others. This later became the basis for the perception among new, regional economic elites that big business enjoyed privileged ties to the state. The combination of an ISI development strategy and heavy state regulation over economic activity produced an Indian business class composed of a handful of large, family-based business houses, which controlled significant portions of the economy,[17] alongside numerous small-scale firms. The state maintained the overwhelming stake in the economy, with over 200 state-owned enterprises operating in all basic industries.

The institutionalization of the license-permit raj is an important backdrop to the adoption of economic liberalization programs beginning in the mid-1980s. In 1987, under Rajiv Gandhi's tenure as prime minister (1984–1989), the government tried – but largely failed – to deregulate and liberalize the economy (Kohli 2004, 282; Sinha 2005, 9). A second round of reforms, introduced in 1991, instituted export promotion policies, facilitated the creation of new firms, streamlined the tax code, eliminated the industrial licensing system for most activities, opened up the banking system and capital markets, and increased restrictions on labor mobilization (Jenkins 1999, 2–3, 12, 18–19; Kochanek 1987, 1299; Kohli 2004, 282; Sinha 2005, 4, fn. 15; Waterbury 1993, 60).[18] In addition, the reforms shifted economic decision making to the state rather than the federal or national levels, granting increased discretionary power over private investment to regional state governments (Frankel 2000, 14).

Reduced regulation of domestic and foreign private investment and increased integration in the global economy reshaped the industrial class. At the same time, the devolution of power to the subnational level also facilitated greater policymaking influence for a broader segment of regional elites, facilitating the rise of new entrepreneurs outside of

---

[17] The top 37 houses belonged to families from the traditional trading communities of India (Marwaris, Gujaratis, Parsis, and Chettiars) and switched from trade to industry in the late 19th century. In 1965, 75 business houses controlled half of all nongovernmental, nonbanking assets in the country. By the late 1970s, wealth became even more concentrated, as two family-based groups – the Tatas and the Birlas – controlled about 40 percent of the assets of the top 20 houses (Kochanek 1987).

[18] The extent of the reforms is debated: Kohli (2004) questions the real extent of liberalization, but Jenkins (1999, 3) argues that it has taken root in India despite many obstacles.

established business elites. Regional capitalists used wealth generated in the post–Green Revolution agrarian sector as well as from kinship and caste networks to create new industrial ventures (Chari 2000). Middle-class professionals also entered the industrial sector. Some new investors in the industrial sector expanded enormously, even taking market share away from big business houses and establishing joint ventures with foreign investors (Baru 2000).[19] Importantly, this new group of investors in the industrial sector was sociologically distinct from the big business houses. While the big business houses traced their origins to trade, commerce, and moneylending, new regional elites were largely drawn from the agrarian economy as well as from middle-class professionals. These relative newcomers began in areas with low barriers to entry, such as apparel, food processing, and other low-tech activities, and later profited from opportunities to establish joint ventures with foreign firms generated from changes in global manufacturing networks in the past two decades (Baru 2000, 226).[20] Thus, the new class of industrial investors exhibited significant parallels in terms of their position in the domestic political economy and relationship to global production circuits as the Moroccan export-oriented entrepreneurs who emerged since the late 1980s.

The new capitalist class was the driving force for change from the mid-1980s onward (Jenkins 1999, 8). Some of these new, regional entrepreneurs developed close linkages to regional political parties by providing funds, thereby ensuring access to policymaking channels, and did not support the Congress Party, which they believed could not represent their interests because it had close ties to big business elites (Baru 2000, 225). While a handful of new industrialists were able to benefit from the licensing system,[21] most were excluded, creating pressure for the dismantling of the license-permit raj and resentment of the privileged business houses (Baru 2000, 209–210; Chibber 2005, 250–252). The preexisting

---

[19] Baru (2005, 215–216) emphasizes that new Indian industrialists emerged in particular regions such as Andhra Pradesh, Gujarat, and other states as a result of several factors, including the policies of particular (subnational) state governments to support local enterprise, federal government decisions on the location of public-sector firms, which gave rise to ancillary private-sector initiatives by generating subcontracting opportunities, and the fact that big business houses had invested in these states, providing additional subcontracting opportunities for local businesses.

[20] Not all of the new economic elites that had emerged from the mid-1980s onward were interested in real trade liberalization, but almost all favored deregulation of access to local economic opportunities. This is because not all had emerged as a result of export opportunities; some had taken advantage of investment opportunities in India's large and growing domestic market (Kohli 2004, 281).

[21] The rise of The Reliance Group is one example (Chibber 2005, 252).

class structure mediated the effects of globalization to produce collective mobilization among new entrepreneurs in India.

Reactive cycles of business mobilization among new entrepreneurs and established elites played out in producer associations. Two well-established associations, the Federation of Indian Chambers of Commerce and Industry (FICCI) and the Association of Chambers of Commerce, had long dominated Indian business representation. FICCI basically represented the well-connected, protectionist elite with strong connections to the ruling Congress Party and the bureaucratic apparatus (Sinha 2005, 1). After trade liberalization measures were instituted, a small, existing association of engineers, the Confederation of Engineering Industry (CEI), evolved to challenge the hegemony of these organizations.

The CEI came to represent export-oriented firms and championed economic liberalization. In 1992, members of the CEI refashioned the organization into a cross-sectoral body and renamed it the Confederation of Indian Industry (CII). The CII leadership, which did not benefit from the license-permit raj, expanded and diversified their membership to represent outward-oriented firms, including many with ties to multinational firms. The CII became an outspoken institutional supporter of liberalization and undertook numerous "developmental" business association activities (Doner and Schneider 2000), including lobbying the state to improve basic infrastructure, fight corruption, and increase access to international markets as well as the provisions of industrial upgrading assistance and market information to member firms.[22] Before the late 1980s, Indian business associations largely sought particularistic benefits for their firms or sectors, but the CII explicitly avoided activities that might be construed as distributive (Sinha 2005, 20).

The rise of the CII spurred cycles of reactive mobilization among different elements of the business community and compelled greater overall institutionalization of business associational life. As the CII became an influential, developmentally oriented association, the FICCI leadership felt pressured to alter its own internal governance and activities.[23] In 1994, FICCI appointed a new secretary general, Dr. Amit Mitra, who openly acknowledged that the CII "helped wake FICCI up" (cited in Sinha

---

[22] Sinha (2005, 10) argues that the state was greatly responsible for the rise of the CII: the coincidence of interests between the CII and Rajiv Gandhi's administration, which used the organization as a platform for promoting its reform agenda in the 1990s, explains the rise of the association. State support undoubtedly helped the CII rise to prominence, but it does not explain its emergence in the first place.

[23] Sinha (2005, 18–19) also emphasizes that internal splits within FICCI in the late 1980s and early 1990s also compelled revitalization of the association.

2005, 21), and henceforth the organization began to offer many of the services that its new competitor had already established, including trade shows and the dissemination of information on quality control. FICCI also undertook a major public relations campaign designed to emphasize its "new economy" credentials and shifted its financial structure to operate on a for-profit basis.

This brief overview of business responses to economic opening corroborates the claim that the historical development of business–government relations mediates collective business responses to economic opening. Changes in business representation in Turkey in the 1990s provide further support for the argument. Thanks to state efforts to promote an indigenous industrial class and ISI policies beginning in the 1950s, a small group of big, domestically oriented capitalists dominated the Turkish economy. In the 1990s, new interest groups emerged and organized collectively explicitly in response to the hegemony of established, protectionist elites. The historical development of large-scale capital with close ties to the state, then, induced reactive collective organization from newer, less privileged capital holders in a subsequent period.

In the mid-1950s, the Turkish government enacted ISI tariff and exchange rate policies. Licensing systems to control imports and investment established a patronage system in which state officials had increased discretionary power to support industrialists. This period also led to important shifts in the composition of the Turkish bourgeoisie. During the interwar period, the state had promoted the rise of a Muslim bourgeoisie, which was largely dependent on the state.[24] Import-substitution industrialization policies in the 1950s attracted investors whose wealth was derived from the provincial economy and foreign credit and who therefore were more independent of the state. In particular, large landowners and merchants shifted capital to the industrial sector, expanding the indigenous industrial class (Pamuk 1981, 27; Waldner 1999, 66–67).

In the 1980s in particular, clientelist networks flourished between bureaucratic elites and elected representatives on the one hand and large, private economic interests on the other hand. Import-substitution industrialization policies enabled some domestic industrialists to amass

[24] Apart from nationalist motivations, the absence of an indigenous bourgeoisie was an important impetus for this policy. The bourgeoisie of the late Ottoman era was largely comprised of Christian and Jewish minorities, who left after modern Turkey was established. The Treaty of Lausanne (1923), which legally established the Republic of Turkey, stipulated a population exchange. As a result, much of the Greek bourgeoisie moved to Greece, while Turks in Greece went to Turkey.

holdings throughout the economy that were organized in family-controlled holding companies. Big commercial and industrial interests were institutionalized in TUSIAD, Türk Sanayicileri ve Işadamlari Derneği, or the Association of Turkish Industrialists and Businessmen, which was established in 1971. It was widely seen as the representative of big capital based in Istanbul, with close ties to the state as well as the military, which shared an antipathy toward the prospect of trade liberalization. Over time, then, the ISI elite that emerged out of ISI policies initiated in the 1950s developed close ties to state officials and enjoyed growing influence on decision-making processes (Arslan 2003; Bianchi 1985, 157; Bugra 1994, 169; Kalaycioglu 1991, 86; Sosay 1999, 247–248).

An economic crisis in 1980 led to the adoption of stabilization and SAPs designed to promote export-led growth. Between 1983 and 1988, the government liberalized the import regime and reduced export subsidies. A 1983 law established free trade zones, and in 1990, quantitative restrictions were eliminated (Greenaway and Sapsford 1996, 53; Taymaz 1999, 3–4; Togan 1994, 3, 226; Yalpat 1984, 19). These policies, along with opportunities on world markets, promoted the rise of export industries, particularly of manufactured goods.[25] While some holding companies and firms that arose under the ISI period diversified into export industries, economic reforms facilitated the rise of many new small and medium-sized firms in activities with low barriers to entry, such as apparel. Some small firms collaborated through Sectoral Foreign Trade Corporations (SFTCs), which group together small export firms in the same industry that share technology and marketing experience to achieve economies of scale (Alagoz and Alagoz 1998; Bugra 1994; Seidman 2004, 6–7; Sosay 1999, 252).[26]

In the 1980s, important new manufacturing hubs arose outside of traditional industrial centers. Small and medium-sized, fast-growing firms from the central Anatolian region were particularly successful and became known as the "Anatolian Tigers." In 1990, a group of industrialists from the region institutionalized their interests in their own association, MUSIAD, which officially stands for Mustakil is Adanleri Dernegi, or the Independent Businessman's Association. In contrast to TUSIAD,

---

[25] The share of manufactured exports in total exports increased from 36.8 percent in 1980 to 88 percent in 1990 (Taymaz 1999, 2).

[26] SFTCs are approved by the Ministry of Trade, which provides financial support, export credit, and technical assistance (Seidman 2004, 6–7).

the MUSIAD membership largely consists of smaller firms created since the 1980s and reflects a much wider diversity of geographic origins (Kristianasen 1997; Onis and Turem 2001; Ozcan and Cokgezen 2003).

The motivations for MUSIAD's creation confirm the argument that global economic integration breeds reactive business mobilization in political economies with dominant ISI elites. MUSIAD's founders explicitly established the association in order to gain greater access to the decision-making channels of the state. A shared sense of exclusion in the context of close ties between big, protectionist capital and the state convinced the future MUSIAD leaders of the need to organize collectively through a formal institution. In interviews with the Turkish press, MUSIAD's founders underscored the importance of increased access to policymakers in citing a particular event as decisive in the formation of the organization: in 1990, they were not allowed to participate in the Association of Foreign Economic Relations (DEIK), an organization composed of the chambers of commerce and industry and TUSIAD, at a meeting in the former Soviet Union (Bugra 1998, 529). This blatant exclusion from an important event bringing together state officials and business leaders was the spark that convinced these central Anatolian investors to form their own interest group.

MUSIAD's member firms arose in a historical moment distinct from that of their counterparts in TUSIAD. The Anatolian Tigers and other relatively new, dynamic firms emerged as a result of economic liberalization, which enabled participation in global manufacturing networks, and many used earnings from worker remittances – and not from state-administered protectionism – as the basis for their initial investments (Bugra 1998, 522–524; Demir, Acar, and Toprak 2004, 170). The tensions between MUSIAD and TUSIAD are therefore, in part, trade-related. But many big holding companies have diversified into the export sector and therefore trade orientation does not provide a complete explanation for shifts in Turkish business politics in the 1990s. The differences between the memberships of the two organizations are also political and cultural. The so-called Anatolian Tigers and MUSIAD have attracted a lot of attention not only because of the high growth rates achieved by member firms but also because of their political-ideological orientations. MUSIAD members are generally more conservative and religious and are associated with the Adalet ve Kalkinma Partisi, or the Justice and Development Party (AKP), the moderate Islamist ruling party headed by Prime Minister Recep Erdogan. In secular, Kemalist Turkey, most MUSIAD members identify themselves as Muslim and feel that their religious orientation has led to discrimination in the form of exclusion from economic opportunities and decision-making channels. A combination of economic success and close ties to the ruling Islamist party gave MUSIAD a greater legitimacy and voice in the system (Bugra 1998; Narli 1999; Ugur and Alkan 2000, 144).

The cases of India and Turkey corroborate the claim that the historical development of business–government relations molds how and why business groups mobilize collectively in response to trade liberalization and global economic integration. In economies that implemented heavily protectionist trade regimes, liberalization may foster and consolidate new private-sector elements linked to the global economy that resent the privileges accorded well-connected ISI elites. A perceived sense of marginalization in the domestic political economy binds new entrepreneurs together, facilitating collective action. Mobilization among new, export-oriented entrepreneurs enables access to decision-making channels and can spur reactive cycles of mobilization among other segments of the industrial class. In places such as India, Morocco, or Turkey, where business associations were largely ineffective or merely masked informal, clientelist ties, reactive business mobilization may fuel greater institutionalization of business representation and even a more developmental role for business associations. The next and final section of the chapter discusses the implications of distinct patterns of business politics for the implementation of industrial development and upgrading strategies in the contemporary world economic context.

BUSINESS POLITICS AND INDUSTRIAL DEVELOPMENT IN THE CONTEMPORARY WORLD ECONOMY

Since the 1980s, the dismantling of trade barriers and changes in global manufacturing compelled firms and policymakers in developing countries to search for new ways to participate and remain competitive in world markets. Upgrading based on sectoral integration[27] and clustering is an important component of contemporary industrial development policy. Pursuing upgrading through clustering and related approaches is more than a technical process. Politics is central to the design and implementation of such approaches: different historical patterns of business–government relations lead to different ways of pursuing cluster-based development and upgrading strategies. Implementing and establishing the

---

[27] Sectoral integration refers to linking upstream and downstream activities in a given supply chain and can occur within a firm or across multiple firms in related industries. For example, sectoral integration might entail cooperation among cloth dyeing, thread spinning, cloth weaving, and apparel assembly firms.

multiple interrelated policies and institutions that are the building blocks of these strategies require extensive coordination across and among firms, interest groups, state agencies, and other relevant institutions, and entail the resolution of collective action problems through non–market-based solutions. Just as they shape the prospect for business collective action, historically constituted patterns of business–government relations affect how relevant actors in different countries pursue industrial upgrading. Basic indicators such as export volume and value added as well as a comparative assessment of institutional and policy measures suggest that Tunisia's state-led approach has been more effective than Morocco's private-sector-led approach, at least in the early stages of industrial upgrading.

Industrial upgrading refers to different processes, including increasing the skill content of local production, moving into market niches that are relatively insulated from competition on global markets, and expanding the range of activities in a given value chain carried out within a firm or cluster of firms (Humphrey and Schmitz 2002, 1018, 1020–1021). The idea of industrial clusters has a long intellectual lineage (Marshall 1919) and often loosely denotes any associational dynamic among firms in related industries. At a basic level, clusters are concentrations of companies and institutions working in the production of related goods or services. Multiple institutions and actors are involved in the functioning of clusters, including firms in related, diverse industries, business associations and labor unions, research and vocational training institutions, government agencies that craft and implement relevant policies, trade associations, certification and standard-setting agencies, and other organizations that boost productivity by disseminating information, providing technical support, or upgrading skills environment (Porter 1998). Clustering can serve at least two distinct purposes – cost reduction through achieving economies of scale in inputs and outputs and promoting innovation through sustained interaction among capitalists.

In its earlier stages, upgrading focuses more on expanding the range of activities carried out within the value chain and moving into market niches rather than on boosting the skill content of local production. Many developing countries, including Morocco and Tunisia, face major obstacles to expanding local research and development capabilities and lack a highly skilled workforce, thus hindering their capacities to pursue more advanced upgrading processes. Similarly, preliminary efforts to promote clusters in developing economies tend to focus more on increasing cost efficiencies than driving innovation through exchanges among firms. State initiative and support therefore may be critical for the initial stages of promoting upgrading and industrial clusters when the primary goal is to achieve economies of scale, particularly among small firms.

Early discussions of clustering, based on European cases, did not highlight the role of the state in either fostering or creating clusters. Firms and networks of firms were the key building blocks and initiators of industrial clusters, while the state played a minor role in fostering their emergence (Piore and Sabel 1984).[28] Increasingly, research on industrial upgrading and clustering points to the importance of state intervention in formulating and executing initiatives to promote interfirm linkages and improve production techniques and processes (Schmitz and Musyck 1994, 903). Proactive government policies can encourage the formation of a skilled and educated workforce, improve infrastructure, and encourage the geographic concentration of firms in complementary activities.

Studies of the origins of "developmental" states show that relationships between business groups and state agencies shape what kinds of industrial policies are adopted as well as the capacity to implement them (Chibber 2005; Doner 1992; Evans 1995; Kang 2002; Underhill and Zhang 2005; Waldner 1999). Similarly, politics and the sociology of power are central to industrial upgrading based on clustering. Different historical configurations of business–government relations are conducive to implementing different policies and institutions associated with clustering. In countries with distant business–government relations, historical state preemption of business interests obviates the need for businesspeople to develop ties to each other and form effective business associations through lobbying activities. Yet interfirm ties through informal networks and formal organizations are at the core of most depictions of industrial clusters (Piore and Sabel 1984; Schmitz and Musyck 1994; Schmitz and Nadvi 1999). Given the relative absence of interfirm ties, the state may take the lead in promoting upgrading through clustering. In countries with close business–government relations, reactive mobilization by new exporters against the perceived privileges of established ISI elites can forge ties among small firms and increase the effectiveness of business associations. Private firms and business associations, then, may proactively push for policies and institutions to promote upgrading. In countries with different historical configurations of business–government relations, the nature of

---

[28] Brusco (1990) depicts two periods of the rise of industrial districts. In the first phase, Mark I, growth was largely sui genesis. In the second phase, Mark II, local and regional institutions supported innovation and market diversification. Some evidence suggests that the state played a larger role in fostering the Third Italy and other European cases of clusters than early research claimed (Schmitz and Musyck 1994, 903).

public–private linkages and interfirm ties varies, and therefore the initiative to upgrade may come from different actors. In either case, clustering requires institutions to coordinate exchanges between all relevant actors and enhance collective capabilities (Perez-Aleman 2000, 50).

To flesh out these propositions more clearly, it is useful to view the formulation and execution of cluster-related policies and institutions in terms of collective action dilemmas. Noble's (1998, 17–22) analysis of industrial policy in Japan and Taiwan highlights different kinds of collective action dilemmas structured around prisoner's dilemma and coordination games. Establishing interfirm consortia to promote research and development or regulating production volume in industries with economies of scale conforms to a prisoner's dilemma model, in which firms have an incentive to free ride or defect. The standardization of industry materials and products, which poses a different kind of collective action problem, requires coordination, which is difficult to achieve but provides little incentive for firms to defect. Resolving these distinct dilemmas requires different kinds of state capacities, including mediation and negotiation skills to facilitate coordination among firms and between business and the state or regulatory and coercive capacity to reward cooperation and punish defection (Noble 1998, 21). While Noble focuses on the state, other institutional actors can also resolve collective action problems. Business associations (as well as less formally structured groups of firms that work together) can also overcome collective action problems relevant to industrial upgrading.

Implementing the policies and institutions central to constructing clusters involves different mixes of state and business initiative. Some require more state-led coordination, while business associations are better suited to take the lead in other policy areas. For example, state agencies may be better equipped to facilitate enterprise creation through "one-stop windows" and business incubators, promote R&D through consortia, encourage the geographic concentration of related firms by creating technology and industrial parks, and improve worker skills by establishing vocational training centers. Countries with distant business–government relations in which the state historically took the lead in establishing industrial policy may be well placed to undertake such initiatives.

In other areas, business associations may be more appropriate institutional brokers to promote interfirm or public–private coordination. For example, producer organizations are well suited to organize joint purchasing of expensive, high-tech machinery among small groups of firms, facilitate production-sharing arrangements among firms, organize trade shows, identify gaps in macroeconomic policies, negotiate production standards and protocols, and generally coordinate interfirm relations. Countries with "developmental" business associations may have an advantage in solving the kinds of collective action dilemmas that require interfirm coordination and firm-level information gathering and aggregation. Of course, all industrial upgrading measures require a mix of public and private initiatives, and state–business cooperation is essential. The exchange of ideas among business, the state, research institutions, and other relevant institutions encourages innovation through knowledge generation, which is at the core of industrial upgrading through clustering. But different types of policies and institutions lend themselves more readily to either state- or business-led solutions.

The examples of Tunisia and Morocco are illustrative. In the mid-1990s, both countries began to prioritize industrial upgrading, in part through cluster promotion. Because of the historical development of business–government relations and, consequently, the ways in which business groups organized in response to global economic integration in the 1990s, the two countries followed different paths to implementing the strategy. In Tunisia, the process was top-down, while in Morocco it was more collaborative, with many initiatives emanating from the private sector rather than the state.

According to the literatures on industrial districts and clustering, which emphasize embeddedness and networks among firms as well as private-sector initiative (Piore and Sabel 1984; Porter 1990), Morocco should be more successful in implementing cluster-based development strategies. Moroccan firms worked together to create institutions promoting product and process upgrading and forged capable developmental business associations that could effectively aggregate and represent producer interests to relevant state agencies. Tunisia's model of state-led export promotion and industrial policy reform seems incompatible with a strategy premised on private-sector initiative. Furthermore, the ineffectiveness of Tunisian producer associations meant that the business community did not have an effective interlocutor to aggregate and represent its interests.

But Tunisia has historically enjoyed greater industrial-sector performance than Morocco, particularly when measured in terms of export volume, and continues to perform better than Morocco and most other countries in the Middle East and North Africa. Tunisia is more integrated in the global economy – with trade as a percentage of GDP amounting to 99 percent in Tunisia versus 77 percent in Morocco (World Development Indicators 2006) and, as figure 2.3 demonstrates, Tunisia continues to have a higher level of exports as a percentage of GDP than Morocco.

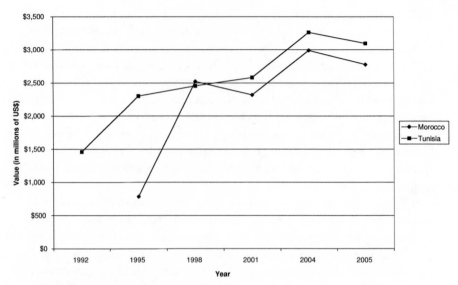

FIGURE 7.1. Total Apparel Exports – Morocco and Tunisia, Selected Years. *Source*: UN COMTRADE Database, various years.

More specifically, as figure 7.1 shows, Tunisia remains a more important supplier of apparel to world markets than Morocco, although Morocco has made substantial gains since the late 1990s and the signing of bilateral free trade accord with the United States in March 2004 may further boost Moroccan apparel exports. Furthermore, the average annual growth rate in the value-added of the textile and apparel industries between 1992 and 2002 was nearly 6 percent in Tunisia and 1 percent in Morocco (UNIDO, "Morocco," 2006; UNIDO, "Tunisia," 2006). Following the dismantling of the MFA in 2005, Morocco suffered even more than Tunisia as apparel exports to world markets from the two countries dropped by 7.4 percent and 5.8 percent respectively (Diop 2006, 4; World Bank 2006, 19).

The Tunisian government established and promoted export-processing zones as far back as the early 1970s and does so currently, while the Moroccan trade regime did not actively promote exports until the mid-1980s. Both countries currently have two export-processing zones, but total employment and firm concentration is much greater in Tunisia than in Morocco.[29]

---

[29] Between 2000 and 2003, total employment in EPZs was 239,000 in Tunisia and 71,315 in Morocco. In addition, 2,503 firms were located in the Tunisian zones, while only 63 firms were located in the Moroccan zones.

Tunisia was also more proactive in creating vocational and technical training institutes and technology parks than Morocco. Each country has one fully operational technology park, both of which focus on information and communication technologies (ICT), but Tunisia has five additional parks targeting diverse sectors under construction. Morocco presently plans to construct additional parks in Marrakesh, Rabat, and Tangiers, which would also focus on ICT (appendix A: I-10; UNIDO, "Morocco," 2006; UNIDO, "Tunisia," 2006).

Trade facilitation, which includes simplifying trade procedures and document processing, improving customs and port systems, promoting quality and safety standards, and streamlining trade logistics, is more efficient and less corrupt in Tunisia than in Morocco (Alavi 2004, 88; appendix A: I-20). As chapter 5 described, Tunisia has had a *guichet unique,* or a "one-stop window," to facilitate firm creation since 1989. In addition, the Customs Authority places agents in individual firms and industrial zones to carry out on-the-spot inspections. Beginning in 1999, Tunisia further simplified and automated the processing of trade documents based on international standards and became the first country in the region to apply ICT to the entire range of trade documents. In 2000, Tunisia established Tunisie Trade Net (TTN), which provides electronic data interchange (EDI) for all relevant parties to expedite trade document flows. The results of these initiatives are tangible, with the average time for clearance of imported goods reduced from an average of 8 days in 1999 to 3 days in 2004 and physical inspections of goods decreased from a range of 50 percent to 80 percent in late 1998 to 15 percent in 2004 (Alavi 2004, 89).

As chapter 6 shows, the Moroccan Customs Authority has also increased the efficiency and transparency of customs-processing procedures since the mid-1990s, although it still lags behind Tunisia. Morocco, too, adopted ICT, but only applied its trade facilitation reforms to customs processing and the ports, overlooking other integral dimensions. Furthermore, unlike Tunisia, the Moroccan government has not implemented an EDI network to process trade documents, although it announced plans to implement a system modeled on the Tunisian TTN (Alavi 2004; appendix A: I-20). Data from the World Bank's Doing Business database (2006), which compares the regulatory environments across 175 economies, confirmed Tunisia's edge over Morocco in facilitating trade in 2006.

Tunisia's relative success in trade promotion partly stems from its implementation of fiscal incentives such as the "1972 Law" over a decade before Morocco and other countries in the region as well as its more proactive establishment of supporting institutions to help companies compete in world markets. For example, the Tunisian government created the API and FOPRODI in 1973 as well as CETTEX and the PMN in the 1990s. This proactive state approach toward industrial policy continued in the new millennium, particularly in response to the dismantling of the MFA. In January 2005, the Tunisian Council of Ministers adopted a series of measures to promote full-package production and the production of higher-value-added goods in the apparel sector. The strategy targeted high-performing firms to help them work directly with global buyers and establishes a "technopole" in Monastir and a textile-finishing zone in El Fejja to promote upstream industries in the apparel cluster (World Bank 2006, 67). The measures also created additional institutions such as the Fonds de Promotions des Exportations (FOPRODEX) and the Fonds d'Accès aux Marchés d'Exportations (FAMEX), which provided market information, loan guarantees, and technical support around trade logistical issues to facilitate export market penetration. Of course, the mere existence of these programs does not attest to their effectiveness, and there is considerable duplication in the goals and activities of these supporting institutions (appendix A: I-2O; Basti and Bechet 2005; Diop 2006; Malouche 2006).

In Morocco, upgrading and cluster promotion in the apparel sector largely came from industrialists and business associations, while active state engagement emerged only later. Starting in the mid-1990s, AMITH pushed for sectoral integration and policies to upgrade local production, as articulated in the *contrat-programme*, and called for the creation of ESITH, a vocational school to train textile engineers. Although the Moroccan government has officially supported clustering since the mid-1990s, from the perspective of local producers, the state did not actively pursue this goal until about 2002, when the government signed the Framework Agreement with AMITH. The agreement established a financial restructuring fund, the Fonds de Soutien aux Entreprises du Secteur du Textile-Habillement (FORTEX), called for reform of the tax system, created an upgrading fund to support firm-level restructuring of technical, capital, and human resources, and required the state to cover 50 percent of employer social security costs and a share of electricity costs. In 2005, the government issued the *programme emergence*, signaling further state commitment to a more proactive stance toward upgrading. The product of a collaborative effort between the ministry of industry and business associations, the *programme emergence* outlined a strategy to promote domestic industries that have the potential to compete successfully on world markets (Royaume du Maroc 2005). The plan prioritized the textile and apparel sectors, calling for reduced customs duties on primary products and key inputs, measures to boost textile and apparel exports by promoting Morocco as an export platform, and the creation of funds such as the Fonds de Garantie de la Restructuration Financière and the Fonds National de la Mise à Niveau (FOMAN) to help firms modernize and restructure their debt (Berrada 2005; Hamri and Belghazi 2005, 40–41). State initiatives were central to the plan, committing the government to improve the educational system, the transportation infrastructure, and the bureaucratic environment for private enterprise. Like the Tunisian strategy adopted in the same year, the Moroccan plan called for the creation of specialized clusters for the upstream textile industry and called on government agencies to "pick winners" among firms based on performance criteria by supporting their upgrading efforts and integration into global production networks (appendix A: I-2O; Royaume du Maroc 2005; World Bank 2006, 67–68).

These data do not definitely demonstrate Tunisia's superiority in implementing industrial upgrading and clustering. Multiple factors determine economic performance, and initiatives, such as the construction of technology parks, frequently fail to achieve their intended goals. Furthermore, officials in both countries adopted cluster-based industrial development strategies relatively recently, while clustering is premised on the longer-term transformation of production incentives and methods. But Tunisia's relative success in implementing and promoting certain aspects of cluster policies and institutions underscores that upgrading and cluster promotion are not only consistent with state-led industrialization but, in the early stages, may *require* state initiative.

The Tunisian and Moroccan cases also highlight different paths toward pursuing and promoting industrial clusters. In keeping with the long tradition of state-led development and high levels of state control over associational activities, the Tunisian government took the lead in proposing and implementing relevant institutional and regulatory changes and creating research and training institutes. For example, the state preemptively established technical support centers for various industries in the 1990s and organized industry trade fairs. At the same time, the absence of representative business associations that could aggregate and articulate interests undercut other aspects of cluster promotion. Industrialists complained that they could not coordinate production-sharing arrangements or joint purchasing of expensive machinery to boost process upgrading.

In Morocco, private capital holders took the initiative to pursue cluster-based development by creating relevant institutions themselves or by lobbying the government to support legal reforms or reallocate subsidies to promote sectoral integration and industrial upgrading. As the previous

chapter showed, in the 1990s Moroccan industrialists forged effective
business associations that took the lead in establishing vocational training institutions, organizing domestic and overseas trade fairs, connecting
international buyers with local firms, disseminating information on local
market structure and international market opportunities, and identifying
key policy areas for reform. Many firm and producer association initiatives, however, could only succeed with state backing. The protracted
efforts of AMITH to gain state support for policy initiatives demonstrate
that state agencies could not always comply, largely because they lacked
the capacity to institute the reforms and, relatedly, because they had to balance multiple competing interests from the private sector as well as from
other social groups. In short, the Tunisian and Moroccan approaches to
cluster promotion reflect different modes of engagement between the state
and industrial capital, each with strengths and weaknesses.

Trends in global manufacturing and the adjustment strategies of states,
business associations, and firms in developing countries are creating a
new politics of industrial development. Studies of the political economy
of industrial development are often premised on a cleavage between the
ISI bourgeoisie and exporters. But the lines between the domestic and
export sectors are blurring in the new global production context. With
mounting competition in global manufacturing industries and pressure
from international retailers to speed up production cycles, cluster-based
strategies have gained appeal. In theory – although not necessarily in reality – clusters accelerate manufacturing processes because factories located
near upstream and downstream industries can access inputs and control
their own manufacturing processes more easily. Thus, if business and the
state in developing countries endorse clustering as an upgrading strategy,
domestic manufacturers and exporters have an incentive to work together
to boost the quality and reduce the costs of local production. The politics
of industrial competitiveness in the evolving global manufacturing context call for attention to the ways in which state agencies and business
associations promote cluster-based industrial development and different
patterns of business–government relations engender distinct paths toward
formulating and implementing industrial upgrading strategies.

Appendix A

Methodological Note and List of Interviewees

DATA COLLECTION

The bulk of the data for this book was collected during 18 months of field research in Morocco and Tunisia conducted in Spring 1998 and 1999–2000. During these extended field visits, I carried out semistructured interviews based on a uniform set of questions in either French or Arabic with over 200 firm owners and managers, business association officials, government officials, labor union leaders and shopfloor representatives, technical support agency representatives, journalists, and academics. Content analysis of these interviews constituted a key source of data. Archival research on documentation from government agencies and ministries, local research centers and libraries, and the economic press in each country also provided crucial sources of information, supplementing and corroborating the data gathered through interviews.

SAMPLING OF INTERVIEWEES

The perceived sensitivity of my research questions at times posed obstacles to the research process and prevented random selection of interviewees. Informants were frequently suspicious of my intentions and unwilling to meet with me without a personal referral from a trusted associate. Access to industrialists was often regulated by governmental and quasi-governmental bodies or producer associations, which tend to direct researchers to more successful firms or relatively uncritical supporters of state policies. By necessity, establishing contacts with informants outside of these channels relied on personal contacts and "snowball sampling," which led to biases in sampling procedures (Biernacki and Waldorf 1981). In some instances, technical factors, such as poor accounting records, also complicated data collection. To compensate, I aimed to construct a sample incorporating firms with varied relevant characteristics, notably industrial activity (cloth, thread, finishing, or knitwear and stitched garment production), firm size in terms of total number of employees, and geographic location. Following is a complete list of informants, identifying occupation, affiliation, industrial activities (where relevant), and the location and date of the interview. Personal names and specific titles are omitted to protect the identities of the informants.

LIST OF INTERVIEWS

Morocco

I-1M: Professor, Department of Economics, Faculty of Law, Université Hassan II, Casablanca, November 24, 1997

I-2M: Professor, Department of Political Science, Faculty of Law, Mohammed V University, Rabat, February 11, 1998

I-3M: Official, American Chamber of Commerce in Morocco, Casablanca, February 13, 1998

I-4M: Official, U.S. Embassy/Morocco, February 17, 1998

I-5M: Official, USAID/Morocco, and analyst, Economic Growth Department, USAID/Morocco, Rabat, February 19, 1998

I-6M: Former advisor to the minister of privatization, government of Morocco, Souissi, Rabat, February 19, 1998

I-7M: Director, investment firm, Casablanca, February 25, 1998

I-8M: Official, International Finance Corporation, Casablanca, February 25, 1998

I-9M: Journalist, Rabat Agdal, February 25, 1998

I-10M: Analyst, investment firm, Casablanca, March 2, 1998

I-11M: Analyst, Office of Economic Growth, USAID/Morocco, Rabat, March 2, 1998

I-12M: Consultant, American consulting firm on private-sector development, Rabat, March 2, 1998

I-13M: Professor, Department of Economics, Faculty of Law, Mohammed V University, Rabat, March 3, 1998

I-14M: Official, U.S. Consulate, Casablanca, March 3, 1998

I-15M: Official, U.S. Embassy/Morocco, Rabat, March 3, 1998

I-16M: Journalist, Casablanca, March 12, 1998

I-17M: Director, multinational bank, Casablanca, March 12, 1998

I-18M: Economist, USAID, Rabat, March 12, 1998

I-19M: Professor, Department of Economics, Faculté de Droit, Université Mohammed V, Rabat Agdal, March 19, 1998

I-20M: Journalist, Casablanca, March 27, 1998

I-21M: Director, multinational bank, Casablanca, March 27, 1998

I-22M: Journalist, Casablanca, March 28, 1998

I-23M: Director, Banque Marocaine du Commerce Extérieur (BMCE), Casablanca, March 31, 1998

I-24M: Official, Conféderation Générale des Enterprises du Maroc (CGEM), April 2, 1998

I-25M: Director, economic think tank, Rabat Agdal, April 6, 1998

I-26M: Official, Caisse de Depôt et de Gestion, Rabat, April 7, 1998

I-27M: Journalist, Casablanca, September 10, 1999

I-28M: Professor, Faculty of Law, Université Mohammed V, Rabat Agdal, September 13, 1999

I-29M: Official, foreign chamber of commerce in Morocco, Casablanca, September 15, 1999

I-30M: Official, CGEM, Casablanca, September 15, 1999

I-31M: Manager, BMCE, Casablanca, September 15, 1999

I-32M: Official, U.S. Consulate, Casablanca, September 16, 1999

I-33M: Journalist, Casablanca, September 16, 1999

I-34M: Former official, AMITH, and former manager, apparel firm, Casablanca, September 20, 1999

I-35M: Manager, Caisse de Depôt et Gestion, Rabat, September 21, 1999

I-36M: Officials, Ministry of Industry, Rabat, September 23, 1999

I-37M: Official, Ministry of Industry, Rabat, September 30, 1999

I-38M: Official, Ministry of Industry, Rabat, October 5, 1999

I-39M: Official, Ministry of Industry, Rabat, March 7, 2000

I-40M: Director, apparel firm, Salé, October 5, 1999

I-41M: Director, integrated textile firm, Ain Sebaa, October 6, 1999

I-42M: Official, AMITH, Casablanca, October 11, 1999

I-43M: Official, FENELEC, October 11, 1999

I-44M: Official, FENELEC, October 26, 1999

I-45M: Former official, AMITH, and former manager, apparel firm, Casablanca, October 27, 1999

I-46M: Businessman, Casablanca, October 27, 1999

I-47M: Director, multinational apparel sourcing firm, London, November 3, 1999

I-48M: Officials, AMITH, Casablanca, November 8, 1999

I-49M: Technical-commercial director, consumer electronics firm, Casablanca, November 10, 1999

I-50M: Financial director, electrical supplies firm, Casablanca, November 10, 1999

I-51M: Director, consumer electronics and household appliances firms, Ain Harrouda, November 12, 1999

I-52M: Director, telecommunications equipment retailer, Casablanca, November 13, 1999

I-53M: Director, multinational electrical supplies firm, Casablanca, November 15, 1999

I-54M: Director, textile firm, Derb Omar/Casablanca, November 16, 1999

I-55M: Assistant director, consumer electronics and household appliances retailer, Casablanca, November 17, 1999

I-56M: Official, Office du Développement Industriel, Rabat, November 23, 1999

I-57M: Director, multinational apparel firm sourcing office, Sidi Maarouf/Casablanca, November 24, 1999

I-58M: Official, Fédération des Industries Metallique, Metallurgique et Electrique (FIMME), Casablanca, November 25, 1999

I-59M: Director, textile firm, Casablanca/Settat, November 25, 1999

I-60M: Commercial director and design director, integrated knitwear and apparel firm, Casablanca, November 25, 1999

I-61M: Director, textile firm, Casablanca, November 26, 1999

I-62M: Director, consumer electronics retail firm, November 26, 1999

I-63M: Director, multinational/Moroccan joint venture textile firm, Settat, November 29, 1999

I-64M: Director, textile firm, Ain Sebaa, December 2, 1999

I-65M: Director, apparel firm, Marrakesh, December 3, 1999

I-66M: Director, apparel firm, Fès, December 6, 1999

I-67M: Director, apparel firm, Fès, December 6, 1999

I-68M: Director, textile firm, Casablanca, January 12, 2000

I-69M: Commercial director, textile firm, Berrechid, January 13, 2000

I-70M: Commercial director, apparel firm, Casablanca, January 18, 2000

I-71M: Director, apparel firm, Ain Sebaa, January 18, 2000

I-72M: Director, textile firm, Ain Sebaa, January 18, 2000

I-73M: Director, textile firm, Casablanca, January 19, 2000

I-74M: Director, apparel firm, Ain Sebaa, January 19, 2000

I-75M: Official, U.S. Consulate, Casablanca, January 20, 2000

I-76M: Commercial director, textile firm, Mohammedia, January 24, 2000

I-77M: Director, apparel firm, Salé, January 25, 2000

I-78M: Official and executive bureau member, CGEM, Casablanca, January 26, 2000

I-79M: Director, textile firm, Ain Sebaa, January 27, 2000

I-80M: Official and executive bureau member, CGEM, Casablanca, January 28, 2000

I-81M: Journalist and member of the Union Maghrébine des Travailleurs (UMT), Casablanca, January 29, 2000

I-82M: Journalist and UMT member, Casablanca, March 4, 2000

I-83M: Director, textile firm, Ain Sebaa, January 30, 2000

I-84M: Financial director, apparel firm, Casablanca, February 1, 2000

I-85M: Director, apparel firm, El-Jedida, February 2, 2000

I-86M: Official, Union Générale des Travailleurs Marocains (UGTM), Casablanca, January 2, 2000

I-87M: Official, Confédération Démocratique des Travailleurs (CDT), Rabat Agdal, February 10, 2000

I-88M: Director, consumer electronics retail firm, Casablanca, February 10, 2000

I-89M: Official, Euro Maroc Entreprises, Casablanca, February 10, 2000

I-90M: Director, textile and apparel firm, Casablanca, February 11, 2000

I-91M: Director, apparel firm, Tangiers, February 16, 2000

I-92M: Director, apparel firm, Tangiers, February 16, 2000

I-93M: Director, apparel firm, Salé, February 17, 2000

I-94M: Director, industrial electronics firm, Casablanca, February 17, 2000

I-95M: Former official, Ministry of Industry, Casablanca, February 21, 2000

I-96M: Director, industrial electronics firm, Casablanca, February 21, 2000

I-97M: Director, textile firm, Meknes, February 23, 2000

I-98M: Director, textile firm, Fès, February 24, 2000

I-99M: Official, UGTM, Fès, February 24, 2000

I-100M: Official, CDT, Fès, February 24, 2000

I-101M: Official, CDT, Fès, March 6, 2000

I-102M: Director, apparel firm, former director, textile firm, Fès, February 25, 2000

I-103M: Director, textile firm, Fès, February 25, 2000

I-104M: Director and selected employees, apparel firm, Fès, February 25, 2000

I-105M: Financial director, consumer electronics retail firm, Casablanca, February 28, 2000

I-106M: Financial director, industrial electronics firm, Ain Sebaa, February 29, 2000

I-107M: Official, Ministry of Industry, Rabat, March 1, 2000

I-108M: Official, AMITH, Casablanca, March 2, 2000

I-109M: Director, apparel firm, Fès, March 6, 2000

I-110M: Director, apparel firm, Fès, March 6, 2000

I-111M: Official, UGTM, Rabat, March 9, 2000

I-112M: Director, multinational industrial electronics firm, Casablanca, March 28, 2000

I-113M: Official, Ministry of Industry, Rabat, March 29, 2000

I-114M: Director, consumer electronics and household appliance retailer, former owner of consumer electronics firm, Casablanca, March 30, 2000

I-115M: Official, CDT, Casablanca, March 30, 2000

Tunisia

I-1T: Official, U.S. Embassy, Tunis, May 4, 1998

I-2T: University Professor, Faculty of Law, University of Tunis, May 5, 1998

I-3T: Former director, nongovernmental agency, and foreign journalist, Tunis, May 8, 1998

I-4T: Director, computer and information systems consulting firm, Tunis, May 12, 1998

I-5T: Official, U.S. Embassy, Tunis, May 14, 1998

I-6T: Professor, Faculty of Letters, University of Tunis, May 18, 1998

I-7T: Director, foreign bank, Tunis, May 19, 1998

I-8T: Director, nonprofit business training organization, Tunis, May 21, 1998

I-9T: Director, investment firm, Tunis, May 21, 1998

I-10T: Professor and institute director, Tunis, May 22, 1998

I-11T: Official, Ministry of Industry, Tunis, May 23, 1998

I-12T: Director, bank and media company, Tunis, May 25, 1998

I-13T: Director, investment firm, Tunis, May 27, 1998

I-14T: Official, UTICA, Tunis, May 27, 1998

I-15T: Industrialist, Tunis, May 28, 1998

I-16T: Director, regional office, BIAT Bank, Sfax, June 8, 1998

I-17T: Director, apparel firm, Sfax, June 8, 1998

I-18T: Manager and commercial services representative, knitwear firm, Sfax, June 9, 1998

I-19T: Manager, knitwear and apparel firm, Sfax, June 9, 1998

I-20T: Manager, apparel firm, Sfax, June 9, 1998

I-21T: Businessmen, medical equipment firm, Sfax, June 13, 1998

I-22T: Deputy director, BIAT Bank, Tunis, June 10, 1998

I-23T: Director, apparel firm, Tunis, June 12, 1998

I-24T: Financial director, apparel firm, Sfax, June 13, 1998 (responses received by fax)

I-25T: Official, Association Professionelle des Banques de Tunisie (APBT), Tunis, June 16, 1998

I-26T: Director, textile firm, Jebel Ouest, June 17, 1998

I-27T: Marketing director, textile firm, Ben Arous, June 18, 1998

I-28T: Director, textile firm, Tunis, June 20, 1998

I-29T: Official, Central Bank of Tunisia, June 22, 1998

I-30T: Banker, Banque Nationale d'Agriculture (BNA), Tunis, June 23, 1998

I-31T: Official, Fédération Nationale du Textile (FENATEX), Tunis, June 26, 1998

I-32T: Economist, Institut d'Economie Quantitative, Tunis, January 12, 2000

I-33T: Officials, U.S. Embassy/Tunisia, Tunis, January 13, 2000

I-34T: Secretary general, FENATEX, Tunis, January 14, 2000

I-35T: Director, ABC Bank, Berges du Lac, Tunis, April 17, 2000

I-36T: Manager, integrated apparel and knitwear firm, Ben Arous, April 19, 2000

I-37T: Director, apparel sourcing office for multinational clothing company, Berges du Lac, Tunis, April 24, 2000

I-38T: Businessman, diverse holdings, Tunis, April 25, 2000

I-39T: Director, consumer electronics firm, Mégrine, May 1, 2000

I-40T: Marketing director, textile firm, Ben Arous, May 11, 2000

I-41T: Director, import/export firm and retail store, Mégrine, May 14, 2000

I-42T: Director, import/export firm and retail store, Mégrine, May 16, 2000

I-43T: Director, apparel firm, Tunis/Charguia I, May 15, 2000

I-44T: Director, STB Bank, Tunis, May 16, 2000

I-45T: Director, apparel firm, Tunis, May 16, 2000

I-46T: Director, consumer household appliance firm and multisectoral group, Megrine, May 17, 2000

I-47T: Official, French Embassy, Tunis, May 18, 2000

I-48T: Official, French Embassy, Tunis, May 18, 2000

I-49T: Director, textile finishing firm, Jebel Ouest, May 18, 2000

I-50T: Director, apparel firm, Ksar Said/Tunis, May 22, 2000

I-51T: Officials, Ministry of Industry, FENATEX, CETTEX. "La 7ème tournée du tour de Tunisie qualité textile." Hotel Abou Nawas El Mechtel, Tunis, May 23, 2000.

I-52T: Professor, Faculty of Law, University of Tunis, May 24, 2000

I-53T: Professor, Faculty of Law, University of Tunis, May 24, 2000

I-54T: Industrialist, Tunis/Charguia, May 25, 2000

I-55T: Director, consumer electronics firm, Ben Arous, May 26, 2000

I-56T: Director, apparel firm, Z. I. Charguia I, May 29, 2000

I-57T: Lawyer, Ferchiou Associates (law firm), Tunis, May 30, 2000

I-58T: Lawyer, Ferchiou Associates, Tunis, May 30, 2000

I-59T: Commercial director, consumer electronics firm, Tunis, May 30, 2000

I-60T: Director, textile firm, Ben Arous, May 31, 2000

I-61T: Director, consulting firm, June 7, 2000

I-62T: Director and technical director, apparel firm, Z. I. Ksar Said, June 7, 2000

I-63T: Official, Agence pour la Promotion de l'Industrie (API), Tunis, May 8, 2000

I-64T: Marketing director, consumer electronics firm, Ben Arous/ Mégrine, June 12, 2000

I-65T: Officials, Ministry of Industry, FENATEX, CETTEX. "La 7ème tournée du tour de Tunisie qualité textile." Hotel Sol El-Mouradi, Port El-Kantaoui, June 13, 2000

I-66T: Director, multinational apparel firm, Jemmal, June 14, 2000

I-67T: Director, multinational apparel firm, Tunis/Charguia I, June 19, 2000

I-68T: Official, Programme de la Mise-à-Niveau, Ministry of Industry, Tunis, June 22, 2000

I-69T: Director, Sfax Chamber of Commerce and Industry, Sfax, June 26, 2000

I-70T: Director of production, apparel firm, Sfax, June 26, 2000

I-71T: Official, Union des Syndicats du Maghreb Arabe (USMA), Tunis, July 8, 2000

I-72T: Professor, Faculty of Letters, University of Tunis, Tunis, July 11, 2000

I-73T: Official and Executive Bureau member, UGTT, Tunis, July 11, 2000

I-74T: Official and Executive Bureau member, UGTT, Tunis, July 12, 2000

I-75T: Former government official, Tunis/Ariana, July 12, 2000

I-76T: Former UGTT official and director of a nongovernmental association, Tunis, July 13, 2000

I-77T: Commercial manager, textile firm, Tunis, July 14, 2000

I-78T: Officials, UGTT, Tunis, July 17, 2000

I-79T: Official and Executive Bureau member, UGTT, Tunis, July 17, 2000

I-80T: Official and Executive Bureau member, UGTT, Tunis, July 19, 2000

I-81T: Official, Centre Technique de Textile (CETTEX), Ben Arous, July 20, 2000

I-82T: Director, textile firm, Tunis, October 12, 2000

I-83T: Official, French Embassy, Tunis, October 13, 2000

I-84T: Director of supplier relations, multinational clothing firm, Les Berges du Lac, October 15, 2000

I-85T: Official, Ministry of Industry, October 31, 2000

I-86T: Officials, FEDELEC/UTICA, Tunis, October 31, 2000

I-87T: Journalist, Tunis, November 1, 2000

I-88T: Professor, Faculty of Law, University of Tunis, November 3, 2000

I-89T: Director, consumer electronics company, Tunis, November 4, 2000

I-90T: Director, multinational apparel firms, La Marsa, November 8, 2000

I-91T: Official, Centre Technique des Industries Méchanique et Electrique, Tunis/Bir Ksaa, November 8, 2000

I-92T: Director, industrial electronics firm, Tunis, November 9, 2000

I-93T: Assistant director and historian, Institut des Recherche sur le Maghreb Contemporain (IRMC), Tunis, October 20, 2000

Other

I-1O: Jean Abinader, Executive Director, Moroccan-American Center for Policy, Washington, DC, December 20, 2006

I-2O: Ndiame Diop, Economist, Trade Department, World Bank, Washington, DC, December 20, 2006

I-3O: Nick Lahowchic, President and CEO, Limited Brands Logistics Services, Inc., Columbus, OH, July 24, 2003

I-4O: Steve Lamar, Senior Vice President, American Apparel and Footwear Association, Arlington, VA, July 2, 2003

I-5O: Bob Zane, Senior Vice President, Liz Claiborne, Inc., New York, NY, July 2, 2003

I-6O: Production director, Roca Wear, New York, July 2, 2003.

I-7O: Designer, Tommy Hilfiger, New York, July 2, 2003.

Appendix B

Standardized Questionnaire for Textile and Apparel Industrialists and Factory Managers

(Translated into French and Arabic)

1. When was your firm established? By whom? When did you acquire it/begin working here?
2. Can you provide some basic information about your firm?

   (a) What is the total capital?
   (b) What do you produce?
   (c) How many machines are in the factory?
   (d) What are your target markets (local, national, export)?
   (e) How has all of this information changed since the firm was first established?

3. What kinds of business and commercial activities were you and/or the founders of the firm involved in prior to establishing your company?
4. Why did the founders decide to go into this business when they established the factory? Was there a long family history of involvement in the industry? Did state policies or incentives influence their decision? Were they responding to perceived sales opportunities?
5. How do you obtain information on sales prospects and potential new markets, both domestic and overseas?
6. How have you obtained your contracts and sales arrangements – through state export promotion or industrial development organizations, through nongovernmental intermediary associations, or personal contacts?
7. What are the greatest difficulties that your firm has faced since it was established, and particularly since Morocco/Tunisia undertook

economic reforms in the mid-1980s and signed the EU Association Agreement in 1996/1995? Specifically, what are your views on the following general policies?

    (a) Reduced duties and nontariff barriers on textile (i.e., thread, cloth) inputs

    (b) Reduced duties and nontariff barriers on finished products (i.e., apparel)

    (c) Streamlined export and customs-processing procedures

8. Conversely, what policies do you favor?

    (a) Reduced duties and nontariff barriers on textile (i.e., thread, cloth) inputs

    (b) Reduced duties and nontariff barriers on finished products (i.e., apparel)

    (c) Streamlined export and customs processing procedures

9. How do you convey your policy preferences to relevant government ministries, organizations, and officials? Which of the following channels do you use?

    (a) Sectoral and national business associations

    (b) Personal contacts with state officials

    (c) Foreign chambers of commerce based in Morocco/Tunisia

    (d) The media, such as the business press or television and radio programs

    (e) Participation in delegations to government ministries

    (f) Other tactics, such as shutting down your factory, participating in producer strikes, or withholding social security payments and other taxes [elaborate]

10. What kinds of relationship do you have with professional associations representing the interests of industrialists in your field? Are you a member of these organizations? Do you attend association meetings? What are the benefits of membership?

11. Do you think that these associations have become more or less effective in the last ten to fifteen years?

12. Have you benefited from government-sponsored industrial *mise-à-niveau* [restructuring/upgrading] programs? If so, in what ways? If not, why not?

13. What kinds of strategies has your firm adopted/will your firm adopt in the new economic climate? Have you tried to integrate upstream and downstream activities within your firm? Have you tried to

establish relationships with other firms in upstream and down-stream activities? Have you tried to establish relationships with firms in the same activity, for example to cooperate in fulfilling large orders?

14. What kinds of relationships or agreements, if any, do you have with labor unions and workers' associations?

Bibliography

JOURNALS AND NEWSPAPERS

Conjoncture, 1996–1998 (Tunisian economic and political publication)
Conjoncture: Revue de la Chambre du Commerce Française au Maroc, 1990–2000 (Monthly publication of the French Chamber of Commerce in Morocco)
Economist Intelligence Unit (EIU) Country Reports on Morocco and Tunisia (various issues)
L'Economiste, 1983–2005 (Moroccan economic and political weekly)
L'Economiste Maghrébin, 1996–2000 (Tunisian economic weekly)
The Guardian, 1999 (London)
Le Journal, 1997–2001 (Moroccan political weekly)
Magazine Maghrébin du Textile, 1995–1997 (periodic publication on the Moroccan textile industry)
Maghreb-Machrek, 1960–1974 (Journal on Middle Eastern and North African Affairs)
Maroc Economie, 1994 (Moroccan economic weekly)
Maroc-Hebdo, 1998–2001 (Moroccan political weekly)
La Nouvelle Tribune, 1992–2000 (Moroccan political and economic weekly)
La Presse, 1995–1999 (Tunisian political daily)
Le Temps, 1997–2000 (Tunisian political daily)
Réalités, 1986–2000 (Tunisian economic and political weekly)
Le Renouveau, 1995–2000 (Tunisian political daily)
Temps du Maroc, 1996–2000 (Moroccan political weekly)
Textile Info, 1995–2000 (AMITH publication)
Textile Magazine, January–August 1997 (Moroccan private textile industry publication)
La Vie Economique (LVE), 1976–2001 (Moroccan economic and political weekly)

GOVERNMENT PUBLICATIONS

République Tunisienne, Ministère du Plan, Institut National de la Statistique. *Annuaire Statistique de la Tunisie* (various years)

Royaume du Maroc (Kingdom of Morocco). *Annuaire Statistique du Maroc* (1983–1998)

Royaume du Maroc, *Bulletin Officiel* (various years)

Royaume du Maroc, Administration des Douanes et des Impôts Indirects, Ministère des Finances, *Cautions*, September 1999.

Royaume du Maroc, Administration des Douanes et des Impôts Indirects, Ministère des Finances, *Régime*, September 1999.

Royaume du Maroc, Administration des Douanes et des Impôts Indirects, Ministère des Finances, *Le Régime Applicable aux Articles Textiles Soumis à Auto-Limitation et Exportées à Destination des Pays de la CEE*, 1981.

Royaume du Maroc, Administration des Douanes et des Impôts Indirects, Ministère des Finances, *Tarif Douanier/Tarifs des Droits de Douane, Droits d'Importation* (various years)

Royaume du Maroc, Ministère de l'Industre et du Commerce. *Les Industries de Transformation* (1989–1998)

Royaume du Maroc. 2005. *Programme Emergence*. Rabat: Ministry of Industry.

BOOKS, ARTICLES, AND REPORTS

Les Accords d'Association entre la CEE, le Maroc et la Tunisie. 1969. *Monde Arabe Maghreb-Machrek* 33:9–12.

Abed, George T. 2003. *Unfulfilled Promise. Finance and Development* 40 (1): 1–10.

Abernathy, Frederick H., John T. Dunlop, Janice Hammond, and David Weil. 1999. *A Stitch in Time: Lean Retailing and the Transformation of Manufacturing – Lessons from the Apparel and Textile Industries.* New York: Oxford University Press.

2003. Globalization in the Apparel and Textile Industries: What Is New and What Is Not? In *Locating Global Advantage*, edited by M. Kenney and R. Florida, 1–43. Stanford, CA: Stanford University Press.

Adam, Andre. 1970. *Les Classes Sociales Urbaines au Maroc. Revue de l'Occident Musulman*, special issue: 223–238.

Aggarwal, Vinod. 1985. *Liberal Protectionism: The International Politics of the Organized Textile Trade.* Berkeley: University of California Press.

Akesbi, Najib. 1986. L'Expérience des Codes des Investissements Industriels au Maroc: L'Evaluation des Investisseurs. *Bulletin Economique et Social du Maroc* 157:51–88.

Alagoz, Selda, and Mehmet Alagoz. 1998. Ihracatta Bir Örgütlenme Modeli: Sektörel Dis Ticaret Sirketleri ve Dis Ticaretteki Performanslari. [A Model of Organization in Exports: Sectoral Foreign Trade Corporations and their Performances in Foreign Trade.] *Çukurova Universitesi Iktisadi ve Idari Bilimler Fakultesi Dergisi* 8 (1): 117–131.

Alaoui, Hassan M. 2000. La Puissance des 'Fassis' Minée par la Reforme. *Arabies* 165:43.

Alavi, Hamid. 2004. Good Practice in Trade Facilitation: Lessons from Tunisia. *Premnotes* 89:87–90.

Alexander, Christopher. 1996. State, Labor and the New Global Economy in Tunisia. In *North Africa: Development and Reform in a Changing Global Economy*, edited by Dirk Vandevalle, 177–202. New York: St. Martin's.

Alladin, Ibrahim M. P. 1993. *Economic Miracle in the Indian Ocean: Can Mauritius Show the Way?* Stanley, Rose Hill, Mauritius: Editions de l'Ocean Indien.

Amin, Ash. 2000. Industrial Districts. In *A Companion to Economic Geography*, edited by Erics S. Sheppard and Trevor J. Barnes. Malden, MA: Blackwell.

Amin, Ash, and Nigel Thrift. 1992. Neo-Marshallian Nodes in Global Networks. *Journal of Urban and Regional Research* 16 (4): 571–587.

Amsden, Alice. 1989. *Asia's Next Giant: South Korea and Late Industrialization*. New York: Oxford University Press.

Anderson, Lisa. 1986. *The State and Social Transformation in Tunisia and Libya, 1830–1980*. Princeton, NJ: Princeton University Press.

1990. Liberalism in Northern Africa. *Current History* 89 (546): 145–175.

1995. North Africa: The Limits of Liberalization. *Current History* 94 (591): 167–171.

Angrist, Michele Penner. 1999. Parties, Parliament, and Political Dissent in Tunisia. *Journal of North African Studies* 4 (4): 89–104.

2006. *Party Building in the Modern Middle East*. Seattle: University of Washington Press.

Applebaum, Richard P., and Gary Gereffi. 1994. Power and Profits in the Apparel Commodity Chain. In *Global Production: The Apparel Industry in the Pacific Rim*, edited by Edna Bonacich, Lucie Cheng, Norma Chichilla, Nora Hamilton, and Paul Ong, 42–64. Philadelphia: Temple University Press.

Arslan, Ali. 2003. Turkish Business Elites, Turkish Economic Elites, Turkish Bourgeoisie, and Business–Political Relations in Turkey. *Is-Guc* 5 (2). Web page (accessed January 28, 2007). Available at http://www.isgucdergi.org/index/php?arc=arc_view.php&ex=147&inc=arc&cilt=5&sayi=28year=2003.

Asheim, Bjorn T. 2000. Industrial Districts: The Contributions of Marshall and Beyond. In *Oxford Handbook of Economic Geography*, edited by Gordan L. Clark, Maryann Feldmann, and Merle S. Gertier, 413–431. New York: Oxford University Press.

Ashford, Douglas E. 1961. *Political Change in Morocco*. Princeton, NJ: Princeton University Press.

Asselain, Jean Charles. 1969. La Réforme des Structures Commerciales en Tunisie depuis 1962. *Annuaire de l'Afrique du Nord* 8:115–143.

Avonde, Charles. 1922. *La Renaissance du Maroc, Dix Aans de Protectorat (1912–1922)*. Rabat: Résidence Générale de la République Française au Maroc.

Ayache, Albert. 1997. *Etudes d'Histoire Sociale Marocaine*. Rabat: Okad.

Azam, Jean-Paul, and Christian Morrison. 1994. *La Faisabilité Politique de l'Ajustement en Côte d'Ivoire et au Maroc*. Paris: Centre de Developpement, OECD.

Bair, J., and G. Gereffi. 2001. Local Clusters in Global Chains: The Causes and Consequences of Export Dynamism in Torreon's Blue Jeans Industry. *World Development* 29 (11): 1885–1903.

Baru, Sanjaya. 2000. Economic Policy and the Development of Capitalism in India: The Role of Regional Capitalists and Political Parties. In *Transforming India: Social and Political Dynamics of Democracy*, edited by F. R. Frankel, Z. Hasan, R. Bhargava, and B. Arora. New Delhi: Oxford University Press.

Bassani, Antonella. 1993. The Political Economy of Trade Liberalization: A Comparative Study of Morocco and Tunisia. PhD diss., School of Advanced International Studies, the Johns Hopkins University, Washington, DC.

Basti, Ahmed, and Charles Bechet. 2005. *Etude sur l'Abolition des Accords Multi Fibres: Etude pour la Tunisie*, 1–119. Washington, DC: World Bank.

Bates, Robert. 1981. *Markets and States in Tropical Africa: The Political Basis of Agricultural Policies*. Berkeley: University of California Press.

Beckert, Sven. 2001. *The Monied Metropolis*. New York: Cambridge University Press.

Bédoui, Abdeljelil. 1998. L'Epuisement d'un Modèle. *Réalites* 633:16–17.

Bégot, M. 1969. Les Industries Textiles à Casablanca. *Revue de Géographie du Maroc* 16:71–95.

Belal, Abdel Aziz. 1964. *L'Investissement au Maroc (1912–1964) et ses Enseignements en Matière de Développement Economique*. Casablanca: Editions Maghrébines.

Belghazi, Saâd. 1997. *Concurrence et Compétitivité Industrielle au Maroc*. Rabat-Agdal: Centre d'Etudes et de Recherches Aziz Belal (CERAB).

Bellin, Eva. 1991. Tunisian Industrialists and the State. In *Tunisia: The Political Economy of Reform*, edited by I. William Zartman, 45–66. Boulder, CO: Lynne Rienner.

———. 1994. The Politics of Profit in Tunisia: Utility of the Rentier Paradigm? *World Development* 22 (3): 427–436.

———. 1995. Civil Society in Formation: Tunisia. In *Civil Society in the Middle East*, edited by Augustus Richard Norton, 120–147. London: E. J. Brill.

———. 2002. *Stalled Democracy: Capital, Labor, and the Paradox of State-Sponsored Development*. Ithaca, NY: Cornell University Press.

Ben Ali, Driss. 1987. Etat et Reproduction Sociale au Maroc: Le Cas du Secteur Public. *Annuaire de l'Afrique du Nord* 26: 117–131.

———. 1991a. Changement de Pacte Social et Continuité de l'Ordre Politique au Maroc. In *Changements Politiques au Maghreb*, edited by Michel Camau, 51–72. Paris: Centre National de la Recherche Scientifique.

———. 1991b. Emérgence de l'Espace Socio-Politique et Stratégie de l'Etat au Maroc. In *Etat: Espace et Pouvoir Local – Réflexions sur le Maroc et les Pays en Développement*, 61–74. Rabat: Gessous.

———. 1993. La Politique Economique Marocaine de l'Indépendance à Nos Jours. In *Analyses de Politique Economique Appliquées au Maroc*, edited by Groupement de Recherche en l'Economie Internationale (GREI), 3–46. Rabat: Faculté de Droit, Université Mohamed V.

Bendourou, Omar. 1996. Power and Opposition in Morocco. *Journal of Democracy* 7 (3): 108–122.

Ben Hamida, Anderson. 1992. Les Bourgeois Tunisiens Face à la Crise Economique de 1929. *Cahiers de la Medite ranée* 45:129–136.

Ben Hammouda, Hakim. 1995. *Tunisie: Ajustement et Difficulté de l'Insertion Internationale*. Paris: L'Harmattan.

Ben Marzouka, Tahar. 1996. Le Role Economique de l'Etat en Tunisie. *Revue Tunisienne de l'Economie* 7:25–43.

Ben Romdhane, Mahmoud. 1986. L'Accumulation du Capital et les Classes Sociales en Tunisie depuis l'Indépendance. PhD diss., Université de Tunis, Tunisia.

Ben Romdhane, Mahmoud, and Pierre Signoles. 1982. Les Formes Récentes de l'Industrialisation Tunisienne, 1970–1980. *Geographie et Développement* 5: 57–98.

Ben Salem, Lilia. 1968. Origines Géographiques et Sociales des Cadres de l'Administration Economique des Offices et Sociétés Nationales en Tunisie. *Annuaire de l'Afrique du Nord* 7:107–127.

1976. *Développement et Problème de Cadres: Le Cas de la Tunisie*. Tunis: Centre des Etudes et des Recherches en Sciences (CERES).

1999. Stratégies Politiques et Formation d'une Elite: Les Premiers Cadres de la Tunisie Indépendante. In *Actes du IXème colloque international sur processus et enjeux de la décolonisation en Tunisie (1952–1964)*, edited by Habib Belaid. Tunis: Institut Supérieur d'Histoire du Mouvement National, Université de Tunis

Benedict, Stephen. 1997. Tunisie, le Mirage de l'Etat Fort. *Esprit* 3–4:27–42.

Benhaddou, Ali. 1997. *Maroc: Les Elites du Royaume – Essai sur l'Organization du Pouvoir au Maroc*. Paris: L'Harmattan.

Berger, Suzanne, and Ronald Dore, eds. 1996. *National Diversity and Global Capitalism*. Ithaca, NY: Cornell University Press.

Berrada, Abdelkader. 1979. Politique Budgetaire et Financement du Grand Capital Privé au Maroc. *Révue Juridique, Politique et Economique du Maroc* 5 (1): 95–122.

1986. La Politique de bas Salaires au Maroc: Ebauche d'Analyse. *Bulletin Economique et Social du Maroc* 157:11–65.

1988. La Marocanisation de 1973: Eclairage Retrospectif. *Revue Juridique, Politique et Economique du Maroc* 20:59–96.

1991. Etat et Capital Privé au Maroc (1956–1980). PhD diss., Faculté des Sciences Juridiques, Economiques et Sociales, Université Mohamed V, Rabat, Morocco.

1992. Etat et Capital Privé au Maroc (1956–1980). *Annales Marocaines d'Economie* no. 2 (Autumn): 29–68.

Berrada, Abdelkader, and Abdelkrim Ben Abdellah. 1980. Analyse Critique du Mémoire de D. E. S. de Noureddine El Aoufi: La Marocanisation et le Développement de la Bourgeoisie. *Revue Juridique, Politique et Economique du Maroc* 7 (1): 213–229.

Berrada, Yassmina. 2005. *Textile: Les Détails de l'Accord-Cadre*. Rabat: Centre de Veille Stratégique, Government of Morocco (October 17). Web page (accessed January 4, 2007). Available at http://www.veille.gov.ma/filinfo/index.php/2005/10/17/710-textiles-les-details-de-laccord-cadre.

Bianchi, Robert. 1985. Businessmen's Associations in Egypt and Turkey. *Annals of the American Academy of Political and Social Science* 482:147–189.

Biernacki, Patrick, and Dan Waldorf. 1981. Snowball Sampling. *Sociological Methods and Research* 10 (2): 141–164.

Bonacich, Edna, Lucie Cheng, Norma Chichilla, Nora Hamilton, and Paul Ong. 1994. The Garment Industry in the Restructuring Global Economy. In *Global Production: The Apparel Industry in the Pacific Rim*, edited by Edna Bonacich, Lucie Cheng, Norma Chichilla, Nora Hamilton, and Paul Ong, 3–17. Philadelphia: Temple University Press.

Bowman, John R. 1989. *Capitalist Collective Action: Competition, Cooperation, and Conflict in the Coal Industry*. New York: Cambridge University Press.

Bowman, Larry W. 1991. *Mauritius: Democracy and Development in the Indian Ocean*. Boulder, CO: Westview.

Bras, Jean-Phillipe. 1996. Tunisie: Ben Ali et sa Classe Moyenne. *Poles* no. 1 (April–June): 174–195.

Bratton, Michael, and Nicolas van de Walle. 1994. Neopatrimonial Regimes and Political Transitions in Africa. *World Politics* 46 (4): 453–489.

Brautigam, Deborah A. 1994. What Can Africa Learn from Taiwan? Political Economy, Industrial Policy, and Adjustment. *Journal of Modern African Studies* 32 (1): 111–138.

Brugnes Romieu, Marie Paule. 1966. Investissements Industriels et Developpement en Tunisie. *Cahiers du CERES, Series Economique* no. 1: 1–167.

Brusco, S. 1990. The Idea of the Industrial District: Its Genesis. In *Industrial Districts and Inter-Firm Cooperation in Italy*, edited by F. Pyke, G. Beccattini, and W. Sengenberger. Geneva: International Institute for Labor Studies.

Bruton, Henry J. 1998. A Reconsideration of Import Substitution. *Journal of Economic Literature* 36 (2): 903–936.

Bugra, Ayse. 1994. *State and Business in Modern Turkey: A Comparative Study*. Albany: State University of New York Press.

——— 1998. Class, Culture, and State: An Analysis of Interest Representation by Two Turkish Business Associations. *International Journal of Middle East Studies* 30 (4): 521–539.

Cairoli, M. Laetitia. 1998. Garment Factory Workers in the City of Fez. *Middle East Journal* 53:28–43.

Callaghy, Thomas. 1984. *The State–Society Struggle: Zaire in Comparative Perspective*. New York: Columbia University Press.

Cammett, Melani. 1999. International Exposure, Domestic Response: Financiers, Weavers, and Garment Manufacturers in Morocco and Tunisia. *Arab Studies Journal* 7/8 (2/1): 26–51.

——— 2006. Development and the Changing Dynamics of Global Production: Global Value Chains and Local Clusters in Apparel Manufacturing. *Competition and Change* 10 (1): 23–48.

Campbell, John L. 1997. Mechanisms of Evolutionary Change in Economic Governance: Interaction, Interpretation and Bricolage. In *Evolutionary Economics and Path Dependence*, edited by Lars Magnusson and Jan Ottosson, 10–32. Cheltenham: Edward Elgar.

Cardoso, Fernando Henrique, and Enzo Faletto. 1979. *Dependency and Development in Latin America*. Berkeley: University of California Press.

Catusse, Myriam. 1999a. Acteurs Privés et Actions Publiques. *Les Cahiers de l'Orient* 55:13–50.

⸺ 1999b. L'Entrée en Politique des Entrepreneurs au Maroc. PhD diss., University de Droit, d'Economie et des Sciences d'Aix-Marseille, France.

Central Intelligence Agency (CIA). 2005. *World Factbook*. Washington, DC: CIA.

Centre National d'Etudes Industrielles (CNEI). 1976. *Note de Synthése de l'Etude Sectorielle d'Industrie Textile (Filature, Tissage, Finissage)*. Tunis: CNEI.

⸺ 1981. *Note sur les Enterprises Exportatrices dans le Secteur Textile-Habillement*. Tunis: CNEI.

⸺ 1984. *Le Niveau de Dévelopment de l'Industrie Textile en Tunisie et les possibilitiés de son Expansion*. Tunis: CNEI.

Chaponnière, J. R., and Marc Lautier. 1998. Industrial Policy for Catching Up: The Case of Taiwan. In *Latecomers in the Global Economy*, edited by M. Storper, S. B. Thomadakis, and L. J. Tsipouri. London: Routledge.

Chari, Sharad. 2000. The Agrarian Origins of the Knitwear Industrial Cluster in Tiruppur, India. *World Development* 28 (3): 579–599.

Charrad, Mounira. 2001. *States and Women's Rights: The Making of Postcolonial Tunisia, Algeria, and Morocco*. Berkeley: University of California Press.

Chaudhry, Kiren Aziz. 1993. The Myths of the Market and the Common History of Late Developers. *Politics and Society* 21 (3): 245–274.

⸺ 1994. The Middle East and the Political Economy of Development. *Items* 48 (2/3): 41–49.

⸺ 1997. *The Price of Wealth: Economies and Institutions in the Middle East*. Ithaca, NY: Cornell University Press.

Cheng, Tun-jen, and Peggy Pei-chen Chang. 2003. Limits of Statecraft: Taiwan's Political Economy under Lee Teng-hui. In *Sayonara to the Lee Teng-hui Era: Politics in Taiwan, 1988–2000*, edited by W.-c. Lee and T. Y. Wang, 113–148. Lanham, MD: University Press of America.

Chibber, Vivek. 2005. *Locked in Place: State Building and Late Industrialization in India*. Princeton, NJ: Princeton University Press.

Chu, Yun-han. 1996. Taiwan's Unique Challenges. *Journal of Democracy* 7 (3): 69–82.

Clairmonte, Frederick, and John Cavanagh. 1981. *The World in Their Web: Dynamics of Textile Multinationals*. London: Zed.

Claisse, Alain. 1987. Makhzen Traditions and Administrative Channels. In *The Political Economy of Morocco*, edited by I. William Zartman, 34–58. New York: Praeger.

Coe, Neil M., Martin Hess, Henry Wai-Chung Yeung, Peter Dicken, and Jeffrey Henderson. 2003. 'Globalizing' Regional Development: A Global Production Networks Perspective. Manchester: School of Environment and Development, University of Manchester.

Collier, David, ed. 1979. *The New Authoritarianism in Latin America*. Princeton, NJ: Princeton University Press.

Collier, Ruth Berins, and David Collier. 1979. Inducements versus Constraints: Disaggregating "Corporatism." *American Political Science Review* 73: 967–986.

1991. *Shaping the Political Arena*. Princeton, NJ: Princeton University Press.

Combs-Schilling, M. E. 1989. *Sacred Performances: Islam, Sexuality, and Sacrifice*. New York: Columbia University Press.

Commission Economique et Monétaire. 1977. *Rapport sur la Crise dans l'Industrie Textile*. Brussels: European Community.

Coram, A. 1972a. The Berbers and the Coup. In *Arabs and Berbers*, edited by Ernest Gellner and Charles A. Micaud, 425–430. London: Duckworth.

1972b. Note on the Role of the Berbers in the Early Days of Moroccan Independence. In *Arabs and Berbers*, edited by Ernest Gellner and Charles A. Micaud, 269–276. London: Duckworth.

Crompton, Rosemary. 1993. *Class and Stratification*. Cambridge: Polity Press.

Cumings, Bruce. 1987. The Origins and Development of the Northeast Asian Political Economy: Industrial Sectors, Product Cycles, and Political Consequences. In *The Political Economy of the New Asian Industrialism*, edited by F. C. Deyo, 44–83. Ithaca, NY: Cornell University Press.

Dammak, O. Kalthoum. 1980. La Sous-Traitance Industrielle. *Cahiers du CERES, Série Géographique* no. 4:73–94.

Darga, L. Amedee. 1998. A Comparative Analysis of the Accumulation Process and Capital Mobilization in Mauritius, the United Republic of Tanzania and Zimbabwe. Geneva: UNCTAD.

Deaux, Kay, and Anne Reid. 2000. Contemplating Collectivism. In *Self, Identity, and Social Movements*, edited by Sheldon Stryker, Timothy J. Owens, and Robert W. White, 172–190. Minneapolis: University of Minnesota Press.

Demir, Omer, Mustafa Acar, and Metin Toprak. 2004. Anatolian Tigers or Islamic Capital: Prospects and Challenges. *Middle Eastern Studies* 40(6): 166–188.

Denieuil, Pierre-Nöel, and Abdelkhalek B'chir. 1996. La PME Tunisienne. *L'Annuaire de L'Afrique du Nord* 35:181–193.

Dicken, Peter. 2003. *Global Shift: Reshaping the Global Economic Map in the 21st Century*. Fourth Edition. New York: Guilford.

Dickerson, Kitty G. 1991. *Textiles and Apparel in the International Economy*. New York: Macmillan.

Dimassi, Hassine. 1983. Accumulation du Capital et Repartition des Revenues: Essai sur la Reproduction de la Formation Sociale Tunisienne Post-Coloniale, Fin des Années 50–Fin des Années 70. PhD diss., Université de Tunis.

Diop, Ndiame. 2006. L'Impact du Démantèlement de l'Accord Multifibre et les Perspectives de Développement du Secteur Textile et Habillement en Tunisie, Maroc, Egypte et Jordanie. *La Lettre d'Information Trimestrielle du Groupe de la Banque Mondiale au Maroc* 2:4–6.

Dlala, Habib. 1989. Etat et Développement Industriel en Tunisie: De l'Investissement Direct au Désengagement. *Revue Tunisienne de Geographie* 17:33–65.

1993. *Structuration et Fonctionnement de l'Espace Industriel Tunisien: Approche Macroscopique*. Tunis: Faculté des Sciences Humaines et Sociales, Université de Tunis.

Donaghu, Michael T., and Richard Barff. 1990. Nike Just Did It: International Subcontracting and Flexibility in Athletic Footwear Production. *Regional Studies* 24 (6): 537–552.

Doner, Richard. 1992. The Limits of State Strength: Toward an Institutionalist View of Development. *World Politics* 44 (3): 398–431.

Doner, Richard, and Ben Ross Schneider. 2000. Business Associations and Economic Development: Why Some Associations Contribute More than Others. *Business and Politics* 2 (3): 261–288.

Donze, Frederic. 2002. Tunisie, une Pionnière en Mal de Confiance. *Le Temps* (May 29).

Dopfer, Kurt. 1994. How Economic Institutions Emerge: Institutional Entrepreneurs and Behavioral Seeds. In *Innovation in Technology, Industries, and Institutions: Studies in Schumpeterian Perspectives*, edited by Yuichi Shionoya and Mark Perlman. Ann Arbor: University of Michigan Press.

Dougui, Nouréddine. 1992. Etat Colonial et Entreprises Concessionnaires en Tunisie (1890–1940). *Les Cahiers de Tunisie* 46 (161): 3–23.

Doumou, Abdelali. 1990. The State and Legitimation in Post-Colonial Morocco. In *The Moroccan State in Historical Perspective (1850–1985)*, edited by Abdelali Doumou. Dakar: Codresia.

DRI/McGraw-Hill, FOCS 1996. *Le Maroc Competitif*. Rabat: Ministère de l'Industrie et du Commerce. Royaume du Maroc.

Duvignaud, Jean. 1969. Classes et Conscience de Classe dans un Pays du Maghreb: La Tunisie. *Cahiers Internationaux de Sociologie* 77:185–201.

El-Aoufi, Nouréddine. 1979. La Marocanisation et le Développement de la Bourgeoisie. PhD diss., Université de Mohamed V.

———. 1990. *La Marocanisation*. Casablanca: Toubkal.

———. 1999. La Réforme Economique: Stratégies, Institutions, Acteurs. *Monde Arabe Maghreb Machrek* no. 164:36–52.

El Malki, Habib. 1980. Capitalisme d'Etat, Développement de la Bourgeoisie et Problématique de la Transition: Le Cas du Maroc. *Révue Juridique, Politique et Economique du Maroc* 8 (2): 207–228.

El Mossadeq, Rkia. 1987. Political Parties and Power-sharing. In *The Political Economy of Morocco*, edited by I. William Zartman, 59–83. New York: Praeger.

Entelis, John P. 1974. Ideological Change and an Emerging Counter-culture in Tunisian Politics. *Journal of Modern African Studies* 12 (4): 543–568.

European Commission. 2004. Trade in Textiles. Europa Press Release, MEMO/04/166 (June 29).

Eurostat. 2003. EU Trade Relations with the 12 Mediterranean Partner Countries. Eurostat News Release 78 (July 4).

Evans, Peter. 1995. *Embedded Autonomy: States and Industrial Transformation*. Princeton, NJ: Princeton University Press.

Fejjal, Ali. 1987. Industrie et Industrialisation à Fes. *Révue de Géographie du Maroc* 11 (2): 55–69.

Feldman, Maryann P. 2000. Location and Innovation: The New Economic Geography of Innovation Spillovers and Agglomeration, In *Oxford Handbook of*

Economic Geography, edited by Gordon L. Clark, Maryann P. Feldman, and Merle S. Gertier, 373–394. Oxford: Oxford University Press.

Fields, Karl J. 1995. *Enterprise and the State in Korea and Taiwan*. Ithaca, NY: Cornell University Press.

Findlay, Allan. 1984. Tunisia: The Vicissitudes of Economic Development. In *North Africa: Contemporary Politics and Economic Development*, edited by R. Lawless and A. Findlay, 217–240. New York: St. Martin's.

Foster, Kenneth W. 2001. Associations in the Embrace of an Authoritarian State: State Domination of Society? *Studies in Comparative International Development* 35 (4): 84–109.

Fox, James W. 2003. Successful Integration into the Global Economy: Costa Rica and Mauritius. Washington, DC: Nathan Associates, Inc.

Frankel, Francine R. 2000. Contextual Democracy: Intersections of Society, Culture and Politics in India. In *Transforming India: Social and Political Dynamics of Democracy*, edited by F. R. Frankel, Z. Hasan, R. Bhargava, and B. Arora, 1–25. New Delhi: Oxford University Press.

ed. 2005. *Transforming India: Social and Political Dynamics of Democracy*. Second Edition. New York: Oxford University Press.

Frieden, Jeffry. 1981. Third World Indebted Industrialization: International Finance and State Capitalism in Mexico, Brazil, Algeria, and South Korea. *International Organization* 35 (3): 407–431.

Frieden, Jeffry A., and Ronald Rogowski. 1996. The Impact of the International Economy on National Policies: An Analytical Overview. In *Internationalization and Domestic Politics*, edited by Robert O. Keohane and Helen V. Milner, 25–47. New York: Cambridge University Press.

Gale, Colin, and Jasbir Kaur. 2002. *The Textile Book*. New York: Berg.

Gallisot, René. 1990. *Le Patronat Européen au Maroc (1931–1942)*. Casablanca: Eddif.

Gamson, William A. 1992. The Social Psychology of Collective Action. In *Frontiers in Social Movement Theory*, edited by Aldon Morris and Carol Mueller, 53–76. New Haven, CT: Yale University Press.

Gasiorowski, Mark J. 1992. The Islamist Challenge: The Failure of Reform in Tunisia. *Journal of Democracy* 3 (4): 85–97.

Geertz, Clifford. 1968. *Islam Observed: Religious Development in Morocco and Indonesia*. New Haven, CT: Yale University Press.

Geissman, Patrick R. 1999. Atelier textile. *Conjoncture* 793 (May).

Gereffi, Gary. 1994. The Organization of Buyer-Driven Global Commodity Chains: How U.S. Retailers Shape Overseas Production Networks. In *Commodity Chains and Global Capitalism*, edited by G. Gereffi and M. Korzeniewicz, 95–122. Westport, CT: Greenwood.

1999. International Trade and Industrial Upgrading in the Apparel Commodity Chain. *Journal of International Economics* 48:37–70.

Gereffi, Gary, John Humphrey, and Timothy Sturgeon. 2005. The Governance of Global Value Chains. *Review of International Political Economy* 12 (1): 78–99.

Gherzi Organisation. 1999. *Etude Stratégique du Secteur Textile-Habillement*. Zurich: Gherzi Consultants.

Gibbon, Peter. 2000. *"Back to the Basics" through Delocalisation: The Mauritius Garment Industry at the End of the Twentieth Century.* Copenhagen: Centre for Development Research.

Gold, Thomas B. 1986. *State and Society in the Taiwan Miracle.* Armonk, NY: M. E. Sharpe.

Gough, Neil. 2004. Made in China: Of Rags and Riches. *Time Asia* 164 (18) (November 1). Web page (accessed January 28, 2007). Availabe at: http://www.time.com/time/magazine/article/0,9171,733846,00.html.

Gramsci, Antonio. 1995. *Selections from the Prison Notebooks.* New York: International.

Greenaway, David, and David Sapsford. 1996. Trade Reform and Changes in the Terms of Trade in Turkey. In *The Economy of Turkey Since Liberalization,* edited by Subidey Togan and V. N. Balasubramanyam, 52–66. New York: St. Martin's.

Guelmami, Abdelmajid. 1996. *La Politique Sociale en Tunisie de 1881 à Nos Jours.* Paris: Harmattan.

Guésquiere, H., K. Enders, P. Alonso-Gamo, P. Duran, and S. Sheybani. 1997. *Tunisia: Selected Issues.* Washington, DC: International Monetary Fund.

Haggard, Stephan. 1990. *Pathways from the Periphery: The Politics of Growth in the Newly Industrializing Countries.* Ithaca, NY: Cornell University Press.

Haggard, Stephan, and Tun-jen Cheng. 1987. The State and Foreign Capital in the East Asian NICs. In *The Political Economy of the New Asian Industrialism,* edited by F. C. Deyo, 84–135. Ithaca, NY: Cornell University Press.

Hall, Peter A. 1986. *Governing the Economy: The Politics of State Intervention in Britain and France.* New York: Oxford University Press.

Hall, Peter A., and David Soskice, eds. 2001. *Varieties of Capitalism: The Institutional Foundations of Comparative Advantage.* New York: Oxford University Press.

Hall, Peter A., and Rosemary C. R. Taylor. 1996. Political Science and the Three New Institutionalisms. *Political Studies* 44 (5): 936–957.

Hamdouch, Bachir. 1978. Le Maroc et les Sociétés Multinationales. *Bulletin Economique et Social du Maroc* nos. 136–137:87–121.

Hammoudi, Abdellah. 1997. *Master and Disciple: The Cultural Foundations of Moroccan Authoritarianism.* Chicago: University of Chicago Press.

———. 1999. The Reinvention of *Dar al-Mulk*: The Moroccan Political System and Its Legitimation. In *In the Shadow of the Sultan: Culture, Power, and Politics in Morocco,* edited by Rahma Bourqia and Susan Gilson Miller, 129–175. Cambridge, MA: Harvard University Press.

Hamri, Jaouad, and Saâd Belghazi. 2005. *Impact du Démantèlement de l'Accord Multifibres sur le Maroc,* 1–57. Washington, DC: World Bank.

Harik, Iliya. 1992. Privatization and Development in Tunisia. In *Privatization and Liberalization in the Middle East,* edited by Iliya Harik and Denis J. Sullivan, 210–232. Bloomington: Indiana University Press.

Held, David, Anthony McGrew, David Goldblatt, and Jonathan Perraton. 1999. *Global Transformations: Politics, Economics and Culture.* Stanford, CA: Stanford University Press.

Henderson, Jeffrey, Peter Dicken, Martin Hess, Neil Coe, and Henry Wai-Chung Yeung. 2002. Global Production Networks and the Analysis of Economic Development. *Review of International Political Economy* 9 (3): 436–464.

Henry, Clement M., and Robert Springborg. 2001. *Globalization and the Politics of Development in the Middle East*. New York: Cambridge University Press.

Hermassi, Elbaki. 1972. *Leadership and National Development in North Africa: A Comparative Study*. Berkeley: University of California Press.

Herrera, Yoshiko M. 2005. *Imagined Economies: The Sources of Russian Regionalism*. New York: Cambridge University Press.

Heydemann, Steven, ed. 2004. *Networks of Privilege in the Middle East: The Politics of Economic Reform Revisited*. New York: Palgrave Macmillan.

Hibou, Beatrice. 1996. *Les Enjeux de l'Ouverture au Maroc: Dissidence Economique et Contrôle Politique*. Paris: Centre d'Etudes et de Recherches Internationales.

———. 1999. *Les Marges de Manoeuvre d'un 'Bon Elève' Économique: La Tunisie de Ben Ali*. Paris: Centre d'Etudes et des Recherches Internationales.

Hines, Tony. 2001. From Analogue to Digital Supply Chains: Implications for Fashion Marketing. In *Fashion Marketing: Contemporary Issues*, edited by T. Hines and M. Bruce, 26–47. Boston: Butterworth-Heinemann.

Hirschman, Albert O. 1970. *Exit, Voice, and Loyalty: Responses to Decline in Firms, Organizations and States*. Cambridge, MA: Harvard University Press.

Hoffman, Kurt. 1985. Clothing, Chips and Competitive Advantage: The Impact of Microelectronics on Trade and Production in the Garment Industry. *World Development* 13 (3): 371–392.

Hoffman, Kurt, and H. Rush. 1984. *Microelectronics and Clothing: The Impact of Technical Change on a Global Industry*. Geneva: International Labour Office.

Hollingsworth, J. Rogers, and Robert Boyer. 1998. *Contemporary Capitalism: The Embeddedness of Institutions*. New York: Cambridge University Press.

Hotz-Hart, Beat. 2000. Innovation Networks, Regions, and Globalization. In *Oxford Handbook of Economic Geography*, edited by Gordon L. Clark, Maryann Feldman, and Merle S. Gertier, 432–450. New York: Oxford University Press.

Houssel, J. P. 1966. L'Evolution Récente de l'Activité Industrielle à Fes. *Révue de Géographie du Maroc* 9:59–83.

Humphrey, John, and Hubert Schmitz. 2002. How Does Insertion in Global Value Chains Affect Upgrading in Industrial Clusters? *World Development* 36 (9): 1017–1027.

———. 2004. Governance in Global Value Chains. In *Local Enterprises in the Global Economy: Issues of Governance and Upgrading*, edited by H. Schmitz, 95–109. Cheltenham: Edward Elgar.

Immergut, Ellen M. 1997. The Normative Roots of the New Institutionalism: Historical-Institutionalism and Comparative Policy Studies. In *Theorieentwicklung in der Politikwissenschaft – eine Zwischenbilanz*, edited by Arthur Benz and Wolfgang Seibel, 325–355. Baden-Baden: NOMOS Verlagsgesellschaft.

1998. The Theoretical Core of the New Institutionalism. *Politics and Society* 26 (1): 5–34.

International Labor Organization (ILO). Various Years. *Yearbook of Labor Statistics.*

Jaidi, Larabi. 1979. *Industrie Textile et Processus d'Industrialisation au Maroc.* Rabat: Editions de la Faculté des Sciences Juridiques, Economiques et Sociales de Rabat, Université Mohamed V.

Jenkins, Rob. 1999. *Democratic Politics and Economic Reform in India.* Cambridge: Cambridge University Press.

Joekes, Susan. 1982. The Multifibre Arrangement and Outward Processing: The Case of Morocco and Tunisia. In *EEC and the Third World: A Survey*, edited by Christopher Stevens, 102–112. London: Hodder and Stoughton.

Joffé, George. 1988. Morocco: Monarchy, Legitimacy and Succession. *Third World Quarterly* 10 (1): 201–228.

Johnson, Chalmers. 1982. MITI and the Japanese Miracle: The Growth of Industrial Policy, 1925–1975. Stanford, CA: Stanford University Press.

Kahler, Miles. 1985. Politics and International Debt: Explaining the Crisis. *International Organization* 39 (3): 11–36.

Kahn, Gabriel. 2004. City Transforms Apparel Industry. *Wall Street Journal*, August 13, p. 131.

Kalaycioglu, Ersin. 1991. Commercial Groups: A Love and Hate Relationship with the State. In *Strong State and Economic Interest Groups: The Post 1980 Turkish Experience*, edited by Metin Heper, 79–88. Berlin: Walter de Gruyter.

Kang, David C. 2002. *Crony Capitalism: Corruption and Development in South Korea and the Philippines.* Ithaca, NY: Cornell University Press.

Katzenstein, Peter J. 1985. *Small States in World Markets: Industrial Policy in Europe.* Ithaca, NY: Cornell University Press.

Katznelson, Ira. 1986. Working-Class Formation: Constructing Cases and Comparisons. In *Working-Class Formation: Nineteenth-Century Patterns in Western Europe and the United States*, edited by I. Katznelson and A. R. Zolberg, 3–41. Princeton, NJ: Princeton University Press.

2003. Periodization and Preferences: Reflections on Purposive Action in Comparative Historical Social Science. In *Comparative Historical Analysis in the Social Sciences*, edited by J. Mahoney and D. Rueschemeyer, 270–301. New York: Cambridge University Press.

Khatibi, Abdelkabir. 1968. Note Déscriptive sur les Elites Administratives et Economiques Marocaines. *L'Annuaire de l'Afrique du Nord* 7:79–90.

Khiari, Sadri, and Olfa Lamloum. 1998. Le Zaïm et l'Artisan ou de Bourguiba à Ben Ali. *L'Annuaire du l'Afrique du Nord* 37:377–395.

Kim, Eun Mee. 1997. *Big Business, Strong State: Collusion and Conflict in South Korean Development, 1960–1990.* Binghamton: State University of New York Press.

Klandermans, Bert, and Marga de Weerd. 2000. Group Identification and Political Protest. In *Self, Identity, and Social Movements*, edited by Sheldon Stryker, Timothy J. Owens, and Robert W. White, 68–90. Minneapolis: University of Minnesota Press.

Klein, Michael, and Bita Hadjimichael. 2003. *The Private Sector in Development: Entrepreneurship, Regulation, and Competitive Disciplines.* Washington, DC: World Bank.

Kochanek, Stanley A. 1987. Briefcase Politics in India: The Congress Party and the Business Elite. *Asian Survey* 27 (12): 1278–1301.

Kocka, Jürgen. 1981. Classes, Interest Articulation, and Public Policy. In *Organizing Interests in Western Europe*, edited by Suzanne Berger, 63–81. New York: Cambridge University Press.

Kohli, Atul. 2004. *State-Directed Development: Political Power and Industrialization in the Global Periphery.* New York: Cambridge University Press.

Kondoh, Hisahiro. 2001. The Effect of Political Change on Economic Policy Coordination Networks in Taiwan and South Korea. Paper read at American Political Science Association, August 30–September 2, San Francisco, CA.

Kristianasen, Wendy. 1997. No Delight for Turkey: New Faces of Islam. *Le Monde Diplomatique* (July). Available at http://mondediplo.com/1997/07/turkey.

Krueger, A. O. 1974. The Political Economy of the Rent Seeking Society. *American Economic Review* 64 (3): 291–303.

Kuo, Cheng-Tian. 2001. Private Governance in Taiwan. Unpublished manuscript. Department of Political Science, University of Wisconsin, Madison.

Kurt Salmon Associates (KSA). 1997. The ABC's of Strategic Alliances. Web page (accessed March 2002). Available at www.kurtsalmon.com/KSA_library.

——— 2001. *Modular Manufacturing.* Kurt Salmon Associates 2001 Web page (accessed May 2003). Available at www.kurtsalmon.com/KSA_library.

——— n.d. Cross Border Capital Flows Increasingly Common: Capital Flows in the Textile Industry. Web page (accessed March 2002). Available at www.kurtsalmon.com/KSA_library.

——— n.d. Quick Response: Meeting Consumer Needs. Web page (accessed March 2002). Available at www.kurtsalmon.com/KSA_library.

——— n.d. Vision for the New Millennium: Evolving to Consumer Response. Web page (accessed March 2002). Available at www.kurtsalmon.com/KSA_library.

Labouz, Marie-Françoise. 1981. Les Codes Maghrébins des Investissements. *Monde Arabe Maghreb Machrek* no. 94:51–77.

Lamrhili, Ahmed El Kohen. 1978. Formation et Développement de la Bourgeoisie Marocaine. *Al Asas* no. 10:31–38.

Lârif-Béatrix, Asma. 1988. *Edification Etatique et Environnement Culturel: Le Personnel Politico-Administratif dans la Tunisie Contemporaine.* Paris: Publisud.

Laroui, Abdallah. 1993. *Les Origines Sociales et Culturelles du Nationalisme Marocain (1830–1912).* Casablanca: Centre Culturel Arabe.

Layachi, Azzedine. 1998. State–Society Relations and Change in Morocco. In *Economic Crisis and Political Change in North Africa*, edited by Azzedine Layachi, 89–106. Westport, CT: Praeger.

——— 1999. Economic Reform and Elusive Political Change in Morocco. In *North Africa in Transition*, edited by Yahia H. Zoubir, 43–60. Gainesville: University Press of Florida.

Leveau, Remy. 1985. *Le Fellah Marocain: Defenseur du Trône*. Paris: Fondation Nationale des Sciences Politiques.

1987. Stabilité du Pouvoir Monarchique et Financement de la Delte. *Maghreb-Machrek* 118:5–19.

1993. Reflections on the State in the Maghreb. In *North Africa: Nation, State and Region*, edited by George Joffé, 247–265. New York: Routledge.

Li & Fung. 2003. Corporate Profile 2003. Web page (accessed August 6, 2003). Available at http://www.apparelandfootwear.org/4col.cfm?pageID/103.

Luebbert, Gregory M. 1991. *Liberalism, Fascism, or Social Democracy: Social Classes and the Political Origins of Regimes in Interwar Europe*. New York: Oxford University Press.

Lynn, Robert, Jalal Jalali, Mohammed Lahouel, Claude Leroy, Kim Murrell, and Mick Riordan. 1996. *Tunisia in the Global Economy*. Washington, DC: World Bank.

Mahjoub, Azzam. 1978. Industrie et Accumulation du Capital en Tunisie: De la Fin du XVIIème Siècle à Nos Jours. PhD diss., Université de Grenoble.

Mahoney, James. 2002. *Legacies of Liberalism: Path Dependence and Political Regimes in Central America*. Baltimore: Johns Hopkins University Press.

Malouche, Mariem. 2006. *Export Promotion and Diversification: The Tunisian Experience*, 1–11. Washington, DC: World Bank.

Mamdani, Mahmood. 1996. *Citizen and Subject: Contemporary Africa and the Legacy of Late Colonialism*. Princeton, NJ: Princeton University Press.

Marshall, Alfred. 1919. *Industry and Trade*. London: Macmillan.

McAdam, Doug. 1999. *Political Process and the Development of Black Insurgency, 1930–1970*. Second Edition. Chicago: University of Chicago Press.

McAdam, Doug, John D. McCarthy, and Mayer N. Zald, eds. 1996. *Comparative Perspectives on Social Movements*. New York: Cambridge University Press.

McAdam, Doug, Sidney Tarrow, and Charles Tilly, eds. 2001. *Dynamics of Contention*. New York: Cambridge University Press.

McBeath, Gerald. 1998. The Changing Role of Business Associations in Democratizing Taiwan. *Journal of Contemporary China* 7 (18): 303–321.

Melucci, Alberto. 1989. *Nomads of the Present: Social Movements and Individual Needs in Contemporary Society*. London: Hutchinson Radius.

Micaud, Charles A. 1964. *Tunisia: The Politics of Modernization*. New York: Praeger.

Miller, Gary J. 1998. Coalitional Instability and Institutional Transformation. *Journal of Institutional and Theoretical Economics* 154:764–773.

Mody, Ashoka, and David Wheeler. 1987. Towards a Vanishing Middle: Competition in the World Garment Industry. *World Development* 15 (10–11): 1269–1284.

Moore, Clement Henry. 1965. *Tunisia Since Independence*. Berkeley: University of California Press.

1977. Clientelist Ideology and Political Change: Fictitious Networks in Egypt and Tunisia. In *Patrons and Clients in Mediterranean Societies*, edited by Ernest Gellner and John Waterbury, 255–273. London: Duckworth.

1993. Political Parties. In *Polity and Society in Contemporary North Africa*, edited by I. William Zartman and Mark Habeeb, 42–67. Boulder, CO: Westview.

Moore, Pete. 2001. What Makes Successful Business Lobbies? *Comparative Politics* 33 (2): 127–147.

2004. *Doing Business in the Middle East: Politics and Economic Crisis in Jordan and Kuwait*. Cambridge: Cambridge University Press.

Mourad, Kamal ed-Din. 1997. Origins of the Moroccan Bourgeoisie. *Journal of International Politics* 7 (3): 88–99.

Munck, Gerardo L., and Jay Verkuilen. 2002. Conceptualizing and Measuring Democracy: Evaluating Alternative Indices. *Comparative Political Studies* 35 (1): 5–34.

Munson, Henry, Jr. 1993. *Religion and Power in Morocco*. New Haven, CT: Yale University Press.

1999. The Elections of 1993 and Democratization in Morocco. In *In the Shadow of the Sultan: Culture, Power, and Politics in Morocco*, edited by Rahma Bourqia and Susan Gilson Miller, 259–281. Cambridge, MA: Harvard University Press.

Murphy, Emma. 1999. *Economic and Political Change in Tunisia: From Bourguiba to Ben Ali*. New York: St. Martin's.

Narli, Nilufer. 1999. The Rise of the Islamist Movement in Turkey. *Middle Eastern Review of International Affairs* 3 (3): 38–48.

Nathan Associates, Inc. 2003. *Successful Integration into the Global Economy: Costa Rica and Mauritius*. Washington, DC: Nathan Associates, Inc.

Noble, Gregory. 1998. *Collective Action in East Asia: How Ruling Parties Shape Industrial Policy*. Ithaca, NY: Cornell University Press.

North, Douglass C. 1990. *Institutions, Institutional Change, and Economic Performance*. New York: Cambridge University Press.

Offe, Claus, and Helmut Wiesenthal. 1980. Two Logics of Collective Action: Theoretical Notes on Social Class and Organizational Form. *Political Power and Social Theory* 1:67–115.

Oliver, Pamela, and Gerald Marwell. 1988. The Paradox of Group Size in Collective Action: A Theory of the Critical Mass. *American Sociological Review* 53 (1): 1–8.

Olsen, Richard Paul. 1978. *The Textile Industry: An Industry Analysis Approach to Operations Management*. Lexington, MA: Lexington Books.

Olson, Mancur. 1965. *The Logic of Collective Action: Public Goods and the Theory of Groups*. Cambridge, MA: Harvard University Press.

Onis, Ziya, and Umut Turem. 2001. Business Globalization and Democracy: A Comparative Analysis of Turkish Business Associations. *Turkish Studies* 2 (2): 94–120.

Organisation for Economic Co-operation and Development (OECD), Development Assistance Committee. 1995. *Private Sector Development: A Guide to Donor Support*. Paris: OECD.

Ozcan, Gul Berna, and Murat Cokgezen. 2003. Limits to Alternative Forms of Capitalization: The Case of Anatolian Holding Companies. *World Development* 31 (12): 2061–2084.

Pamuk, Sevket. 1981. Political Economy of Industrialization in Turkey. *Middle East Report* no. 93:26–32.

Pennell, Richard. 1993. Libya and Morocco: Consensus on the Past. In *North Africa: Nation, State, and Region*, edited by George Joffé, 203–220. London: Routledge.

Perez-Aleman, Paola. 2000. Learning, Adjustment and Economic Development: Transforming Firms, the State and Associations in Chile. *World Development* 28 (1): 41–55.

Perrault, Giles. 1990. *Notre Ami le Roi*. Paris: Gallimard.

Pierson, Paul. 2000. Increasing Returns, Path Dependence, and the Study of Politics. *American Political Science Review* 94 (2): 251–267.

Piore, Michael J., and Charles F. Sabel. 1984. *The Second Industrial Divide: Possibilities for Prosperity*. New York: Basic Books.

Poncet, Jean. 1970. L'Economie Tunisienne depuis Indépendance. *L'Annuaire de l'Afrique du Nord* 9:93–114.

———. 1980. La Tunisie: La Politique d'Industrialisation. *Cahiers du CERES, Série Géographique* 4:369–381.

Porter, Michael E. 1990. *The Competitive Advantage of Nations*. New York: Free Press.

———. 1998. Clusters and the New Economics of Competition. *Harvard Business Review* 76 (6): 77–90.

———. 2000. Location, Competition, and Economic Development: Local Clusters in a Global Economy. *Economic Development Quarterly* 14 (1): 15–34.

Richards, Alan, and John Waterbury. 1996. *A Political Economy of the Middle East*. Second Edition. Boulder, CO: Westview.

Rozhon, Tracie. 2005. A Tangle in Textiles. *New York Times*, April 21, C1 and C11.

Rueschemeyer, Dietrich, Evelyn Huber Stephens, and John D. Stephens. 1992. *Capitalist Development and Democracy*. Chicago: University of Chicago Press.

Ruf, Werner. 1984. Tunisia: Contemporary Politics. In *North Africa: Contemporary Politics and Economic Development*, edited by Richard Lawless and Allan Findlay, 101–119. New York: St. Martin's.

Saâdi, Mohamed Saïd. 1983. Eléments d'Analyse de la Concentration Financière dans le Secteur Privé Marocain. *Révue Marocaine de Droit et d'Economie du Développement* 5:116–122.

———. 1989. *Les Groupes Financiers au Maroc*. Casablanca: Okad.

———. 1992. Concentration et Pouvoir Economique dans l'Industrie du Maroc. *Economie et Socialisme* 12:7–19.

Sabah, Saadia. 1987. The Interface between Family and State. In *The Political Economy of Morocco*, edited by I. William Zartman, 117–140. New York: Praeger.

Saxenian, AnnLee. 1994. *Regional Advantage*. Cambridge, MA: Harvard University Press.

Sayer, Andrew, and Richard Walker. 1992. *The New Social Economy: Reworking the Division of Labor*. Cambridge, MA: Blackwell.

Schmitter, Philippe C. 1974. Still the Century of Corporatism? *Review of Politics* 36:85–131.

Schmitz, Hubert, ed. 2004. *Local Enterprises in the Global Economy: Issues of Governance and Upgrading.* Cheltenham: Edward Elgar.

Schmitz, Hubert, and Bernard Musyck. 1994. Industrial Districts in Europe: Policy Lessons for Developing Countries? *World Development* 22 (6): 889–910.

Schmitz, Hubert, and Khalid Nadvi. 1999. Clustering and Industrialization: Introduction. *World Development* 27 (9): 1503–1514.

Schneider, Ben Ross. 2005. *Business Politics and the State in Twentieth-Century Latin America.* New York: Cambridge University Press.

Schrank, Andrew. 2004. Ready-to-Wear Development? Foreign Investment, Technology Transfer, and Learning-by-Watching in the Apparel Trade. *Social Forces* 83 (1): 123–156.

———. 2005. Entrepreneurship, Export Diversification, and Economic Reform: The Birth of a "Developmental" Community in the Dominican Republic. *Comparative Politics* 38 (1): 43–62.

———. 2007. "Asian Industrialization in Latin American Perspective: The Limits to Institutional Analysis." *Latin American Politics and Society* 49 (Spring).

Schulpen, Lau, and Peter Gibbon. 2002. Private Sector Development: Policies, Practices and Problems. *World Development* 30 (1): 1–15.

Scott, Allen J. 1998. *Regions and the World Economy.* New York: Oxford University Press.

———. 2002. Competitive Dynamics of Southern California's Clothing Industry: The Widening Global Connection and Its Local Ramifications. *Urban Studies* 39 (8): 1287–1306.

Scott, Allen J., and Michael Storper. 1986. *Production, Work, Territory: The Geographical Anatomy of Industrial Capitalism.* Boston: Allen and Unwin.

Seidman, Lisa. 2004. Textile Workers in Turkey, 1922–2003. Paper read at the Textile Conference, IISH, Istanbul, Turkey, November 11–13, 2004.

Sethom, Noureddine. 1992. *L'Industrie et le Tourisme en Tunisie: Etude de Géographie du Developpement.* Tunis: Faculté des Lettres et Sciences Sociales, Université de Tunis I.

Shadlen, Kenneth C. 2002. Orphaned by Democracy: Small Industry in Contemporary Mexico. *Comparative Politics* 35 (1): 43–62.

———. 2004. *Democratization without Representation: The Politics of Small Industry in Mexico.* University Park: Pennsylvania State University Press.

Shafer, Michael. 1994. *Winners and Losers.* Ithaca, NY: Cornell University Press.

Signoles, P., M. Bouthier, and J. M. Miossec. 1980. Une Approche de l'Espace Industriel Tunisien. *Cahiers du CERES, Série Géographique* 4:13–54.

Singleton, John. 1997. *The World Textile Industry.* London: Routledge.

Sinha, Aseema. 2005. Understanding the Rise and Transformation of Business Collective Action in India. *Business and Politics* 7 (2): 1–35.

Sluglett, Peter, and Marion Farouk-Sluglett. 1984. Modern Morocco: Political Immobilism, Economic Dependence. In *North Africa: Contemporary Politics and Economic Development,* edited by Richard Lawless and Allan Findlay, 50–100. New York: St. Martin's.

Smith, A. 2003. Power Relations, Industrial Clusters, and Regional Transformations: Pan-European Integration and Outward Processing in the Slovak Clothing Industry. *Economic Geography* 79 (1): 17–40.

Snow, David, and Robert Benford. 1992. Master Frames and Cycles of Protest. In *Frontiers in Social Movement Theory*, edited by Aldon Morris and Carol Mueller, 133–155. New Haven, CT: Yale University Press.

Snow, David, and Doug McAdam. 2000. Identity Work Processes in the Context of Social Movements. *Self, Identity, and Social Movements*, edited by Sheldon Stryker, Timothy J. Owens, and Robert W. White, 41–67. Minneapolis: University of Minnesota Press.

Snow, David, E. Burke Rochford, Jr., Steven K. Worden, and Robert D. Benford. 1986. Frame Alignment Processes, Micromobilization, and Movement Participation. *American Sociological Review* 5:464–481.

Sobh, Samir, et al. 2000. Capitalisme Marocain: Le Choc des Titans. *Arabies* 165:36–42.

Sosay, Gul. 1999. External Pressures, Domestic Choices: A Comparative Analysis of Trade Liberalization in Spain and Turkey. PhD diss., Department of Political Science, Ohio State University.

Spinanger, Dean. 1991. The Effects of Trade Liberalization: Experiences with Liberalization Policies, the Case of Textiles. *European Economic Review* 35(2–3): 543–551.

Stallings, Barbara. 1990. The Role of Foreign Capital in Economic Development: A Comparison of Latin America and East Asia. In *Manufacturing Miracles: Patterns of Development in Latin America and East Asia*, edited by G. Gereffi and D. L. Wyman, 55–89. Princeton, NJ: Princeton University Press.

Stengg, Werner. 2001. The Textile and Clothing Industry in the EU: A Survey. European Commission Papers No. 2. Web page (accessed February 2006). Available at http://www.ers.usda.gov/publications/so/view.asp?f/field/cws-bby/.

Storper, Michael. 1997. *The Regional World*. New York: Guilford.

Streeck, Wolfgang, and Kathleen Thelen. 2005. *Beyond Continuity: Institutional Change in Advanced Political Economies*. New York: Oxford University Press.

Stryker, Sheldon. 2000. Identity Competition: Key to Differential Social Movement Participation? In *Self, Identity, and Social Movements*, edited by Sheldon Stryker, Timothy J. Owens, and Robert W. White, 21–40. Minneapolis: University of Minnesota Press.

Sturgeon, Timothy J. 2002. Modular Production Networks: A New American Model of Industrial Organization. *Industrial and Corporate Change* 11 (3): 451–496.

Taymaz, Erol. 1999. Trade Liberalization and Employment Generation: The Experience of Turkey in the 1980s. In *Turkey: Economic Reforms, Living Standards, and Social Welfare Study*, edited by Ana Revenga, Vol. II, Technical Papers, 1–29. Washington, DC: World Bank.

Tessler, Mark A. 1982. Morocco: Institutional Pluralism and Monarchical Dominance. *Political Elites in Arab North Africa: Morocco, Algeria, Tunisia, Libya, and Egypt*. New York: Longman.

Tessler, Mark A., John P. Entelis, and Gregory W. White. 1995. Republic of Tunisia. In *The Government and Politics of the Middle East and North Africa*, edited by David E. Long and Bernard Reich. Third Edition, 369–393. Boulder, CO: Westview.

Thelen, Kathleen, and Sven Steinmo. 1992. Historical Institutionalism in Comparative Politics. In *Structuring Politics: Historical Institutionalism in Comparative Analysis*, edited by Sven Steinmo, Kathleen Thelen, and Frank Longstreth, 1–32. New York: Cambridge University Press.

Thompson, E. P. 1963. *The Making of the English Working Class*. New York: Vintage Books.

Todaro, Mike. 2003. The Land of Not-China. American Apparel Producers' Network. Web page (accessed August 2003). Available at http://aapnetwork.net/main.html?page/notchina.

Togan, Subidey. 1994. *Foreign Trade Regime and Trade Liberalization in Turkey During the 1980s*. Aldershot: Avebury.

Toyne, Brian, Jeffrey S. Arpan, Andy H. Barnett, David A. Ricks, and Terence A. Shimp. 1984. *The Global Textile Industry*. London: George Allen and Unwin.

Trabelsi, Mohsen. 1985. L'Industrie Manufacturière Tunisienne et sa Place dans l'Economie Nationale. *Cahiers du CERES, Séries Géographique* 5:1–225.

Tsai, Ming-Chang, 2001. Dependence, the State and Class in the Neoliberal Transition of Taiwan. *Third Word Quarterly* 22 (3): 359–379.

Ugur, Aydin, and Haluk Alkan. 2000. Türkiye'de Isadami-Devlet Iliskileri Perspektifinden MÜSIAD. [MÜSIAD from the Perspective of Businessmen–State Relations in Turkey.] *Toplum ve Bilim* 85 (3): 133–155.

Underhill, Geoffrey R. D., and Ziaoke Zhang. 2005. The Changing State–Market Condominium in East Asia: Rethinking the Political Underpinnings of Development. *New Political Economy* 10 (1): 1–24.

UNESCWA (United Nations Economic and Social Council for Western Asia). 2002. Technology Capacity-Building Initiatives for the Twenty-First Century in ESCWA Member Countries. Beirut: UNESCWA.

UNIDO (United Nations Industrial Development Organization). 2001. *Development of Clusters and Networks of SMEs*. Vienna: UNIDO.

2006a. Technology Parks: Morocco. Web page (accessed April 1, 2006). Available at http://www.unido.org/doc/26497.

2006b. Technology Parks: Tunisia. Web page (accessed April 1, 2006). Available at http://www.unido.org/doc/26821.

United Nations. Various Years. Comtrade Database. Available at http://comtrade.un.org/.

van de Walle, Nicholas. 2001. *African Economies and the Politics of Permanent Crisis, 1979–1999*. New York: Cambridge University Press.

Vogel, Ezra F. 1991. *The Four Little Dragons: The Spread of Industrialization in East Asia*. Cambridge, MA: Harvard University Press.

Vogel, Steven K. 1996. *Freer Markets, More Rules: Regulatory Reform in Advanced Industrial Countries*. Ithaca, NY: Cornell University Press.

Wade, Robert. 1990. *Governing the Market: Economic Theory and the Role of Government in East Asian Industrialization*. Princeton, NJ: Princeton University Press.

Waldner, David. 1999. *State-Building and Late Development*. Ithaca, NY: Cornell University Press.

2003. On the Non-Institutional Origins of Institutions. Unpublished paper. Department of Politics, University of Virginia. Available at http://www. people.virginia.edu/%7Edaw4h/articles.html.

Waltz, Susan. 1999. Interpreting Political Reform in Morocco. In *In the Shadow of the Sultan: Culture, Power, and Politics in Morocco*, edited by Rahma Bourqia and Susan Gilson Miller, 282–306. Cambridge, MA: Harvard University Press.

Waterbury, John. 1970. *The Commander of the Faithful: The Moroccan Political Elite, a Study of Segmented Politics*. London: Weidenfeld and Nicolson.

1972. The Coup Manqué. In *Arabs and Berbers*, edited by Ernest Gellner and Charles A. Micaud, 397–424. London: Duckworth.

1991. Twilight of the State Bourgeoisie? *International Journal of Middle East Studies* 23:1–17.

1993. *Exposed to Innumerable Delusions: Public Enterprise and State Power in Egypt, India, Mexico, and Turkey*. New York: Cambridge University Press.

1994. Democracy Without Democrats?: The Potential for Political Liberalization in the Middle East. In *Democracy Without Democrats?: The Renewal of Politics in the Muslim World*, edited by Ghassan Salamé, 23–47. London: I. B. Tauris.

1999. The Long Gestation and Brief Triumph of Import-Substitution Industrialization. *World Development* 27 (2): 323–341.

White, Gregory. 2001. *A Comparative Political Economy of Tunisia and Morocco: On the Outside of Europe Looking In*. Albany: State University of New York Press.

Woo-Cumings, Meredith, ed. 1999. *The Developmental State*. Ithaca, NY: Cornell University Press.

World Bank. 1996. *Tunisia's Global Integration and Sustainable Development: Strategic Choices for the 21st Century*. Washington, DC: World Bank.

2002. *Private Sector Development Strategy – Directions for the World Bank Group*. Washington, DC: World Bank, April 9.

2003. *Unlocking the Employment Potential in the Middle East and North Africa: Toward a New Social Contract*. Washington, DC: World Bank.

2006. *Morocco, Tunisia, Egypt and Jordan after the End of the Multi-Fiber Agreement*, Report No. 35376 MNA, 1–85. Washington, DC: World Bank.

Various years. *World Development Indicators*. Washington, DC: World Bank.

Various years. Doing Business Database. Available at http://www. doingbusiness.org/.

World Trade Organization. 2001. ATC: Agreement. Web page (accessed October 8, 2002). Available at http://www.wto.org/wto/english/thewto_e/ whatis_e/eol/e/wto02/wto2_37.htm.

Wright, Erik Olin. 1997. *Class Counts: Comparative Studies in Class Analysis.* Cambridge: Cambridge University Press.

Yalpat, Altan. 1984. Turkey's Economy under the Generals. *MERIP Reports* 122: 16–24.

Young, Crawford. 1976. *The Politics of Cultural Pluralism.* Madison: University of Wisconsin Press.

Zartman, I. William. 1987. King Hassan's New Morocco. In *The Political Economy of Morocco*, edited by I. William Zartman, 1–33. New York: Praeger.

    1990. Opposition as Support of the State. In *The Arab State*, edited by Giacomo Luciani, 220–246. London: Routledge.

Zysman, John. 1983. *Governments, Markets, and Growth: Financial Systems and the Politics of Industrial Change.* Ithaca, NY: Cornell University Press.

Index

Abdallah, Ibrahim, 92n28
Act of Algéciras, 92
Adalet ve Kalkinma Partisi (AKP) (Justice and Development Party), 208
Admissions Temporaires (AT) system, 34–35, 99, 102, 155–158, 160–162, 164, 166–167, 177, 185–186; *Campagne d'Assainissement* and, 155–156, 157n16, 180
Agence pour la Promotion de l'Industrie (API), 73, 75n32, 128, 135, 139, 145, 216
Agreement on Textiles and Clothing (ATC), 40
agriculture, 63, 65, 68, 72, 90, 91, 195
Algeria, 39
Ali, Prince Moulay, 87
Alioua, Khalid, 183, 188
Al-Nahda, 62
AMITH, 149–167, 170, 173, 175, 177, 178, 179–180, 181–185, 186–188, 216, 218; *Admissions Temporaires* system and, 156–157; black markets and, 155n12
Ammar, Ferdjani bel Hadj, 68
Amor, Ali, 155n11
Anatolian Tigers, 207–208
Annual Quality Textile Tour, 1999; Tunisia, 114

antidumping laws, 47n29
apparel sector: automation of, 30n4, 39, 43; competitiveness, 38–41, 44–45; computerized systems, 42–44, 45, 49; délocalisation, 29–41, 99, 116, 166–167; electronic data interchange and, 42, 44; fashion cycles, 41–45, 75, 76; floor-ready merchandise, 43, 45; geography and, 28–29, 41, 44–47, 48, 49, 52, 142; global supply chain, 25–52, 186, 188n51; manufacturing process, 26–28, 193, 218; social origins and, 13, 101–102, 136, 137, 171–172, 177; subcontracting, 6, 20, 29, 30, 31–32, 44–45, 69n24, 76, 78, 94, 98, 99, 100–101, 141, 166
Asia: Asian financial crisis, 39, 157–158; competition with, 4, 39–41, 109, 144, 146, 147, 157–158
Association Agreements. *See* EU Association Agreements
Association Marocaine de l'Industrie du Textile (AMIT). *See* AMITH
Association Marocaine des Industries du Textile et de l'Habillement. *See* AMITH
Association of Chambers of Commerce (India), 205

Association of Foreign Economic
Relations (DEIK) (Turkey),
208
AT system. *See Admissions
Temporaires* (AT) system

Banque Tunisienne de Solidarité, 36;
as instrument of social control,
117–118
Barcelona Declaration of 1995, 11
Basri, Driss, 102n42; *Campagne
d'Assainissement* and, 154–155,
157
Bel Hadj Ali, Mondher, 125
Ben Achour, Ezzedine, 68
Ben Ali, Zine el-Abidine, 60–62, 78,
118–120, 124–125, 126–127, 138
Ben Salah, Ahmed, 68, 71, 72,
98n37
Berbers, 96n36, 98; political loyalties
of, 83
bey, 56–57, 58, 63; beylical elite,
62–63, 67
black market, 39–40, 150n2, 154–157,
160, 171, 174
bled al-makhzen, 81
bled al-siba, 81
bourgeoisie: close business–
government relations and, 92; Fassi,
84n8, 85–86; Istiqlal and, 84, 90;
Moroccan industrial, 80–81, 85,
88–90; Moroccan monarchy and
the, 96; Moroccan nationalist
movement and, 84, 90;
Neo-Destour Party and, 64, 65n19,
72; Tunisian industrial, 58, 70,
71n27, 78; Turkish Muslim,
206
Bourguiba, Habib, 57–60, 64, 67,
68
Brigades Economiques, 117
business associations, 4, 6, 18, 209,
210, 211–213, 216, 218; business
collective action and, 6, 9, 22, 145,
179–180; developmental, 22, 205,
213; importance of, 152–153, 179,
182n46; Indian, 201, 202, 205–206;

industrial upgrading and, 212–213;
lobbying and, 111, 193; Moroccan,
185, 218; state control of, 121–130;
Taiwan and, 198, 200; Tunisian,
110, 111, 145, 217. *See also*
AMITH; CETTEX; CGEM;
FENATEX; UTICA
business collective action: business–
government relations and, 13–23,
22t1.3, 190–195, 210; business
passivity in Tunisia, 110–117,
135–136, 141–147; coordination
and, 212–213; dual-market system
and, 140–147; effect of state power
on, 17; group identity and, 13,
18–23, 168, 173–174, 177–178,
192–193, 209; Olsonian theory, 16,
136n22, 193; prisoner's dilemma
model and, 212; social movements
theory and, 18; theoretical models
of, 13–23, 15t1.2. *See also* business
associations; business–government
relations; business mobilization;
lobbying
business–government relations, 4,
6–7, 9, 11, 15t1.2, 17, 22, 55, 64,
79, 112, 118, 125, 148–149,
178–183, 187, 190–195, 209–213,
218; degree of capital concentration
and, 7; dimensions and
configurations of, 6–7, 191–192
economic liberalization and, 9–13;
industrial development strategies
and, 48, 209–218;
postindependence Morocco and,
80–84; state power and, 7–8
business mobilization: associations as
sites of, 6; definition of, 4n1; effects
of, 4; impact of global economic
integration on, 8–9; India, 201–206;
societal factors and, 135–147; state
responsiveness and, 130–135;
Taiwan, 195–201; Turkey, 206–209.
See also business associations;
business collective action;
business–government relations;
lobbying

Campagne d'Assainissement,
154–157, 167, 180, 186
capital structure, 7–9, 11–13, 22, 51,
139–141, 145, 191–192, 194, 197,
199–200, 201–203
Centre Marocain pour la Promotion
des Exportations. *See* CMPE
Centre pour la Promotion des
Exportations. *See* CEPEX
Centre Technique des Industries
Méchanique et Electrique, 130
Centre Technique du Textile. *See*
CETTEX
CEPEX, 111, 139
CETTEX, 115, 127–130, 13, 133–34,
216
CGEM, 149–150, 152, 154n8,
156–157, 159n19, 170, 180,
182n46, 184n49, 186
Chaibi group, 138
Chamber of Commerce: French, 162,
170n34; Tunisian, 112, 139n26;
Tunisian-British, 145. *See; also*
Association of Chambers of
Commerce; Federation of Indian
Chambers of Commerce and
Industry (FICCI)
Chamber of Counselors (Morocco),
82
Changement, 126–127
Chang-Kai Shek, 196
chemicals sector: textile industry and,
26
Cherif group, 138
China: competition with, 3, 32,
46–47, 109, 157; EU-China
Shanghai Accord, 40; Taiwan and,
196–197
civil liberties, 21, 82, 83
civil society, 21; state control of, 62,
82, 116, 127
class analysis: value and limitations of,
19n22
clientelism, 4, 9, 58, 83, 64, 206, 209.
See also networks of relations
cloth-finishing industry, 71,
75–76

clustering, 22, 25, 37, 41, 46, 47–52,
75, 147, 164, 167, 189, 209–213,
216–218; definition of, 210;
different paths to, 217–218; state
support for, 210–212. *See also*
industrial upgrading; sectoral
integration
CMPE, 97, 171, 173, 175
COGESPAR, 87
collectivization (Tunisia), 68, 70, 71,
73
colonial period, 17, 22t1.3; Morocco,
80–82, 84, 87–88, 90; Taiwan,
197n6; Tunisia, 56–57, 62-64
Commission Supérieure
d'Investissements, 36
commodity products, 44
Communist Party, 57
"companies in difficulty" law, 134
competitiveness, 4, 21, 45n27, 48, 49;
Morocco, 21, 157, 160n22,
166–167, 168, 174, 187n50,
188n51; Tunisia, 111–112, 113, 116,
131, 133, 144–145
Conféderation Générale des
Enterprises du Maroc. *See* CGEM
Confederation of Engineering Industry
(India), 205
Confederation of Indian Industry,
205
conglomerates: Morocco, 87; Taiwan,
197–198; Tunisia, 138. See also
groupes; holding Companies
Congress Party, 201, 202, 204–205
constitution (Morocco), 82–83
Constitutional Democratic Rally. *See*
Rassemblement Constitutionel
Démocratique
contrat-programme, 165–167,
182–183, 187–188, 216
Cooperation Accords of 1976, 31
cooperative spirit: lack of, in Tunisia,
111–112
corruption, 64, 125, 141, 154, 200,
202–203, 205, 215. *See also*
clientelism; networks of relations;
state repression

COTEF, 158
coutourriers: Moroccan apparel
  manufacturers as, 175–176
"cozy capitalism," 86, 200
credit, 8, 34, 36, 68, 76–77, 86, 96,
  102, 113, 130, 137, 139, 150n2,
  188n51, 186, 192, 195, 197n7, 206
cross-sectoral disputes, 158–164, 168
culture of production, 173
currency, 73, 97, 162, 167, 182,
  183n47, 187; devaluation of Asian,
  39, 158; "export dirham," 165
Customs Authority: Morocco, 153,
  155n11, 162, 180, 185–187, 215;
  Tunisia, 109, 120–121, 215
customs policies: Morocco, 91–92, 97,
  154–157, 161–163, 165, 167n33,
  175n39, 177, 180, 185–187, 215,
  216; Tunisia, 66, 70, 73–74,
  108–109, 120–121, 130, 141, 143,
  215

Debt Crisis, 10
Decathlon, 100
délocalisation: apparel and textile
  sectors, 29–41, 166–167
Democratic Bloc (Kutla
  Democratiyya), 84
Democratic Progressive Party (DPP),
  199
denim jeans: Moroccan black market
  and, 39n18
Destour Party, 57–58, 61. *See also*
  Neo-Destour Party
developing countries, 3–5, 8, 9–11,
  13–15, 17, 23, 25–26, 28–33, 71,
  78, 115, 136, 140, 145, 147, 190,
  209, 210, 218; "bread riots" in,
  10n12; competition among, 37–39;
  employment growth in, 30; growth
  in apparel exports from, 29–30;
  industrial development in, 46–51;
  textile vs. apparel sectors in, 14–15
dirigisme, 66–72. *See also* statist
  models
Djelani, Hédi, 123–127, 136n23;
  marriage strategies of, 124–125

Dominican Republic, 8n10
dual-market system: Morocco, 11, 21;
  Tunisia, 78–79, 140–147

East Asia: exports from, 29–30, 32,
  46, 149
economic liberalization, 5–6, 9–13,
  16–17, 19, 21, 23, 79, 190–192,
  199, 201, 203, 205, 208
El Fassi, Abbas, 188
El Mossadeq, Abderrazaq, 185,
  186–187
electoral system: Morocco, 82;
  Taiwan, 199, 200; Tunisia, 58,
  61
Electronic Data Interchange (EDI), 42,
  43, 44; trade facilitation and, 215
elites, 7, 8, 21, 191, 194, 195; India,
  202, 205; Morocco, 6, 11, 13, 16,
  22, 80, 81, 84–86, 89–90, 91,
  95–96, 98–99, 102, 104–106,
  168–169, 172, 174, 178, 188–189;
  Taiwan, 198; Tunisia, 12, 55,
  56–57, 62–65, 68, 72, 136, 140;
  Turkey, 207. *See also* bourgeoisie
employment, 14, 28, 30, 62, 73, 74,
  99, 141, 165, 170, 173, 214. *See
  also* labor
energy costs, 152, 162, 165, 167, 187,
  216
Entente Nationale, 83
entrepreneurship, 36, 76–77, 134,
  136–137, 148n1
EPZ. *See* export processing zones
Erdogan, Recep, 208
EU. *See* European Union
EU Association Agreements (EUAA),
  6, 14, 31, 88, 93–94, 108–109, 112,
  113, 120, 131, 157, 159, 162–163,
  174
EUAA. *See* EU Association
  Agreements
EU-China Shanghai Accord, 40
Euro-Mediterranean Association
  Agreements, 11
Europe: Chambers of Commerce, 145;
  clients from, 100, 151, 158, 187n50;

délocalisation and, 31–32, 37, 38,
40, 99, 116, 166–167; Eastern, 32,
38, 42, 44, 46, 47n30, 142; free
trade zone with, 114; industrial
investment from, 39, 40, 46, 66, 76,
89, 141, 166; industrial training in,
101; largest apparel importer, 45;
markets in, 4, 5, 31, 76, 93–94, 109,
140; Moroccan economic
dependence on, 94; proximity to,
41, 46, 47n30; trade agreements
with, 31, 88, 93–94, 157n17; wages
in, 94. *See also* EU Association
Agreements; European Union (EU)
European Union (EU), 5, 6, 120, 149,
151, 154, 160, 167, 190; grants
from, 131; trade policies; of, 150n4.
See also EU Association
Agreements; Europe
export class. *See* industrial class
structure
Export Code: Moroccan, 97
export processing zones (EPZs), 10,
196n4, 214

family groups: economic power of,
86–87, 88–89; *groupes* and,
95–96
fashion cycles, 44, 45, 75–76. *See also*
global supply chain
"fat cats," 168, 169, 173, 174,
193
Fédération Nationale du Textile. *See*
FENATEX; Federation of Indian
Chambers of Commerce and
Industry (FICCI), 205–206
FENATEX, 114, 127–130, 133,
144–145, 146; "Livre Blanc" and,
128–129
fiber manufacturing, 26
FILCOF, 158
Finance Law (Morocco), 1998–1999,
163; 1999–2000, 163n28
flexible specialization, 47n31
Fond pour la Promotion du
Developpement Industriel. *See*
FOPRODI

Fond pour la Promotion et
Décentralisation Industrielle (Fund
for Industrial Promotion and
Decentralization), 73
Fonds d'Accès aux Marchés
d'Exportations (FAMEX), 216
Fonds de Garantie de la
Restructuration Financière, 217
Fonds de Promotions des Exportations
(FOPRODEX), 216
Fonds National de la Mise à Niveau
(FOMAN), 217
Fonds National de Solidarité: as
instrument of social control,
117–118
food-processing sector, 89
FOPRODI, 77, 137, 216
foreign investment, 37, 40–41, 46;
Morocco and, 34, 92, 97–98, 182;
Taiwan and, 196, 199; Tunisia and,
36–37, 73, 76, 78, 136, 140–144
Framework Agreement (Morocco),
216
France: textile education in, 69
free trade agreements: U.S.-Morocco,
214. *See also* Agreements on Textile
and Clothing; EU Association
Agreements; Euro-Mediterranean
Association Agreements; GATT;
Multi-Fiber Agreement; NAFTA;
WTO (World Trade Organization)
free trade zones, 207
full-package production, 25, 37, 41,
43n26, 46, 50, 51, 216

Gandhi, Indira, 202
Gandhi, Mohandas K., 202
Gandhi, Rajiv, 203, 205n22
Gap International, 71, 100, 142n32,
173
GATT, 6, 120, 157n17, 159
General Agreements on Tariff and
Trade. *See* GATT
geographic proximity: value of,
142
Gherzi Organisation: "Livre Blanc,"
114–115, 128–129

global commodity chain framework,
49–50
global economic integration, 6–7, 16,
190; business mobilization and, 9,
18, 21, 23, 208–209, 213;
periodization of, 9–11
global supply chain, 5, 26–28;
clustering and, 48; core and
peripheral regions of, 49–50;
management of, 41–47, 51, 186. *See
also* clustering; fashion cycles;
full-package production; industrial
upgrading; management models
Grand Conseil, 63
Great Britain: textile industry and, 28
group interests, 4n1, 4n2, 9, 12,
18–20, 110, 121, 123, 163–165,
170, 179–180, 189–191, 199, 200.
See also business collective action;
business mobilization; policy
preferences
groupes, 66, 77, 95–96
guichet unique system, 134–135, 215
Gulf War (1990–1991), 39, 149, 150,
151, 173

Hassan II, King of Morocco, 83, 96,
154n9
holding companies: Morocco, 77, 80,
86–87; Tunisia, 12, 77, 137–138,
192; Turkey, 207–208. *See also*
conglomerates; *groupes*
Hong Kong, 29, 32
House of Representatives (Morocco),
82

Icomail, 160n22
ICOSE, 158
IMF, 32–33
import-substitution industrialization
(ISI): business–government relations
and, 8–13, 15, 192–193, 194–195,
201, 209, 211, 218; India, 201–203;
Morocco, 16, 20–22, 79, 92–93,
192–193; Taiwan, 196; Tunisia, 67,
71–72, 140, 192; Turkey, 206–209.
See also protectionism

in-bond trade regime, 34, 141, 186,
160–161. See also *Admissions
Temporaires* (AT) system
India, 201–206; business associations,
201, 202, 205–206; corruption in,
202–203; family-based economic
powers, 203; "license-permit raj,"
202–203, 204, 205; middle class,
204; nationalist movement, 202
Indian National Congress (INC), 202
individualism: Tunisian industrial
sector and, 115
industrial class structure, 7, 8–9,
11–12, 17, 18, 21, 78–79, 117, 194,
201, 209; export class, 8–9, 11–12,
13, 22–23, 99, 191; Indian, 203;
Taiwanese, 195; Tunisian, 12, 23,
55, 65–72, 79, 117, 136–140, 145,
147; Turkish, 206. *See also*
clustering; import-substitution
industrialization; industrial
upgrading; sectoral integration
industrial upgrading, 22, 50, 130, 133,
173, 205, 209–214, 216–218. *See
also* clustering; import-; substitution
industrialization; sectoral
integration
Industrie Cottonière du Oued Zem, 97
infitah, 72
Institut Arabe des Chef d'Enterprise
(IACE), 114, 125n15
institutionalist models, 16–18, 193;
"varieties of capitalism" approach,
15t1.2, 16–17
International Labor Organization
(ILO), 13n17
International Monetary Fund. *See* IMF
investment codes: Moroccan, 34, 36,
92, 93, 95, 97, 172; Tunisian, 71,
73
ISI. *See* import-substitution
industrialization
Istiqlal, 83–84, 90–91

Japan, 29, 32, 44, 196–197, 212
Jettou, Driss, 163
Jeunes Entrepreneurs law, 34, 36

Kettani group, 87n18, 98, 149, 170, 175
Khodorkovsky, Michael, 8n9
Kuomintang (KMT), 196–200
Kutla Democratiyya, 84

labor, 47n31, 90n24, 91, 92–93n33, 94, 107, 113, 116, 121, 129–130, 142, 163n28, 176, 210; activism, 13n17, 165, 188, 203; costs, 29–30, 44, 109–144, 166, 184; low-wage, 27–28, 44, 146; movement, 57; unions, 58, 123, 182, 184, 188, 210. *See also* Union Générale des Travailleurs Tunisiens (UGTT); Union Morocaine du Travail (UMT); wages
labor code: Morocco, 152, 165; Tunisia, 113, 135
Lahjouji, Adberrahman, 156
land reform: Morocco, 91, 96–97; Taiwan, 197; Tunisia, 68
Latin America, 12n14, 32, 46, 195n3
Law 74–74, 73; 1974 Law Companies, 73n30
Law of Ill-Gotten Gains, 58, 63
Law of National Indignity, 58, 63
leadership: group identity formation and, 20–21
Levi's, 71, 76, 141, 142n32, 143
Li & Fung, 47n30
Libya, 39–40
lobbying, 4n1, 6, 8–9, 15–17, 20, 23, 190, 211; India, 205; lack of, in Tunisia, 107–113, 115–117, 130, 134; media and, 181–183; methods of, 110; Morocco, 20, 153–154, 159, 162–164, 165, 167–171, 177–189, 193, 217–218; Taiwan, 198–201
Lyautey, Louis Hubert Gonzalve, 81

makhzen families, 81, 85–86
management models: modular manufacturing, 42, 45; quick response (QR), 41–43

marabouts, 81
Maroc Compétitif, 167
marriage-based alliances, 85–86, 124–125
Mauritius, 8n10
media, 6, 110, 111, 130–131, 134, 181–183, 185
merchandising, 43–44, 45
Mestiri, Ahmed, 61
Mexico, 46n28
MFA. *See* Multi-Fiber Agreement
middle class: economic liberalization and, 10n12; Indian, 204; Moroccan, 96, 101–102, 171; Tunisian, 65, 67, 76–77, 137
Middle East, 82, 195n2; export sector, 3, 11, 32, 39, 213
Ministry of Commerce (Morocco), 188n51
Ministry of Finance: Morocco, 162, 187n50; Tunisia, 117, 133
Ministry of Industry: Morocco, 162, 166n31, 167, 180n44, 183, 186, 216; Tunisia, 113–114, 115, 129, 130–131, 133–134
Ministry of Labor (Morocco), 183–184
Mitra, Amit, 205–206
Mohamed V, King of Morocco, 90
Mohamed VI, King of Morocco, 154n9, 154n10
monarchy: Moroccan, 12, 13, 21, 64n15, 81–83, 87, 90, 91, 95–96, 148, 181
Moroccanization, 34, 94–99, 102
Mouadda, Mohamed, 61
Mouvement des Démocrates Socialistes (MDS), 61
Mouvement Ettajdid, 61n11
Mouvement National Populaire (MNP), 83
Movement Populaire (MP), 83
Multi-Fiber Agreement (MFA), 30–31, 46; abrogation of, 3–4, 5, 31, 40, 214, 216; EU Association Agreements, 31; "transitional safeguards," 40

multinational companies (MNCs), 25,
27–28, 47n29, 49, 51–52, 71, 73,
77, 116, 142, 144, 187, 205;
Admissions Temporaires system
and, 99–101, 180; API and, 139;
supply chain management and,
41–42, 44
multipartyism, 61–62, 83
Mustakil is Adanleri Dernegi
(MUSIAD) (Independent
Businessmen's Association),
207–209
Mzabi group, 138

Nabisco, 142n33
NAFTA, 11
National Commission for Simplifying
Procedures (Morocco), 180n44
National Constitutive Assembly,
60
National Federation of Industry and
Commerce (Taiwan), 200
National Pact, 61
Nehru, Jawaharlal, 202
Neo-Destour Party, 57–62, 64–65, 66,
72, 121. *See also* Destour Party
networks of relations, 9, 124–125,
177, 204; informal, 14, 16, 20, 21,
48, 211; patronage, 58, 64, 86, 148,
168–170, 179, 189, 198, 206–207.
See also clientelism; 1972 Law, 30,
73, 74, 78, 114–115, 137, 141, 142,
215
North American Free Trade
Agreement. *See* NAFTA
Nouira, Chakib, 125n15, 136n23
Nouira, Hédi, 72, 73, 78, 125n15

Office Chérfienne des Phosphates
(OCP), 162n26
Office du Developpement Industriel,
97
Office National du Textile, 69–70
Olson, Mancur: theory of collective
action, 16, 136n22, 193
Omnium Nord Africain (ONA),
86–87

opposition parties: Moroccan, 83–84;
Tunisian, 60–62. *See also*
multipartyism
Organisation de l'Action
Démocratique et Populaire (OADP),
84

parliament: Moroccan, 82–83,
163n28, 181, 186; Tunisian, 60,
137
Parti de l'Unité Populaire (PUP), 61n11
Parti du Progrés et du Socialisme
(PPS), 83, 84
Parti National Démocratique (PND),
83
Parti Socialiste Destourian (PSD),
60n10
Parti Social Libéral
Party of Justice and Development
(PJD), 84
PBK, 158
peak-level business association, 58,
118, 131, 159. *See also* AMITH;
CGEM; UTAC; UTICA
Plan Emergence Textile-Habillement,
188n51
Playtex, 139n26
PMN, 130–134, 216
policy preferences, 6–7, 14–16, 17, 84,
107–110, 113, 159, 164, 178, 181,
190, 193; as different from group
interests, 19–20. *See also* business
collective action; group interests
political economy, 18n21, 209, 218;
India, 202, 204; Morocco, 12, 13,
21, 86, 87n18, 91, 94–95, 98,
148–149, 168, 178, 188; Taiwan,
199; Tunisia, 22, 64, 72, 107, 125,
136
political-sociological approach,
193–195
Poulina group, 77, 137n24, 138
prices, 36, 69, 146, 158, 159, 163,
169, 173, 197
Programme Emergence, 216–217
Programme pour la Mise à Niveau.
See PMN

protectionism, 9, 190; India, 202, 205; Morocco, 13, 18, 20, 33, 80, 91–93, 94, 98–99, 102, 149, 159, 161, 164, 166, 168, 170, 173–174, 188, 193–195; Taiwan, 196; Tunisia, 35–36, 71, 73–74, 78–79, 136, 140, 144; Turkey, 206, 208–209. *See also* import-substitution industrialization (ISI)
Protectorate: Moroccan, 81, 89, 90–91; Tunisian, 63, 64n15. *See also* colonial period
Putin, Vladimir, 8n9

qaids, 56, 81, 90
quick response management system (QR), 41–43

Rassemblement Constitutionel Démocratique (RCD), 60, 62. *See also* Neo-Destour Party
Rassemblement National des Indépendants (RNI), 83
Rassemblement Socialiste Progressiste, 61n11
rational-choice models, 108, 109–110
RCD. *See* Rassemblement Constitutionel Démocratique
recession, 149, 150; 1970s, 29; 1980s, 31–32; 1990s, 38
reference prices, 159–163, 169–170, 173, 177
regions: global economy and, 47–48
rentier industrialists: Moroccan textile manufacturers as, 168–169
Résidence Général, 56, 81
Royal Council, 86n14

Salon du Vêtement Marocain. *See* VETMA
SAP. *See* structural adjustment programs
Sara Lee Group, 139n26
SATFIL-LAGE, 158
Sebti family, 39–40n18

Secretary of State of the Presidency (Tunisia), 59
Sectoral Foreign Trade Corporations (SFTCs) (Turkey), 207
sectoral integration, 209; Morocco, 22, 161–162, 164–166, 189, 216, 217; Tunisia, 114–116, 128, 147. *See also* clustering; Gherzi Organisation; industrial upgrading
"self-made men," 78, 149, 168, 173, 177, 193
SETAFIL, 158
sharifian families, 85
SICAF, 137–138
SIHAM, 87
single-party state: Taiwan, 198–199; Tunisia, 12, 56, 58–60, 79, 107. *See also* state repression
Siter, 69, 71, 75n33, 115
SITEX, 69n24
small- and medium-sized enterprises, 28, 44, 72, 79, 96, 136n22, 192–193; Morocco, 96, 153, 159n19, 165, 180; Taiwan, 197–198, 200–201; Tunisia, 124, 125–126, 136; Turkish "Anatolian Tigers," 207–208
social inequality: Tunisia, 57
social movement theory, 18–19
social policy: Tunisian, 65–67, 136
social security system: Moroccan, 102, 150n2, 165, 166, 169, 183–184, 188, 216
Société d'Investissement du Capital Fixe. *See* SICAF
Société Générale du Coton. *See* Sogitex
Société Générale du Textiles. *See* Sogitex
Société Nationale d'Investissement, 87
Sogicot. *See* Sogitex
Sogitex, 69–70, 71
South Asia, 32
South Korea, 7, 29, 32, 38t2.1, 194, 197, 199n12
state corporatist model, 121n10, 198

state-owned enterprises: India, 203;
  Taiwan, 197; Tunisia, 69–70
state repression, 11, 17, 79, 107,
  116–130, 135, 147. *See also* business
  collective action;
  business–government relations
statist models, 17, 66–68, 72,
  193–194, 199, 200
Stefanel, 173
stock-keeping units (SKUs), 41
structural adjustment programs
  (SAPs), 3, 5–6, 10, 35, 92, 97, 126,
  149, 157, 195n2, 207. *See also*
  World Bank
subcontracting, 6, 20, 29, 30, 31–32,
  44–45, 69n24, 76, 78, 94, 98, 99,
  100–101, 141, 166

Taiwan, 29, 32, 38t2.1, 46, 194–201,
  212; business associations and, 198,
  199–201; business passivity and,
  196–200; capital structure of,
  197–198; democratization of, 195,
  199–201; model of distant
  business–government relations,
  194–201; protectionism and, 196
Tazi, Alami, 167n33
technical contraband, 156n14
technology, 39, 49, 50n38, 75, 207;
  information and communication
  technology (ICT), 215; parks, 212,
  215, 217; supply chain management
  and, 42–44
textile sector: "fat cats" and, 18,
  168–171, 193; industrial upgrading,
  73–76, 114–116, 161–162, 217;
  manufacturing process, 26–28;
  1972 Law and the Tunisian, 73–76;
  noncompetitiveness of Tunisian,
  70–76, 173–174, 178–179; textile
  lobby, 162–164, 169–170, 178–179;
  trade liberalization and, 113–116,
  143–144, 146–147; Tunisian statism
  and, 69–72. *See also* Agreement on
  Textiles and Clothing; CETTEX;
  EU Association Agreements;
  FENATEX; import-substitution

industrialization; Multi-Fiber
  Agreement; protectionism
trade facilitation, 215–216
trade fairs, 217, 218
trade liberalization, 5–10, 12–15, 20,
  23–33, 168, 190–194, 195, 201;
  India, 201, 205, 209; Morocco,
  33–35, 88, 92, 99, 102–103,
  149–151, 157–159, 177n42;
  Taiwan, 200–201; Tunisia, 22–23,
  33, 35–37, 76, 78–79, 107,
  109–110, 113, 126, 128–129, 135,
  137, 143–144; Turkey, 201, 207,
  209. *See also* import-substitution
  industrialization; protectionism
Tunisie Trade Net (TTN), 215
Türk Sanayicileri ve lsadamlari
  Dernegi (Association of Turkish
  Industrialists and Businessmen)
  (TUSIAD), 207–208
Turkey, 206–209
2626 Fund: as instrument of social
  control, 117–118

UGTT. *See* Union General des
  Travailleurs Tunisiens
ulema, 81n2
Uniform Commercial Code, 42
Union Constitutionnelle (UC), 83
Union Démocratique Unioniste, 61n11
Union Générale des Travailleurs
  Tunisiens (UGTT), 58, 64, 122–123
Union Marocaine du Travail (UMT),
  184
Union Socialistes des Forces
  Populaires (USFP), 83, 84
Union Tunisienne de l'Artisanat et du
  Commerce (UTAC), 58
Union Tunisienne de l'Industrie, du
  Commerce et de l'Artisanat. *See*
  UTICA
Universal Product Code (UPC), 42
UTAC. *See* Union Tunisienne de
  l'Artisanat et du Commerce
UTICA, 113, 114, 118, 144, 121–127;
  organized labor and, 123; small-
  and medium-sized enterprises and,

123–124, 125–126; wage
negotiations and, 122–123

VETMA, 150–151, 175, 163n28
vocational training, 127, 183n47, 188,
210, 212, 215, 216, 217, 218

wages, 27–28, 28–29, 41, 44, 46, 49,
67, 94, 102, 116, 122–123, 127,
144, 147, 182, 184, 188. *See also*
labor

World Bank, 4, 33, 35, 69n24, 92,
159, 167, 180n44; Doing Business
database, 215
WTO, 120, 163n27; Agreement on
Textiles and Clothing (ATC), 40;
WTO Accords, 11

Youssoufi, Abderrahman, 83, 86n13,
185

Zghal family, 77